We Have Taken A City

We Have Taken A City

The Wilmington Racial Massacre and Coup of 1898

By
H. Leon Prather, Sr.

Dram Tree Books
A JEF Publications Company

First Edition 1984
Second Edition 1998
This Edition 2006

Published in the United States of America by Dram Tree Books,Inc.

Publisher's Cataloging-in-Publication
(Provided by DRT Press)

Prather, H. Leon, 1921-
  We have taken a city: the Wilmington racial massacre and coup of 1898 / by H. Leon Prather, Sr.
   p. cm.
   Includes bibliographical references and index,
   "Updated with additional photographs."
   ISBN 0-9723240-8-9

1. Wilmington (NC) -- Riot, 1898. 2. Wilmington (NC) -- Race relations. 3. Afro-American -- North Carolina -- Wilmington -- History -- 19th century. I. Title.

F264. W7P72 2006
975.6'27

Dram Tree Books
549 Eagle Lane
Southport, N.C. 28461
(910) 538-4076
dramtreebooks@ec.rr.com

Discounts available
for educators.
Call or e-mail for terms.

Contents

Preface

The phenomena known as race riots have persisted throughout much of this nation's history; often they have exploded into cataclysmic proportions. At Wilmington, North Carolina, on 10 November 1898, the most ghastly racial massacre of the Progressive Era erupted. Following in its wake was a hurricane of violence directed primarily against the black community. This event, a legacy, has a graphic connection between the past and present, as shown by the noted case known as the *Wilmington 10*. Certainly, in a symbolic sense, the American tragedy of 1898 should have become a cause célèbre, for the events were so horrendous that even President William McKinley and his cabinet became involved. And for the first time in the history of the American republic there occurred a coup d'état.

In 1981, Professor Arthur S. Link of Princeton University, one of America's foremost historians, with other renowned scholars concurring, wrote: "Armed Democrats in Wilmington, North Carolina, in 1898 overthrew the duly elected Republican government, an event which, had it occured elsewhere on the globe, would have been called a *coup d'état*. Instead, it is known in history books as the Wilmington race riot."[1]

Reporting this event, the *New York Herald* proclaimed, "WHITES KILL NEGROES AND SEIZE CITY OF WILMINGTON."[2] Leading Democrats instigated the violence as a smoke screen for the revolutionary seizure of the municipal government from the legally elected Republican administration. Significant to an explanation of the coup was the devastation of black political leadership through violent means to assure the return of white supremacy. In the wake of the excitement, a militia with fixed bayonets, amid jeering crowds, banished forever from the city leading white Republicans and Negro leaders. One of the whites drummed out of town was almost lynched. Next, there ensued an economic coup, as the whites took over the black trades, municipal jobs, and even the menial occupations traditionally viewed as Negro monopolies. Thus, the Wilmington racial massacre was part of the nation's only coup.

In the historical context of American race relations, the Wilmington racial conflict is significant. Comparing its seriousness with that of other conflicts by death toll, the episode was one of the most ruthless and brutal riots in the nation's history.

The event attracted wide attention both nationally and in Europe. It also inspired two works of fiction. David Bryant Fulton, under the pseudonym of Jack Thorne, authored *Hanover; or, The Persecution of the Lowly;* and the famous black novelist Charles W. Chesnutt wrote *The Marrow of Tradition.* Both authors tried to prick the conscience of white America by pillorying before the world the monstrosity of the crime.

The Wilmington riot was a major racial disturbance. It is therefore surprising that it has been ignored by scholars and that there has not been a single sound scholarly book on the subject. In researching the literature concerning race riots, some brief references to the event can be found, but there is a paucity of detailed accounts, and most histories are completely silent about it. In seeking more information, one soon runs into a dead end. The scholar attempting to probe the event quickly becomes aware of the similarity in the accounts.

One may logically ask: What was the genesis of this book? As a young social science teacher (1948–58), I was a member of the faculty of the historically black Elizabeth City State Teachers College, located in the North Carolina Black Belt, about 210 miles from Wilmington. Intermittently during my tenure there, some of the students from Wilmington and other places in New Hanover county would inquire about my knowledge of the race riot. I became more fascinated with the topic while researching and writing the book, *Resurgent Politics and Educational Progressivism in the New South: North Carolina, 1890–1913.*[3] My interest continued to grow as I realized that the existing literature had dealt with the theme inadequately. Equally important was my familiarity with the history of North Carolina during this era. I began by both discussing the problems and seeking the advice of authorities, who would very much like to see studies done on this horror. Their names and contributions appear in the Acknowledgments.

All the actors in the Wilmington drama of 10 November 1898 have gone to their graves. The audience, except for a very few, has also gone to its grave. Yet today there are crucial questions surrounding the tragic drama that still demand answers:

1. What sociopolitical forces created the catastrophe?
2. Did the white citizens create the immediate conditions that ignited the violence or were they merely responding to the violence of the Civil War and Reconstruction?.
3. Did the black citizens create volatile conditions in the city?
4. Did certain prominent white citizens catalyze the Wilmington rebellion for personal gain?
5. Was the intensity of the riot fed by the subculture of racism and by white poverty?
6. Were there larger political and economic issues involved?

These questions and others will be answered in this book. An important point must be made here: Social scientists need a new term for what has been called a race riot. The traumatic episode in Wilmington, like many others, was largely one-sided: a white massacre of defenseless blacks with a macabre mixture of carnage and carnival. These racial conflicts are generally recorded in American historiography as *riots*. Such nomenclature may be incomplete, and the significance of the Wilmington events can be enhanced if the words *massacre, revolution* and *rebellion* are added to describe the situation. *Webster's New Collegiate Dictionary* defines *massacre* as the "killing of a number of . . . human beings under circumstances of atrocity or cruelty." It defines *rebellion* as an instance of "defiance of or resistance to . . . one in authority or dominance"; and *revolution* as a "sudden, radical or complete . . . overthrow or renunciation of one government . . . and the substitution of another by the governed." In spite of this, however, the terms *riot, massacre, revolution,* and *rebellion* will be used interchangeably in this narrative.

In the Wilmington racial massacre, blacks were the people to whom things happened. This situation is still somewhat true as blacks today struggle for survival and development. For this reason, black Americans are possessed of a stronger sensitivity toward racial violence than may be found among whites. The oral tradition, an indispensable link with the past, has contributed to this sensitivity. Would not this same sensitivity be true of Jewish survivors of the brutal and genocidal processes that occurred in the Nazi concentration camps?

Some scholars believe that whites write from an elitist perspective, which makes obtuse their conceptualization of the black experience. Professor William M. Tuttle, Jr., put it well when he wrote in *Race Riot: Chicago in the Red Summer of 1919:* "Unfortunately much that has been written about black Americans by whites has been written from the point of view" of guilt-ridden liberalism. "This is true, for example, of much of the literature on racial violence." Professor Tuttle goes on to point out the propensity for distortion among white authors, who tend to interpret the black experience from their own middle-class perspective.[4] The white perspective to which Tuttle was referring was that of many white liberals—that is, people who want to deal sympathetically with the Negro problem. Notwithstanding, a wealth of history has been written from this perspective. But much too often, scholars have tended to treat blacks as passive victims and not as actors. Their focus, furthermore, has been on victimization, as reflected by lynchings and race riots—rather than on black successes, such as the creation of flourishing black institutions, the enduring black family and the cultural contributions to the nation.[5]

The definitive pen of the black scholar is needed to correct the distortions and to fill in the glaring omissions. *We Have Taken a City: The Wilmington Racial Massacre and Coup of 1898.* is not wholly black history; it is essentially a treatise on American race relations, focusing upon pervasive institutional racism and is a singularly appropriate study for a black historian, who has a unique perspective. In the delineation and analysis of the political and socioeconomic forces that generated this American tragedy, every effort was made to capture the spirit and the drama along with the personalities of the characters. Some of the events have the ingredients of fiction, but the narrative is documented. Equally important, the extensive research is based on a number of previously unexplored sources—new documents, archival data, manuscripts, interviews, private letters, official correspondence, diaries, and cartoons.

Finally, writing both as a scholar and a humanist, I made every effort to capture the spirit of the drama, and my scholarship does not overtax the lucidity of the study or neglect its provocativeness. Given the book's theme and the intrinsic interest it might hold for scholars, I constantly kept two goals in view. The first one was to present an accurate account of this American tragedy, one that would stand the scrutiny of other scholars. Moreover, since history contains explicit humanistic elements and values, it is the responsibility of scholars to communicate with the public, and transcend that false dichotomy between a 'democratic' or an 'elite' enterprise. Accordingly, the second goal was to write a book that would be accepted by the general reading public. This study is a personal commitment, and I hope that it will make a distinctive contribution to historiography in American race relations.

Acknowledgments

Financial assistance was indispensable in the development of the manuscript for this book. I might not have been able to write it at all had it not been for assistance of the Moton Center for Independent Studies. The center provided the fellowship and research facilities that enabled me to devote nine months (1976–77) to travel, research, and writing. In particular, I must thank Miss Louise Coursey, our librarian, now holding a similar position at the University of Pennsylvania, who went beyond the call of duty in securing long-distance research sources, which saved me both time and money; and Raymond Trent of Biddle Library at the University of Pennsylvania. While in residence at the center, I was able to exploit two fellows and friends— Daphne D. Harrison of the University of Maryland, Baltimore County, and Allen B. Ballard of the City University of New York—who took time out from their research and responded generously to my requests for assistance. I must mention here that I am indebted to Professor Ballard for the introduction and for setting up the first interview with Milo Manly of Philadelphia.

I have discussed the theme of this study with numerous scholars and other interested persons, who shared ideas and significant materials with me in the formative stages. An early version of this theme was presented in a paper under the title "The Day the River Ran Red: The Wilmington Racial Massacre, November 10, 1898" at the annual meeting of the Association for the Study of Afro-American Life and History in Philadelphia on 25 October 1974. Charles Crowe of the University of Georgia critiqued it and later supplied me with a list of pertinent sources. Lawrence C. Goodwyn of Duke University also knows much about the Wilmington bloodshed from his own works and sources. I have conferred with him and, in addition to significant insights, he gave me invaluable suggestions on how to overcome what appeared to be insurmountable obstacles and offered leads to some rare sources. Likewise, William M. Tuttle, Jr., of the University of Kansas, gave me encouragement and supplied leads to significant data in the National Archives in Washington, D.C., and for his valuable comments on the final section of the manuscript. Through Professor Joel Williamson of the University of North Carolina, I became acquainted with the still neglected work of Charles W. Chesnutt. He suggested that I probe it for its sociological sensitivity toward the Wilmington event. I am indebted in several ways to Alton Hornsby, Jr., Chairman of the Department of History of Morehouse College and current editor of the *Journal of Negro History*.

It was George B. Tindall, Kenan Professor of History at the University of North Carolina, who raised such pointed questions as, Was the riot spontaneous or planned? Did certain persons have something to gain from the riot? When I remarked that I was going to expose those perpetrators, Professor Tindall's parting words were, "Just tell the truth."

It was my longtime acquaintance, Leon Weidman, Librarian, American History Division of the New York Public Library, who first suggested the theme of coup d'état, following his perusal of the original prospectus.

For expert guidance and unmistakable courtesy, I want to thank the staffs of the following libraries and archives: the New York Public Library; the Schomburg Center for Research in Black Culture; the University of Pennsylvania; the Manuscript Division of the Library of Congress; the National Archives; the Southern Historical Collection and the North Carolina History Room in the Wilson Library, University of North Carolina, Chapel Hill; the Manuscript Division, William R. Perkins Library, Duke University; and the North Carolina Department of Archives and History.

More personally, I must thank my departmental colleagues, who make research a joy in academics. I wish to thank Samuel H. Shannon for reading the original draft and offering constructive criticism. I am also indebted to Joseph Udelson for his suggestions and corrections made throughout the revised manuscript. My thanks are also due Bobby L. Lovett, a young scholar who proofread the entire finished manuscript. I also wish to express my appreciation to Katharine Turok, Managing Editor of Associated University Presses, for her valuable suggestions and skilled copyediting of the manuscript. It is not their fault if some errors might still appear.

I also want to thank Mrs. Janie R. Ganaway for the skillful and conscientious typing of the rough drafts and of the final manuscript, and Mrs. Evelyn Cannon, who had the responsibility of typing various key revisions.

And finally, I must express gratitude to my wife, Audrey Minga Prather, Assistant Professor of Chemistry at Tennessee State University, who over the years has evolved into a skilled editorial assistant. While I did not always follow her advice (notwithstanding her intermittent heedings with sailor's language), she still found time to review each chapter and to offer countless suggestions and corrections, as well as to rewrite some awkward sentences in the longhand drafts.

We Have Taken a City

Prologue: The Psyche of a Southern City

1

ON the Cape Fear River, about thirty miles from the East coast of North Carolina rests the beautiful city of Wilmington. At the dawn of the twentieth century, it was the largest and the most important city of the Old North State. Country folks referred to it as the "big city," with electric lights, streetlights, and streetcars. Situated on the east bank of the river, it extended mainly north to south. "Market Street, the centre and the main thoroughfare of the city, wide and beautiful, begins at the river front and gradually climbs a hill eastward, so persistently straight."[1]

Wilmington was also one of the chief seaports of the Atlantic Coast. Its snug harbor was a strategic facility for commerce, a logical site for inland traders carrying their produce to market. And for many generations it had served as the port of entry for Americans of English, Irish, Scotch-Irish, German, and Jewish ancestry.

To the west of Wilmington, within the eyeshot, is Eagles Island, an immense swamp. The northeast and southeast branches of the Cape Fear River come together at the southeast point of the island. During the colonial era, the island was partly drained and converted to cultivation by a number of "rice-planters."[2] And according to oral tradition, its swamp provided a haven for runaway slaves.

The purpose herein is to provide a sense of history and familiarity with Wilmington. This is more than a prologue and includes the setting of things to come. For without this background, the theme might be somewhat parochial or even vacuous.

During the days of slavery, Wilmington was an anomaly in the South. For example, no slave revolt occurred in the state of North Carolina. The fact that the slave population was relatively small was probably largely responsible for this peaceful situation. It is also interesting to note that North Carolina's laws against nonwhites were among the harshest in the United States—as is described by Winthrop D. Jordan in *White Over Black*. Jordan reminds us that castration, for example, was legally sanctioned until re-

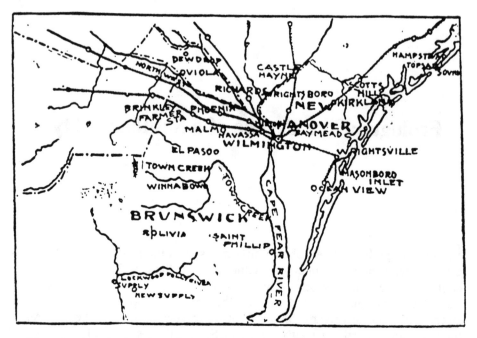

Map showing the location of the City of Wilmington, North Carolina. New York *Herald*, **November 11, 1896 (file, New York Public Library).**

pealed in 1764, and that this form of punishment "was reserved for Negroes and occasionally Indians" (pp 154–55). But it is also worth noting that free blacks were permitted to vote in North Carolina until 1835. Meanwhile a viable black middle class of artisans was emerging in Wilmington.

The port city of Wilmington is steeped in history and tradition. In antebellum days its source of wealth was in the naval stores industry—those products of turpentine known as spirits, rosin, tar, pitch, and crude turpentine. American turpentine was extracted mainly from the longleaf pine, then abundant in the Cape Fear region, lining every river, estuary and creek in the eastern part of North Carolina. Wilmington was the turpentine capital of the world.[3]

An abundant supply of slave labor was its lifeblood. Then outnumbering the whites, the slave population was growing throughout eastern North Carolina, later to become a political power to be reckoned with by Wilmington and the entire region.

After the firing on Fort Sumter that opened the Civil War, the awe-inspiring Fort Fisher guarded Wilmington's harbor. Fort Fisher was one of the most formidable fortresses ever contrived. Throughout the duration of the war, Wilmington (aided by blockade-runners) thrived as never before as a port. Its capture by the Union was delayed until nearly the end of the war, and then only after a most difficult land and naval attack, involving a huge armada and a force of nearly eight thousand men.[4] Some of the most terrific bombardments of the Civil War took place at Fort Fisher.

The clash between the U.S.S. *Monitor* and the Confederate *Merrimack* was more than the first skirmish between two armored warships; this contest demonstrated that wooden ships, so dependent on Wilmington's naval supplies, were obsolete. Hence, the Civil War snapped the former economic lifeline of Wilmington and marked the decline of the naval-store industry.

The stillness at Appomattox, as throughout the South, was a watershed for Wilmington, and the post–Civil War era witnessed the emergence of a new city, accompanied by a spirit of civic improvement and economic growth. The city became a major railroad center, served by five lines. At the same time, some of its leading boosters were predicting that Wilmington would become another Atlanta, Charleston, or New Orleans.

Industries that were quite profitable during the antebellum era were revived. One was the sawmill industry, which expanded in volume. In 1897, for example, the city business directory listed seven lumber companies. The rice industry was also revived, with large quantities of rice being shipped to Northern ports. Peanuts also came into Wilmington to be shipped to distant places. And with the Navassa Guano Company being organized in 1869, the fertilizer business assumed extensive proportions. But after the postwar economic adjustment was completed, Wilmington remained a colonial economy—industrial products fell under the general pattern of economic imperialism and had to be shipped elsewhere for "final processing before going to the consumer." Worse still, such products fell victim to the "one general type—the 'low wage–low value'" type of industry that added the lowest value of product per wage earner.[5] This production required not skilled labor, but large supplies of cheap and unskilled labor, and there was more than enough to be found among both the white and black populations.

If industrialism was to dawn upon the New South, stimulated by Northern capitalism, Wilmington's "new order" would disregard it. Antebellum Wilmington had been a commercial city, and it would remain one far into the twentieth century. New capitalists appeared on the scene to shape the economic character of Wilmington. A novel commercial enterprise was introduced with the cotton-presser trade in 1866; the moving force behind this was Alexander Sprunt, founder of the firm of Alexander Sprunt and Son, which employed numerous black laborers. During the race riot, a stirring drama would be acted out at this establishment.

2

After the Civil War, Wilmington's new leaders, the middle-class blacks and the freedmen, assisted one another in bringing order out of chaos. Post-Reconstruction Wilmington reflected a new breed of Southern city, yet Wilmington was, in some ways, still committed to the cult of the Lost Cause.

Relics of Civil War cannons marked many of the downtown street corners, not only as decorations but also to prevent the drays, wagons, and carriages from cutting the corners. Almost every town exhibited that standard pictur- esque monument "in the courthouse squares—usually the figure of a soldier facing North, gun in hand."[6] But Wilmington had erected its monument in a more appropriate location; the impressive granite Confederate statue (fifteen feet, three inches high) had been erected in Oakdale Cemetery and dedicated on 10 May 1872.[7] In 1889, the United Confederate Veterans was organized at New Orleans, and annual reunions and parades became common throughout the South. Wilmington became a mecca for such parades, with hosts of ragged Confederates thronging annual reunions, singing "Tenting Tonight on the Old Camp Ground."

The majority of Wilmington's population were members of Methodist and Baptist churches. Other groups included Presbyterians, Lutherans, Catho- lics, Jews, Episcopalians, and two undenominational sects. There were also the secret orders that were secular in nature, such as the Knights of Pythias, the Independent Order of Odd Fellows, the Knights of the Golden Eagle, the American Legion of Honor, and the Independent Order of B'nai B'rith.

Saloons, anathema to many churches and Christians, operated throughout the city. The city directory of 1897 listed eighteen white saloons. Included among them were cafés, such as the French Café on Princess Street. With little or no regulation, such businesses made it easy for the more pious of the public officials to observe their baneful influence in the city, as swinging doors opened and closed for as many hours as the saloon keepers desired. In those days, no standard codes were applied to these establishments. Citi- zens who did not care to patronize saloons could purchase their wine, beer, or liquor at grocery stores, entering them with their families through the family entrance. In the rear were the swinging doors leading to where whis- key was sold and drunk over the counter. Sometimes women and children would take a peek out of curiosity; the hum of men's voices was audible as they huddled together drinking in clouds of smoke.[8]

During this era, red-light districts were also common, especially in port cities. In Wilmington, the infamous district was called Patty's Hollow, and it flourished near the Sprunt Cotton Compress. Brothels for whites and blacks were openly and defiantly operated in various parts of the city, with the underworld exercising a baneful influence over the official and private lives of some city and county authorities. This district was frequented by poor whites and "wild and daring blacks."[9] Prominent white men did not have to visit this section of town; according to black oral tradition, some white men of status had comely black mistresses, a legacy of the antebellum era. Dur- ing the riot, one well-known Republican would be drummed out of town for living with a Negro woman.

Every city had its slum; in Wilmington it was known as 'Dry Pond,' the southern section of town. This was originally an area of low sand hills and ditches between where rainwater collected. As people moved in, the ditches were drained or filled up, and with time, homes were built farther and farther south. The expression "run and jump" (i.e., running and jumping over ditches to get where one wanted to go) has been passed down in both the literature and oral tradition. Mostly poor whites who were identified with Dry Pond, although there were also Negro shanties there. Dry Ponders were a group to be "feared and shunned," and if an outside group of boys was looking for a fight, it came to this community. An individual Dry Ponder was not particularly dangerous, but many townsmen agreed that two, four, six or more was a thing to be careful of and avoided if possible. Then there were the infamous "degraded and shiftless . . . the meaner sort of poor whites, possessing few redeeming qualities."[10] They made life hideous on Dry Pond with their brawls and frolics.

The Irish made up a sizable element of the population in Dry Pond. Animosity between Irish and blacks has deep taproots; in fact, blacks were the first to call the Irish *buckra,* sometimes spelled *bocra,* meaning "white nigger." A name of contempt, *buckra,* as used by the average aristocrat of Wilmington was likely to apply indiscriminately to the poor whites. "The people," Professor June Nash wrote, "they did not consider for many years white, [and] they would have to go around to the back door to these aristo-crats who live up the street there."[11] Settling in the cities, the Irish sought any kind of employment and competed with blacks for jobs, regardless of wages or conditions. Young Frederick Douglass thought them the most bigoted element in American society, and their economic status placed them in direct competition with the blacks they despised. In many cities they rapidly moved in on jobs traditionally performed by blacks: heavy labor shipyard work, carting and even domestic service.[12]

White laborers alleged that Wilmington white employers preferred blacks, a situation that heightened tensions among blacks, Irish, and other whites in need of jobs. The whites channeled their frustrations and anger into hatred of blacks and found comfort in the doctrine of white supremacy.[13] They later became a tool for designing politicians during the days before the race riot. In view of the fact that an unemployed Irishman surfaced as the organizer and leader of the Redshirts in 1898, it is important to ask: To what extent did Dry Ponders, along with the Irish, comprise the mobs during the riot?

It appears that many of the influential blacks lived in integrated neighbor-hoods. Wilmington had a predominantly black community, however. It was known as Brooklyn and occupied the entire northern section of the city. No one actually knows how it got this name. Brooklyn was separated by the Wilmington and Weldon railroad tracks, which lie in a deep cut spanned by two bridges, built jointly by the railroad company and the city at a cost of $13,000—a good price during this era.[14] Like many things that disappear with progress, today the bridges are not there, and perhaps most of the older citizens do not remember them ever being there.

Brooklyn grew rapidly after the Civil War. "The tides of Negro migration that had set in during Reconstruction, as the first and most characteristic expression of freedom," wrote Professor Woodward, "continued to move in the same direction for some years. One of these movements was from the country to the towns."[15] No doubt some former fugitive slaves on Eagles Island after the Civil War scampered through the swamps and marshes to settle in Brooklyn. Like some of the poor whites in the Dry Pond section, some were of the meaner sort, but it appears safe in saying that most of the blacks, as most of the Dry Ponders, were law-abiding citizens. Many of the houses were gaudy, baked two-room shanties. Here and there, like museum pieces, were the houses of the black bourgeoisie. White capitalists maintained some businesses in Brooklyn, but they did not reside in this ghetto. From their labors in the heavy industries—cotton presses, the wharves, sawmills, construction sites, and railroad maintenance yards—black men brought their meager wages into the community.

Brooklyn in the daytime looked cheerful. Seemingly happy children played in the yards and the dusty streets. A wash line flung like a gay flag across the yard, while women sang as they washed. Black violence was there to be sure—not against whites, but against blacks. As the slaveholder feared slave revolts, it appears that the Wilmington whites feared violence from blacks in 1898. The black community of Brooklyn became the scene of the tragic race riot. Some whites also lived in Brooklyn, and this was a major factor in the riot.

3

In most parts of the New South, blacks continued to vote in large numbers for almost two decades after Reconstruction and to hold office as well.[16] After the Populist revolt, their situation worsened. They were already being subjected to a maze of jim crow laws, and total disfranchisement was becoming a reality. Wilmington was an exception to this trend.

The year before the race riot, blacks were very visible in public office in the city. In 1897, for example, there were three blacks on the ten-member Board of Aldermen, which elected the mayor. Another black was a member of the powerful five-constituent Board of Audit and Finance.

Other public jobs held by blacks included justice of the peace, deputy clerk of the superior court, and even the coroner (a barber by trade).[17] There were also the black Superintendent of Streets, and Cattle Weigher, two black fire departments, and an all-black health board. And to this list can be added the black policemen and, in federal patronage, the mail clerk and mail carriers.[18]

William McKinley appointed twice as many blacks to federal positions as previous presidents. One of his foremost appointees was John Campbell Dancy in 1897 as collector of customs at the Port of Wilmington. Not only

John Campbell Dancy (1857–1920). Courtesy of Livingstone College.

was he black and not a native of Wilmington, but he replaced a prominent white Democrat. "Dancy's salary as collector of customs was approximately $4,000 per year; $1,000 more than the annual salary of the Democratic Governor Elias Carr; $2,000 more than Charles M. Cook received as secretary of state; $1,000 more than Worth received as state treasurer; and $1,500 more than the Supreme Court judges received."[19] As an outsider who enjoyed an economic status above most people in Wilmington, Dancy was understandably resented by many whites as well as some local blacks.[20] Thomas W. Clawson, editor of the *Wilmington Messenger* (which was recognized as the official organ of the Democrats), made a practice of referring to Dancy as "Sambo of the Custom House."[21]

Never before and never since had blacks occupied such a central place in a city's political and economic life as they did in Wilmington from 1865 to 1897. It was in the area of black economics more than any other that this city moved toward democratization.

Wilmington's black entrepreneurs were unique. Contrary to the general practice in both the South and the North, black business establishments dotted the downtown streets, suggesting that in some instances all their patrons were white.

Blacks dominated the restuarant business. For example, only one owner in eleven of the city's eating houses was white. More significant was the almost complete monopoly blacks had in the barber trade: twenty of the twenty-two barbers listed in the city directory were black, most pursuing this occupation in shops on the principal downtown streets. Blacks also greatly outnumbered the white boot and shoemakers.

The establishment of Bell and Pickens was listed in the WILMINGTON BUSINESS DIRECTORY (1897) as among the four dealers and shippers of fish and oysters. Among the provision dealers (butchers and meat sellers), three of the nine were black. At the same time, two blacks were listed among the city's four tailors. They were also conspicious in such functions as dyers and scourers, druggists, grocers and bakers. Both Negroes and Whites had a lot of faith in the efficacy of medicinal roots. The only person listed as a dealer under this heading was black, with an office located downtown.[22]

Thomas C. Miller was certainly the most unique of the black businessmen. He plays a minor but memorable role in this narrative. He was one of Wilmington's three real estate agents and auctioneers, and the only person listed under "pawnbrokers" in the city directory.[23] In addition, he owned extensive real estate holdings throughout the city. He did not seek public office; nevertheless, Miller's affluence made his presence in the city seem undesirable to most whites. According to black oral tradition, too many whites owed him money. Numerous poor whites were envious of successful blacks in business; sometimes in the countryside, night riders would drive away a prosperous black farmer by burning him out. The whites did not burn Miller out; yet his fate during the riot reflected the plight of the Southern black middle class of this era.

Still another important black entrepreneur was Frederick C. Sadgwar, a contractor in addition to a "financier and architect."[24] His two-story residence still stands majestically after several generations, a monument to his competency in both carpentry and architecture.

Wilmington was one of the few Southern cities with a black newspaper— the *Daily Record*. Owned and operated by the Manly brothers, it was headed by the militant and progressive editor, Alexander L. (Alex) Manly. He was an octoroon without the slightest earmark of negroid features. One of his parents was the acknowledged offspring of a former governor of the state. He was also deputy registrar of New Hanover County. The youngest child of an affluent family that lived in the residential section of a prominent white family recalled much later that during his childhood the *Daily Record* "was the only Negro daily in the world."[25] With offices located in the heart of the downtown section, it had liberal support from white merchants in the form of paid advertisements. The paper was a force in the community and circulated throughout the state. The irony of it all was that the white leaders of the city, the region, and even the nation charged that Manly used the paper to inflame the whites to riot—a recurring theme in this narrative.

Wilmington in the 1890s could boast a large number of Negro professionals. Prominent among this class were four black lawyers.[26] Just how successful they were in terms of economics is questionable, the assumption being that their clients were all black, with the majority being members of a depressed economic class. To what extent, if any, did black lawyers supplement their income from nonlegal sources? Some may have been public school teachers. The black attorneys were in competition with the twenty-one whites in the legal profession and what was true of the black lawyers may have been true of some white ones, whose clients were also poor.

Included in the black lawyers' ranks was Armond W. Scott, a brilliant graduate of Shaw University in Raleigh, who was admitted to the bar at the age of twenty-one. He was later appointed by President Franklin D. Roosevelt as judge of the Twelfth Municipal District of Washington, D.C.[27] As will later be shown, he was entrusted with a crucial task that could have prevented the riot, and why he acted in the manner he did is still shrouded in mystery. Scott was not Wilmington's most outstanding lawyer, however—L. A. Henderson was, and for this role he, too, was among the prominent blacks banished from town the day after the coup.

A significant number of Wilmington's craftsmen were blacks, including such diversified occupations as mechanics, furniture makers, jewelers and watchmakers, painters, plasterers, plumbers, blacksmiths, stonemasons, brickmasons, and wheelwrights.[28] The successful black artisans in Wilmington were considered middle class, and this fact greatly enhanced their prestige within black society. Along with the professional classes, the small businessmen and the politicians shared the leadership of the black community.

After Reconstruction, the black artisan had significantly lost ground to white competitors, who tended to close ranks and successfully proscribe further increase in numbers of blacks within the trades. The caste system along color lines was basically the same throughout most of the South. In 1870, for example, the New Orleans "city directory had listed 3,460 Negroes as carpenters, cigar makers, painters, clerks, shoemakers, coopers, tailors, bakers, blacksmiths, and foundry hands; not 10 percent of that number were employed in the same trades in 1904. Yet the Negro population had gained more than 50 percent.[29] In Wilmington, on the other hand, the efforts to exclude blacks from the skilled trades did not have the cooperation of white employers. The white craftsmen even complained that most of the city's artisans were black and were given preference in employment. This situation, along with acute unemployment within the white ranks, did indeed generate racial tension.

In accordance with Southern tradition, blacks maintained a monopoly of the service occupations: cooks, janitors, porters, messengers, and waiters. Blacks were in most instances given preference in these occupations—a legacy of the antebellum era. Such business establishments as hotels, private clubs, and banks tacitly required persons with particular cultural traits. During slavery days, both free blacks and slaves had worked in the private clubs of the aristocrats or in affluent homes, had learned to emulate the manners of their employers and owners and had passed the knowledge on to their children. Some had a cultivation that exceeded their formal education, and they performed as messengers, bellhops, and waiters with an aristocratic appearance and proper speech patterns, which many of Wilmington's poor whites had yet to acquire.

It is important to remember that there was acute unemployement among the poor white population. The Wilmington capitalist had traditionally preferred to hire blacks in the heavy industries—cotton presses, lumber mills and camps, seaports, railroads, shipyards, and warehouses. It is wrong to believe, as some social scientists have suggested, that blacks were given preference in the menial occupations because of their willingness to work for lower wages than their white competitors. Both the landlords and the captains of industries looked upon the creation of a reasonable surplus of labor as a good thing, and they gave whites the same terms given to blacks. The late W. J. Cash expressed aptly this sentiment when he wrote: "Give them [the whites] special advantages? We shall do nothing of the kind. We shall give them the same terms we give the Negro. We shall carry over into our dealing with them very much of the attitude toward labor fixed by slavery."[30]

Evidence strongly suggests that the New Order had left behind in Wilmington as throughout the New South, a large body of whites without any definite place in the economic order or any settled means of livelihood. The most numerous element in the Southern population was the five or six millions of poor whites scattered throughout the South. "Northern visitors . . . found some difficulty in accounting for other millions of Southerners of approximately the same economic status who were not black."[31] White racism fed on poverty, a factor that produced a smoldering fire of resentment among Wilmington's numerous poor whites. On the other hand, there were masses of blacks at loose ends, more than enough to fill Wilmington's quota of unskilled occupations. Just thirty-three years out of slavery, blacks had been accustomed to poverty and did not carry their economic status across racial lines. But now, whites were in competition with them for survival. "To reflect their own superiority, the whites insisted on caste demarcation and demanded that blacks be kept down in their place—this place had to be defined realistically as under themselves."[32] It would, indeed, be a mistake to assume that the race riot of 1898 was only politically oriented. More jobs, skilled and unskilled, at the expense of blacks were to be among the top priorities demanded by the leaders of the coup.

4

It should be recalled here that most positive historical descriptions of the South are from the point of view of whites. Indeed, John Campbell Dancy's recollections are unique in that they provide both a dynamic cameo and keen insight into the psyche of Wilmington on the eve of the race riot from a black perspective. His father was a man of national—even international—prominence and by the standards of the time, a wealthy man.[33]

In the 1960s Dancy wrote in his *Memoirs:* "Though Gershwin's *Porgy and Bess* was set in Charleston, so much of it reminds me of my Wilmington boyhood. There was always, for example, someone like 'Sportin' Life, the fellow who had been away to the big town and had come back, flashily dressed, to impress the folks back home." He also recalled that Wilmington was a very pretty place at the turn of the century, and this is still true today. The outside world, including New York, was a mystery to him and in his early years he could not understand why anyone would want to leave North Carolina; as far as he was concerned, "everything about it was fine."[34]

Dancy's recollections revealed his keen sociological eye. He was able to see the mass unemployment in Wilmington, especially among his people. A large number of blacks worked in the cotton press and on the cotton boards, hauling bales to the wharves and loading them onto ships, but this was seasonal employment that "lasted only about three months," and this was all the work they did. Thus, many blacks only "made about $90.00 a year."[35]

The black woman of Wilmington was often the sole support of the family, and many of the black men's wives worked as domestics for such meager wages as "$1.50, $2.00 or $3.00 a week."[36] With legacy of slavery looming in the background and a mere thirty-three years of freedom, these black women were often looked upon as part of the house, part of the furniture, and in a sense, they belonged to their employers. They were forced through a depressed system of Southern economics, which they did not comprehend and over which they could not exercise any control, to provide for their family. To them it was a matter of survival.

With the black community cursed by perpetual unemployment, men naturally turned into loafers. With nothing for them to do, no place to go, the loafers gathered in groups on the corner streets or by the railroad tracks. And many just sat—preferably in the shade, because Wilmington is a hot place in summer, full of sand which is baked by the sun until it will scorch if you touch it.

While the standard of living appeared to have been very low in Wilmington, the industrious and thrifty individual could live comfortably. Recalling the experiences of his grandfather, Dancy wrote: "He worked hard, sometimes on the railroad and sometimes in a tannery, and I am confident that he never made more than $6.00 a week in his entire life." With such small earnings, however, his grandfather was able to buy a "cozy house" with some acreage on which he grew everything his family needed for food; they had a "cow, hogs, chickens and all kinds of vegetables."[37]

Wilmington, according to Dancy, was noted for its excellent record in race relations. It was singled out as one of the places where blacks were doing well in the south. There were blacks on the police force and in other municipal jobs. There were blacks who had stalls in the marketplace, a thing that was not done in other Southern towns. Moreover, Dancy lived in an integrated community: his neighbor on one side was black, and the remainder of the people in the block were whites. "Nobody thought anything about it; at least nobody said anything about it. There's no consistency about it, but this is the kind of relationship that could exist, and still can, in some southern towns."[38]

Reflecting on his early boyhood, Dancy confessed that his father's position in the community and his relative affluence had brought him many advantages. His memories of childhood were mostly pleasant ones—of good friends and games and adventurous trips of exploration along the hot, sandy North Carolina beaches, lying out in the sun, digging oysters and clams, and catching fish with a seine and eating them within an hour after they were caught—"and what a paradise it all seems."[39]

Then came the unpleasant memories that jolted his boyish dreamworld, giving him an object lesson in what it means to be a Negro in the South. It was Thursday, 10 November 1898. About eight-thirty in the morning; excited and wide-eyed children rushed up the streets and warned, "There's something going on, you'd better stay in the house."[40] The office of the *Daily Record,* the black newspaper, was burned. And about eleven o'clock, Winchesters began to crack, a cacophony persisting intermittently throughout the day. Angry mobs, including the Redshirts and the military, roamed the black community of Brooklyn. "The main target," wrote Dancy, "were men like my father, whose crime was that they were successful and prosperous beyond the condition of the average white man." Dancy was ten years old at the time and was left with memories of being bundled into a horse-drawn carriage by his stepmother (his mother had died when he was four and his father had married again). His father was out of town, and he and his half-brother were alone with his stepmother. Recalling the wild dash, he points out that there were "no automobiles in town; there were no telephones in Negro homes, except for perhaps those of the doctor and the undertaker; and it was taking your life in your hands to go out of the house." He never knew how his stepmother did it, but somehow she managed to make the arrangements, and the rig drew up to his house at dusk. They were driven to the Atlantic Coastline Railroad, only an eight- or ten-block ride, and were stopped several times by white men who searched the buggy. They were not molested, however, and were allowed to board the train. They rode to Tarboro where they joined his father, who "refused to be intimidated by the warnings that had been directed at him."[41] A dauntless man, he returned to Wilmington to live in peace for three more years. There is a postscript here: President Theodore Roosevelt named him recorder of deeds for the District of Columbia, at an annual salary of "about $6,000, a truly munificent sum for those days."[42] He held the position until 1910.

Dancy himself returned to Wilmington as an adult some fifty years later to visit some friends in his old neighborhood. Right next door to the home he visited lived a white family, and his friend told him that he and his family had been living there for years without the slightest adverse reaction from anybody. While they were visiting, the white woman next door went out and got a gardenia off her tree and gave it to Dancy's wife. She said, "Now this will go bad after a time, but take and press it in a book and it will give a good scent to your book." Dancy recognized that this was a small thing, scarcely worth mentioning; however, to him, it was indicative of the kind of race relations that he had "often observed in places where racial tensions are not fanned by current events."[43]

But with the riot, the harmonious race relations that had traditionally prevailed in Wilmington vanished like a fog attacked by the sun. And it all began with Fusion politics.

1
The Turning Point: The Critical Mayoralty Election of 1897

1

"SOUTHERN Politics," V. O. Key wrote, "is no comic opera. It is a deadly serious business."[1] Considering the series of farcical events associated with the Wilmington municipal election of 1897, however, there is material here for a comedy, which makes Key's thesis only partly true. For example, four politicians claimed to be the legal mayor—unprecedented in American history. Intense legal maneuvering ensued as the controversy worked itself through the state superior court and into the state supreme court.

Students of Southern politics and other persons knowledgeable on the subject might recall Key's thesis, "Whatever phase of the southern political process one seeks to understand, sooner or later the trail leads to the Negro." This proposition was especially true in the Southern Black Belt, a region of contiguous counties with populations 40, 50, 60, or more percent black. Here the crux of the problem was the maintenance of political control by a white minority bent upon maintaining white supremacy.[2] But the problem was deeper: with white Republicans and sometimes Democrats trying to control and manipulate the black voters, the real conflict was essentially a struggle between white men—those of the uplands (Piedmont) against those of the lowlands (Black Belt)—for supremacy in the house of North Carolina politics.

In seeking the genesis of the Wilmington race riot, it is necessary to consider the city's political traditions, beginning with its relations with the North Carolina General Assembly. North Carolina's political order is deeply rooted in geopolitics.

After North Carolina achieved what is euphemistically called Redemption and better known as home rule, the "Redeemers" (Bourbon Democrats)

30

built the HOUSE OF NORTH CAROLINA POLITICS and laid the foundation for its perpetuation. This goal was accomplished through such devices as the centralization of the state's election machinery and the complex county election laws throughout North Carolina's three distinct physiographical regions.[3] These regions are the Carolina highlands (made up of the Blue Ridge counties in the extreme west), the Piedmont plateau (the intermediary region lying between the fall line and the base of the Blue Ridge), and the coastal plain (a part of the eastern seaboard). Not only do these three regions coincide with three distinct socioeconomic classes, they also reflect political differences. Historically, these three regions have interacted like jealous and independent states.[4]

Tentacles of the Democratic machinery reached down to the municipal levels, notably in the coastal plain (also known as the east, the black counties, and the Black Belt), embracing the cities where there was a greater Negro than white population. The city of Wilmington, where the Negro voting population significantly exceeded that of the whites, was one of these cities.

On the eve of the twentieth century, North Carolina was basically rural in character. In 1900, for example, there was not a single city of 25,000 people. Excluding Wilmington, the largest in the state, only two other cities (Asheville and Raleigh) had populations above 10,000, while twenty-three others had populations between 2,500 and 10,000.[5] The majority of these were located in the Piedmont region and were inhabited by country folk come-to-town. Furthermore, only seven towns had populations between 2,000 and 2,499; thirty-one had populations between 500 and 1,999; and over two hundred had populations of fewer than 500 inhabitants. Wilmington had a population of 20,055—blacks outnumbering whites by 11,324 to 8,731.[6] The black voting majority was estimated at 1,400.

It was in the coastal plain region that the plantation system, with its economic, social, and political ideals and institutions, developed to its highest degree. After home rule, it remained an area composed predominantly of blacks. The heart of the coastal plain, both geographically and symbolically, was New Hanover County. It was also one of the contiguous eighteen black counties, so labeled because their Negro population exceeded 50 percent. Wilmington was the county seat; it was there that the courts sat and the governmental business of the county was conducted.

Wilmington, with its large population, was the natural leader of the Black Belt's conservatism in the General Assembly; and its conservative representation generally got what it wanted. This was especially true in the establishment of the election machinery to maintain the hegemony of the Democratic party and to checkmate the formidable Negro vote in the Black Belt counties. The process began with gerrymandering, which has a long history of limiting the voting power of blacks. In many Southern and Northern cities, blacks generally lived in one quarter of the town, and their houses were small and close together, making it quite simple to draw lines and put all or most of the black population in one ward. Unlike most residentially segregated cities, however, Wilmington was perhaps the most integrated city of the New South. Blacks were to be found in each of the wards.

The practice of gerrymandering in Wilmington was a legacy of the Redeemers, who gave the General Assembly constitutional power to divide cities into wards. By its charter, Wilmington was divided into five wards in the 1890s. Notwithstanding that the wards were unequal in population, the legislature gave each an equal representation on the city council.[7] Through gerrymandering, the city was so divided as to give the whites a majority in three wards; the single black First Ward had three times more voters than the predominantly white Second, Third, and Fourth wards.[8] The Fifth Ward was another thorn in the Democrats' side, since the majority of its voters were black. The Wilmington policy of gerrymandering was a clear violation of the principle of one man–one vote; it was also an obvious violation of the fundamental principles of apportionment of representation of the Constitution. Hence, the whites by having a majority in three wards, were able to elect seven of the ten aldermen.

By charter, the corporate powers of the City of Wilmington, as granted by the General Assembly in the 1890s, called for a ten-member Board of Aldermen, two to be elected biannually by the voters of each ward. The ten-member Board of Aldermen, having been elected, would in turn elect one of their number as mayor. Then they would proceed to elect or appoint some citizen to the vacancy on the board. It is important to remember this arrangement.

The General Assembly held sway over the cities. The state constitution mandated that the General Assembly "shall have full power by statute to modify, change or abrogate any or all . . . charters, ordinances and provisions relating to municipal corporations . . . [and to] substitute others in their stead."[9]

The General Assembly appointed Wilmington's most powerful organ of government—the Board of Audit and Finance. Created by the Redeemers during the 1875–76 legislature, its enacting law read:" The governor is empowered to appoint five discreet and proper persons . . . one from each of the five wards . . . who shall constitute . . . the Board of Audit and Finance." Under the broad powers given to the board, it had the authority to elect one of its members as chairman, who was also to be "the Commissioner of the sinking fund of the City of Wilmington." The chairman had powers to administer oaths and to issue subpoenas for witnesses to appear and testify before the board, "under like pains and penalties as if summoned by the Superior Court." At the same time, the board had exclusive powers to audit all claims before they were paid, and no contract, bond, or obligation would be valid unless approved by it. Furthermore, the board possessed the power to fix salaries or compensation for the mayor, city clerk, and city treasurer, city attorney, city physician, and all other city officers and employees.[10]

Typical of the numerous cities throughout the nation on the eve of the Progressive movement, an officeholding clique had evolved in Wilmington. It was comprised of a few Democrats—the city bosses. Knowing the art of ward politics, they saw to it that two of their friends always ran for alderman in each ward, and they in turn elected the mayor. These politicians also dominated the Board of Audit and Finance, which enabled them to hold Wilmington's purse strings. In the words of Benjamin F. Keith, they ran Wilmington "as if they owned it." They had a vested interest in conservatism and obtained much of their private money by controlling the affairs of the city. They made politics a matter of financial gain rather than a civic duty.

In one way or another, most city employees were obligated to the city's political order. Beginning with the police force, fire department, and those who worked in the streets, all municipal employees were appointed by the Board of Aldermen, and once appointed such public servants could be removed only at the pleasure of the Board of Audit and Finance and by no other authority.

In the 1890s, the police department was comprised of a chief of police, one captain, three sergeants, and twenty-five regular policemen.[11] The wages for a regular policeman was a mere one dollar per day. The city maintained five fire companies (one in each ward), two of which were black. Policemen and firemen, like other city employees, lived a precarious existence. The term of appointment was not less than one year and never more than two.

Election time was of great importance, because the change of the political party in power inevitably meant a complete change in the police department, from the chief of police down to the lowest member. As employment opportunities were exceedingly limited, the appointees tended to hold on for dear life. They thus became discernible boosters of the old regime during each municipal election. The same was true of the appointed professionals—mayor, city attorney, physician, and clerk, among others.

It could be argued that the Redeemers intended for their political order to last the millennium, but history has often demonstrated that what some men hope to establish permanently, other men may speedily tear down. In the 1890s, salient forces began to prevail against the house, when a farmers' movement triggered an outburst of agrarian radicalism, which found expression in the Populist revolt. The glue that had held the poor whites to the Democratic party came unstuck, as they bolted their party and supported Populism, later to unite under the banner of Fusionism. Wilmington became trapped in the hellishness of battle, as a power struggle ensued between the Fusionists and the Democratic forces. The farmers got control of the legislature and set Wilmington's government on a new course from that charted by the Redeemers. And the ghost of the Negro past was to walk again, not only in Wilmington, but throughout the Black Belt.

2

In 1894, after a reign of almost twenty years, the Democrats were toppled from power by the so-called Fusion coalition of Populists (disgruntled Democrats) and Republicans. The Fusionist-dominated legislature (69 to 49 in the House; 41 to 9 in the senate) was implacably determined to change things. With the Republicans calling the shots, it abolished Wilmington's powerful Board of Audit and Finance and bestowed its authority upon a still more powerful body named the Police Board.[12] The board chairman also served as chairman of the sinking fund. With the cooperation of the Board of Aldermen, the salary of the mayor was fixed and was not to exceed $1,000 per year. In addition, for all work of a permanent nature done on city streets (such as paving, grading, claying, or placing shells), compensation and contracts were to be approved by concurring action of the Board of Aldermen and the Police Board. Then to top it all, the legislature staffed the Police Board entirely with Republicans, including such active party members as William H. Chadbourn, John R. Melton and Silas P. Wright. It is important to remember these three men, for they will play a significant role in this narrative.

The repeal of the undemocratic county election laws had been the major plank of the Republican platform during the campaign; accordingly, the 1895 legislature embarked on the task of dismantling the Democrats' election machinery. A new county election law was carefully designed to restore to the people local self-government and home rule. Succinctly stated, it abolished the Democrats' policy of appointment of local offices and made them all subject to popular elections. The law also meant a change for blacks. Under the Democrats' strict interpretation of election laws, they had been excluded from the polls, primarily in the Black Belt counties. With the more liberal Fusion election laws, it appeared that the floodgates were thrown wide open for black voter participation in government, estimated in some quarters at 120,000 Republican votes. Ironically, this occurred at a time when the South was taut with pervasive racism, and when white supremacy was being refortified by movements for the disfranchisement of blacks and by the new jim crow status. The Fusionists' voter registration laws led to the democratization of the ballot throughout the Black Belt. Once again the black man constituted a formidable element within the Republican party, and his voting power, which had been dormant since Reconstruction, reappeared as a force to be reckoned with. The 1894 Fusionist triumph startled the Democrats, but even more surprises were in store for them. By the time of the gubernatorial election of 1896, the Democratic party was in shambles.

The Republicans passed over Oliver H. Dockery, heavily favored by many blacks, and named as the standard-bearer Daniel L. Russell of Wilmington. Russell owned a large plantation just opposite Wilmington and had for years supplied the city with milk. He began his career as a leader in this vicinity, and was the organizer of the Cape Fear blacks into a powerful political machine.[13] Working closely with G. Z. French, a former carpetbagger, the two men provided leadership for the blacks of Wilmington—at least, such was the belief of the Democrats.

With the Populist defection, the Negro vote being rejuvenated en masse, and the fusion of Populist-Republican forces, the chance of a Democratic victory on the state level was almost hopeless. When the campaign ended and the results were tabulated, Russell emerged victorious and became the first Republican governor since the era of Reconstructuion. He had scored heavily over Cyrus Watson, the Democratic candidate, in the Black Belt region. Factionalism, along with the resurrection of the formidable black Republican vote, had cracked the walls of white solidarity in the Black Belt, where Wilmington was the leading metropolis.

Black voters were the force behind the political upheaval in 1896. Negro majorities in the Black Belt, referred to as "King Numbers," voted en masse for the Republican ticket. It was becoming evident that the political power of the state would be in the hands of those who controlled the Negro vote, thus assuring the Republican officeholders a continuance in office—a grim prospect for the Democratic party of North Carolina.

Black voter participation in government came with a price tag: Negro public officeholdings. Exactly how many blacks held office under Fusion rule has never been determined. An often repeated claim was that there were at least a thousand Negro office-holders in the state after the complete Fusion victory in 1896.

When the 1897 General Assembly convened, it was composed as follows: 39 Populists, 54 Republicans, and 24 Democrats in the house and 25 Populists, 18 Republicans, and 7 Democrats in the senate. With the Republicans in the saddle, the Fusionist forces undertook the task of revising the character of the cities of Wilmington, Raleigh, Goldsboro, New Bern, and Elizabeth City. With Governor Russell working behind the scene, Wilmington was made the exceptional case. Giving no reasons for their actions, the Legislature abolished the Police Board and recreated the Board of Audit and Finance.

Under the influence of Governor Russell, the legislature, on 5 March 1897, enacted a controversial law that amended the Wilmington city charter. The law read: "There shall be elected by the qualified voters of each ward one alderman only, and there shall be appointed by the governor one alderman for each ward and the board of aldermen thus constituted shall elect a mayor according to laws declared to be in force by this act."[14] The act also empowered the governor to fill by appointment any vacancy resulting from the failure to hold an election in a particular ward.

The new law of 1897 was designed to make municipal elections more democratic. According to the original law, there were to be biennial elections, but the Democrats had stayed in power by not holding primary elections. For example, the year the Police Board was created (1895), no municipal election was held. The clothing merchant, S. H. Fishblate, was mayor; he and his Board of Aldermen were held over as required by law until their successors could be duly elected. But in December a somewhat strange political maneuver occurred. Mayor Fishblate (perhaps after an agreement at some caucus or nocturnal meeting) resigned, and the Board of Aldermen elected as mayor William N. Harriss.[15] It is important to remember this political maneuver, for the Democrats had used this stragegy to hold on to the office of mayor for years. Under the unamended city charter, it was the duty of the administration to hold the offices of mayor and aldermen until their successors were "legally elected and qualified."

All of Wilmington's political factions went into action immediately following the publication of the act of 1897, particularly the wily political clique whose bosses had ruled the city for about fifteen years and had determined the election of the mayor and all other public officers. Benjamin F. Keith dubbed that political circle the Old Fox Crowd and the Old Pro Crowd. At the same time, the Democrats' ranks were pervaded with factionalism between the regulars and the reformers.

The regulars were comprised mostly of the Old Fox Crowd and the party conservatives. The reformers wanted to wage a campaign based on white supremacy; they had the united support of white Democrats, whose sights were set on taking over the job of blacks. The reformers were toying with the idea of running two candidates in the wards instead of one as required by law under the new city charter, with the objective of challenging the 1897 act in the courts. Then there were the independent Democrats (not Populists) who were tired of seeing the Old Fox Crowd run the city as if it belonged to them. Keith was the apparent leader of this faction.

City officials, predominantly Democrats, had not been scheduling primary elections, and the act of 1897 mandated biennial primary elections. Naturally, there ensured a lot of political activities in each of the five wards, as caucuses and "owl (nighttime) meetings became quite common with the Fox Crowd, the reformers, and the like. The following description of events was supplied by Keith. Key political personalities were observed frequenting offices and going up and down rear stairs so as to attract as little attention as possible. On a particular night, for example, in a smoke-filled room, a group of thirty or forty men were seen seated on benches and planks supported by boxes. The hum of male voices was clearly audible, and several subjects were discussed. Now and then laughter rang out in different spots. Several times Keith went up and down the stairs. Becoming more and more impatient, he went down to the sidewalk, and saw two men coming in a "gait between a walk and a trot." His countenance lit up as he recognized them.

The men handed him two packages of tickets, but he gave one package back and asked that they help him distribute them quietly to all anti-Democrats before or during the upcoming primary. Every anti-Democrat in each ward was well known. Keith and a friend drew up a list of twelve names—candidates agreed upon for the coming municipal elections, and among these candidates were some blacks. A caucus was called and Keith "explained the object of the call." Then each in attendance was asked to start out and see every "anti" man in the ward.[16] Political history was about to be made in Wilmington by a movement destined to surpass the city's Reconstruction politics.

Under the amended Charter of the City of Wilmington, registration was mandated to be "open for ten days previous" to each biennial election. Thus, on 10 March 1897, for the first time that many people could remember, the Board of Aldermen called for an election to be held fifteen days later. They also appointed people to act in the several wards of the city as registrars and inspectors of elections.

The next day a notice appeared in the *Wilmington Messenger* "which . . . set out in full the 'Facts Agreed,' giving notice that 'an election would be held at the various polling places for the purpose of electing one alderman from each of the five Wards of the city.' " This notice failed to state when the election would be held and was not signed by anyone.[17]

On 12 March a notice appeared in the *Wilmington Messenger* from H. M. Green, chairman of the Democratic Executive Committee of New Hanover County. He exhorted all Democrats to unite their forces and present a solid, aggressive front to the enemy. Urging all Democrats to go to the meetings and work together for the redemption of the city and for the common good, he asked that there be no "reformers and no regulars in the fight." He emphasized that the new city charter would be tested in the courts. "Whether the act is overthrown or not," he maintained, "it behooves the citizens of Wilmington to go to the polls and enter, by their votes, a powerful protest against such a monstrous interference with the people's rights." He closed with these words: "Fie on the dastard who fritters away/A vote that his country is needing today."[18] Green's main purpose, however, was to give notice that an election would be held on Thursday, 25 March 1897 and to specify that the Democratic primaries would be held at eight o'clock in the evening at the following places:

First Ward: At Old Phoenix Hall, Sixth and Brunswick streets
Second Ward: At Audit and Finance Room (City Hall)
Third Ward: At the City Hall (Upstairs)
Fouth Ward: At City Courtroom
Fifth Ward: At Fifth Ward Truck House

The Republicans were not idle either. Following a caucus, a notice was sent out by F. B. Rice, chairman of the Republican Executive Committee of New Hanover County, that on 16 March the Republicans would hold primary meetings in all wards except the Second. Republicans of the First Ward met at the Mount Calvary Baptist Church (black) at Ninth and Bladen streets. Here Andrew J. Walker (black) was nominated by acclamation, while attorney Thomas H. Sutton was unanimously endorsed for mayor. A similar action was taken in the Third Ward, where a meeting was held at Lowrey's Carriage Shop at Eighth and Princess streets. The meeting in the Fourth Ward was held over a grocery store at Seventh and Nun streets. Republican Chairman Rice was endorsed for city clerk and treasurer. Sutton received his second unanimous endorsement for mayor. And finally, the Fifth Ward primary was held at Ruth Hall. Elijah M. Green (black) received the nomination for alderman. David Bryant (black) offered a resolution endorsing Sutton for mayor, and it was adopted with some opposition. At this point Sutton had been endorsed for mayor in three of the wards.[19]

Meanwhile, on 25 March 1897 the Democrats of the First Ward assembled as scheduled at Old Phoenix Hall and Reel Hall and nominated by acclamation C. L. Spencer for alderman. At the same hour, the meeting of the Second Ward was held in the room of the Board of Audit and Finance at City Hall. Prominent citizens included Frank H. Stedman, Colonel Roger Moore, and Thomas W. Clawson, editor of the *Messenger*. With the course of action already agreed upon and with the goal of challenging the special act of 1897, the nomination of two aldermen was immediately declared in order. On the motion of Stedman, the presiding secretary, Clawson was instructed to cast the unanimous votes for James C. Munds and William E. Springer, and "the vote was so cast."[20]

In contrast, a real fight between the regulars and the reformers was taking place in the Third Ward. Some of the more prominent citizens in the Third Ward were S. H. Fishblate (former mayor), William N. Harriss (mayor, 1895–97), Benjamin Keith, Edward F. Johnson, asnd Owen Fennell. Fishblate and his cabal were set on playing the old game of ward politics. It is significant that he had resigned from the office of mayor in December of 1896, and the board of aldermen had elected Harriss to the position. The regulars, with their sights set on the ultimate position of mayor, prearranged a caucus, and Mayor Harriss placed Fishblate's name in nomination. Keith and his group remained silent. Upon taking the rostrum, Fishblate said that "he thought he was out of politics entirely, but at a conference of the executive committee and citizens, they urged him, for the sake of harmonizing the two factions of the party, to become a candidate with E. F. Johnson as his colleague . . . [and] he had consented for the sake of peace and harmony." Putting it bluntly, he told his listeners that their choice was "white or negro rule," and stressed the need for both factions "to pull together and work in harmony for the rule of the white man." In conclusion, Fishblate said that he was willing to do anything to unite the Democratic party, and "if any man makes statements to the contrary and will come to my face, I will tell him he lies." Making it unequivocally clear that he was a candidate, he said: "I am here to ask you to vote for me. I only desire to be a candidate for peace and harmony."[21]

Nevertheless, to challenge the legality of the act of 1897, the reformers appeared resolved to run two candidates. After Fishblate's speech, Johnson was nominated. He took the rostrum and said that "there had been talk of his connection with the nomination in a manner he did not like." He reminded his audience that at a "conference of [the] Executive Committee, it was agreed for the sake of harmony that each faction in the ward put up one man for alderman." Under this arrangement, Fishblate was selected from the regulars and he was selected from the reformers. He claimed that he had conferred with thirty representatives of his faction and they approved of that course. "I announced myself as a candidate," Johnson continued. "I ask the support of no man. I heard of another caucus to select two candidates and I went to it, but got there too late. I do not propose to back down from my position, but I wish to explain my connection with the nomination."

Keith sat quietly through the spirited discussion, and at the proper time he arose and made a crucial proposal on motion that two challengers be appointed. The motion was carried, and the balloting proceeded. When the time came to count the votes, Keith's faction won over Fishblate and Johnson. Afterward, Fishblate took the rostrum and said that "he wished to reiterate that the most important question in this election was whether there shall be white rule or negro rule." "As for me," he declared, "I am with the white man every time."[22] According to Keith, this was the first time that the Fox Crowd had been defeated in fifteen years, and this meant that Fishblate would not be mayor next term. Soon afterward Keith wrote: "Members of the fox group were off to Raleigh and camped at the Capitol, pleading with Governor Russell to appoint mayor Harriss as one of the alderman, or at least as one of his group."[23] A similar struggle occurred in the Fifth Ward. But the real struggle was in the Fourth Ward, where lived such Democrats as H. M. Green, chairman of the Democratic Executive Committee, attorney John W. Bellamy, Jr., attorney Iredell Meares, Colonel Thomas W. Strange, John J. Fowler (former mayor), Walter G. McRae, and Walter E. Yopp.

Meanwhile the Republicans were having a disagreement over who would be mayor—Wright or Sutton. These two, along with William H. Chadbourn, returned from Raleigh where they had gone to consult the governor; later, following a Republican conference, prominent Republicans informed a *Messenger* reporter that Wright, not Sutton, had been decided on for mayor. In denying this rumor, Sutton sent the following message, dated 22 March, to the *Messenger:*

I hear since my return to the city from Raleigh this evening that Dr. Wright is slated for mayor, and that Governor Russell sanctions this move. I saw Governor Russell last night and know that he does not bite his tongue for anyone. If he was for Dr. Wright he would have told me so. The statements current that he is for Dr. Wright . . . are simply false.[24]

In light of the special act of 1897, who did Governor Russell contemplate appointing as aldermen in Wilmington? According to Keith, daily there were rumors of different delegations at the state capital, badgering Governor Russell "to appoint this one or that one and it was the fox crowd that was generally before him."

And who would Governor Russell appoint to the Board of Audit and Finance? Rumor had it that he had intended to appoint all Democrats to the board; but angered at the action of the Democrats in their determination to run two aldermen in each ward and to carry the act to amend the city charter to the state supreme court, it was rumored that Governor Russell was now resolved to appoint all Republicans to the powerful Board of Audit and Finance, and would likewise appoint five Republicans to the Board of Aldermen.

Beginning with the aldermen, Governor Russell appointed Silas P. Wright (white, Republican) in the First Ward; John G. Norwood (black, Republican) in the Second Ward; Benjamin F. Keith (white, Silver party) in the Third Ward; Andrew J. Hewlett (white, Republican) in the Fourth Ward; and D. J. Benson (white, Republican) in the Fifth Ward. To the Board of Audit and Finance, the governor appointed C. W. Yates and H. C. McQueen (Democrats); and James H. Chadbourn, Jr., H. A. DeCove, and John H. Webber (Republicans).[25] Webber was the first black ever to serve on this board. As required by law, the registrars and inspectors of elections issued the certificates of election to the proper officials and "declared them hereby elected."

On 25 March, election day dawned, and the *Messenger* predicted "AN INTERESTING FIGHT PROMISED TODAY." Seventeen extra policemen had been sworn in for duty at the polls. Naturally, there was more than usual interest in the election, and all the wards buzzed with activity. The reformers did not run two candidates as they had previously threatened. Other than one or two ballots upon which two names appeared, the electors, when voting, voted ballots with one name for aldermen. Election day passed off in an exceedingly quiet and orderly manner. The alderman elected were two black Republicans, Andrew J. Walker and Elijah M. Green; and three Democrats, William E. Springer, Owen Fennell, and Walter E. Yopp. It is important to remember the last three names.

The Board of Aldermen was now made up of six Republicans, three Democrats, and one member of the Silver party. The election of the mayor was now the duty of this new board. With a Republican majority, it was a foregone conclusion that the aldermen would elect a member of that party as mayor. In accordance with a previous understanding, the Republicans had, on the night of the election, held a caucus at the courthouse and agreed on that course of action. The disappointed Democrats had not been idle, however, and had also met.

The new aldermen were to be sworn in the next day at noon; then they would proceed to elect one of their members as mayor. Nevertheless, there were rumors that the old Board of Aldermen would meet at ten o'clock and hold their seats, thereby preventing the new aldermen from assuming office. To forestall this action, the Republicans decided to organize in advance; they assembled in the room of the board at City Hall at 9:05 A.M.[26] It quickly became evident that their ranks had been thinned by a defection of three to the Democrats.

Nevertheless, assuming that a quorum was present, the Republicans continued with their plans. The Republican committee chairman city clerk, F. B. Rice, was in attendance, and the aldermen present filed their commissions and certificates of election with him. Justice of the Peace G. Z. French swore in the members of the board. They then signed the oath of office in the clerk's book and filed their individual oaths with the clerk. Then the group organized themselves into a Board of Aldermen. On motion, the election of mayor was by ballot, and Wright won by a six to one margin, with Keith voting in place of the absent Fennell. Board chairman Keith declared Alderman Wright duly elected mayor of the city of Wilmington. The new mayor tendered his resignation as alderman from the First Ward and it was accepted. Justice French then administered the oath of office to the new mayor. Next, the board elected H. C. Twining to fill the vacancy created by the resignation of Wright. Having taken the oath of office, the new mayor and Board of Aldermen immediately took possession of the office of mayor and control of City Hall. Appointing the Populist John R. Melton as chief of police and all other officers and members of the police force was the board's most significant move—at least until the regular meeting of the board on the first Monday in April. Then, on the motion of Alderman Green, the board adjourned.[27]

"Things grow complicated," the *Messenger* reported, and Keith later explained what happened. A few minutes after the new Board of Aldermen had entered City Hall, some Democrats were seen walking quickly toward the building. Three of them (Keith failed to supply names of individuals involved in the scheme) marched up the steps of City Hall, "each one taking one of the elected Democrats by the arm on the street, persuading them not to qualify, as it was all unconstitutional and would be so held by the higher courts. These disappointed politicians, after pleading earnestly for ever so long, finally succeeded in getting them not to qualify. This was their first successful move in bringing about what was their ultimate aim."[28]

Because of the unexpected hour at which the board met, "not more than two dozen spectators were in attendance." As was to be expected, the crowd had increased by the time the Republican board adjourned. The curious spectators did not have to wait long before the defeated mayor, William N. Harriss, and six of the Democratic members of his Board of Aldermen put in their appearance at City Hall with their counsels—attorneys George G. Rountree and Iredell Meares. They hurried into the former mayor's office and immediately went into caucus. Rountree, with Meares concurring, told Harriss and his board that he had given the matter careful consideration with its important demands, and there were grave constitutional questions involved to be determined by the highest judicial tribunal, and it was their duty to bring the matter to the test of judicial decision once and for all. He emphasized that if the act of 1897 was unconstitutional, then no one had been "duly elected and qualified according to law under it, stressing that no one could succeed either Mayor Harriss or his Board of Aldermen; hence it was their "duty to hold over."[29] This advice was just what the Democrats wanted to hear.

News soon circulated around town of the peculiar happenings at City Hall, and by eleven o'clock quite a number of spectators were looking on. Fifteen minutes later, following the caucus with their attorneys, Harriss called the old Board of Aldermen to order. He announced that a quorum was present and stated that the board was ready for any business that might come before it. Then Alderman Thomas D. Meares arose and said:

As you are aware, an election [was] held in the city yesterday, under an act of the General Assembly, for members of the Board of Aldermen. There are also parties holding certificates of appointment from the Governor as Aldermen of the several wards, it being intended that those elected and those appointed should constitute the new Board of Aldermen for the city. The members of this Board having reason to believe that a contest will be made over the constitutionality of this act of the Legislature.[30] In making the board's intention clear, Meares told the crowd that Mayor Harris had resolved not to surrender the city government to claims by anybody of citizens until required to do so by the courts. The terms of the city clerk, treasurer, and chief of police having expired, this board filled all three positions with former chief of police R. W. Clowe, who was elected unanimously. Completing these measures, the board adjourned at 11:45 A.M.[31]

Meanwhile, the crowd around City Hall had grown larger, and voices from the gathering filled the streets with murmurs and rumors. According to the *Messenger,* "it was a good natured crowd of both white and black, and all seemed amused at what was in the wind."[32]

On that same morning of 26 March, a new development occurred in the Office of Audit and Finance. The three defeated members of Mayor Wright's Board of Aldermen—Springer, Fennell, and Yopp—now appeared at City Hall, accompanied by counsel, John W. Bellamy, Jr., Thomas W. Strange, and Junius Davis. After holding a caucus, the three aldermen held a regular meeting with the five Democratic runners-up from the five wards who claimed (on the gorunds of the unconstitutionality of the act amending the city charter) to have been elected on Thursday. All received their certificates of election and were sworn in as aldermen by Justice of the Peace John J. Fowler. At noon they were called to order, with Springer being in the chair. Then they organized themselves into a Board of Aldermen and nominated H. M. Green and Walker Taylor for mayor,[33] with the former being elected and sworn in by Justice of the Peace Fowler.

"A pretty kettle of fish," noted the *Messenger,* pointing out that Wilmington now had three mayors simultaneously. In the meantime, Green began a search for Wright, in order to demand the keys to the offices. He finally found the mayor at the Orton Hotel where he took his meals. It was 1:25 P.M., and Mayor Wright had just come out of the dining room; he was accosted by Green, who handed him the following letter:

Dear Sir: I hereby notify you that I was today elected Mayor of the city of Wilmington by the lawfully constituted board of aldermen of said city composed of C. L. Spencer, alderman from the First ward and W. E. Springer and James C. Munds, aldermen from the Second ward, Owen Fennell and Washington Catlett, aldermen from the Third ward, Walter Yopp and H. McL. Green, aldermen from the Fourth ward and W. E. Mann, alderman from the Fifth ward, all present and voting. Having been informed that you have taken possession of said office by force of arms under some pretended authority, I demand that you surrender the same to me at once.[34]

The next day, Saturday, 27 March, another claimant for the office of mayor surfaced. On this day, aldermen Spring, Fennell, and Yopp, who had the day before participated in the organization of the board that elected Green as mayor, notified the two black aldermen—Walker from the First Ward and Elijah M. Green from the Fifth Ward—to meet at three o'clock at City Hall for the purpose of organizing themselves into a Board of Aldermen. The three defeated aldermen met at the designated time, but aldermen Green and Walker failed to appear. Claiming to represent the people's interest, the three defeated aldermen organized themselves into an alleged Board of Aldermen. Completing this move, they elected Taylor as mayor, and he then took the oath of office.[35]

On the next Monday, 29 March, at eight in the morning, Mayor Wright and his Board of Aldermen met to complete the city's governmental organization. "Regular Meetings of the Board of Aldermen," the *Messenger* announced, notifying the public that city officials would be elected to the highest-paying positions, and appointments would be made—from policemen down to street workers. A large and orderly crowd milled outside while some people filed into the courtroom, in which an iron railing divided the room from east to west. The room was packed with people standing outside the railing. There were cheers and applause when Mayor Wright entered. City Clerk Rice was already at his post. Also present were the board's attorneys—Marsden Bellamy, A. G. Ricaud, and E. K. Bryan. Mayor Wright arose and informed the spectators that before calling the Board of Aldermen to order he desired to issue some instructions for Chief of Police Melton. Then Melton was ordered not to permit anyone to enter the enclosure while the mayor's court was in session, with the exception of city officials having business with the board, attorneys, reporters of the city newspapers, defendants, and witnesses as they were called to testify.

After calling the board to order, Wright told the audience that the object of

Dr. Silas P. Wright, deposed mayor of Wilmington. From *Collier's Weekly*, **November 26, 1898 (Library of Congress).**

the meeting was to elect the various city officials. There was another out-burst of applause and cheers. Immediately Mayor Wright countered the uproar by ordering the police to clear the hall if there were any more inter-ruptions.

The first order of business was the election of the city clerk and treasurer. Failing after four ballots, the election was deferred until the board's next regular meeting. The body then proceeded to nominate Melton as chief of police. On motion by Alderman Walker, the entire police department was elected as a body. By a vote of six to one (Keith voted for Z. P. Thomas), the board elected an all-black health board, headed by Dr. William D. McMillan, who was elected superintendent of health. L. H. Bryant was elected superin-tendent of streets. Alderman Hewlett again took up the caucus list and nominated Charles Schnibben (of Howard Relief Steam Fire Engine Com-pany No. 1) for fire chief. Some of the other blacks elected were John Carroll (day janitor at City Hall), Thomas E. Scott (messenger at City Hall), and Thomas Rivers (cattle weigher).[36] It is significant that the persons filling these positions were basically new to public office and were Republicans. If this new party remained in power, they could become an exclusive officeholding group, reminiscent of the old Democratic clique.

From the outset, the Democratic leaders were resolved to challenge the act of 15 March 1897 in the courts; accordingly, an unusual legal maneuver followed in the wake of Wilmington's mayoral elections of 1897. Most of the legal talent in the city became involved and lined up behind either the defendants or the plaintiffs.[37] On 14 April 1897, with Judge J. D. McIver presiding, there began three days of long winded quo-warrantos of eloquence.

The Democratic plaintiffs had three chances in four to oust the Republicans. First, the court could hold that the entire act was unconstitutional and that the election held under it was invalid. In this event, there would be no legally qualified aldermen to succeed Mayor Harriss and his board. Since they had refused to surrender their offices voluntarily, they could legally be reinstated to power. Second, the court could hold that the act was unconstitutional as to the appointive power of the governor, but was constitutional in other respects. The unconstitutional clause could then be eliminated or restructured under the old charter, which could be amended by reducing the aldermen to one for each ward instead of two for each ward. In this event, the three Democratic aldermen recently elected—Springer, Fennell, and Yopp—and the two Republicans elected from the First and Fifth wards would constitute the Board of Aldermen of the city, who would then elect the mayor. Third, the court could hold that the entire act was unconstitutional, but that the election was valid as having been held under the provisions of the old charter, and that the ten men receiving the highest vote totals would constitute the Board of Aldermen. For the Republicans, the court could hold that the act amending the city charter, whereby the governor was given the power to appoint the five aldermen, was constitutional, and that the election was indeed valid. If so, Mayor Wright and his board would remain in office.

The opening argument for the Democrats was presented by John D. Bellamy, Jr., counsel for Green and his associates. He spoke for nearly two hours, attacking the act of 1897 and declaring that it was an absolute infringement of the principle of local self-government. He also quoted numerous authorities to show that the bill under which five aldermen were elected and five appointed was contrary to the inherent rights of the people. Referring to the right to revolt, as demonstrated during the Stamp Act crisis, he declared that "it was quite in the order of things for Wilmington to be resisting the infamous legislation by which her citizens are deprived of local self-government, for it was the citizens of this city who first resisted the odious British stamp act."

Bellamy closed at 11:55 A.M. and was followed by Frank McNeill, counsel for Taylor and his group. Speaking for one hour, he argued for the elimination of the unconstitutional clause—the governor's power to appoint the five aldermen. If the clause were eliminated, he said, the five aldermen elected under the act of 1897 would constitute the Board of Aldermen. He was followed by William B. McKoy, another counsel for Green. Much of his argument was concerned with the denunciation of the appointing powers of

Governor Russell. He also contended that the Republican aldermen who had sat with the five appointed aldermen and had elected Wright to be mayor had forfeited their right as elected aldermen. Following the same line of reasoning, he said that the three Democratic aldermen who met and organized with the board that elected Green, and who subsequently met by themselves and elected Taylor had also "forfeited their election by that action."

Thomas W. Strange, yet another counsel for Green's group, who had been speaking when the court took a recess, resumed his argument and spoke for an hour and three-quarters. His line of argument was replete with references to the unconstitutionality of the act of 1897. Employing numerous citations from legal authorities to support his points, he closed dynamically with quotes from the Bill of Rights.

Junius Davis, also counsel for Green, speaking for exactly half an hour, made a very able argument along the same lines as John D. Bellamy, Jr., had earlier.

Attorney E. K. Bryan's argument for Mayor Wright was brief, lasting only eighteen minutes, and stressed the absolute constitutionality of the act of 5 March 1897. Marsden Bellamy, counsel for Wright, controverted the arguments of his brother, John D. Bellamy. Speaking for an hour and a half, he argued that the legislature had full power to pass the acts of 1895 and 1897, and he held that both were absolutely constitutional. He quoted a host of authorities and argued that under the constitution the legislature has absolute control of every branch of a municipal government, except that of finance. A. G. Ricaud, also counsel for Wright, spoke for two hours and ten minutes, and his citation of authorities was exhaustive and very strong in support of his position. Like Bryan, he maintained that the act of 5 March 1897, under which five aldermen were elected and five were appointed, was constitutional in whole, and that the election of five aldermen and the appointment of five under its provisions was valid.

ᴖ Then followed Herbert McClammy, counsel for Harriss and his board, speaking for three-quarters of an hour. Of the arguments in Mayor Harriss's behalf, that of George Rountree was the most notable and extended over two days. In his argument, he fortified himself with many citations of eminent authorities. He also discussed the act establishing the Board of Audit and Finance. After speaking for about an hour and a half he suspended his argument, because court was adjourned for the day, but he informed the court that he would continue the following morning. The next day, his arguments were along the line that the act of 1897 was "wholly unconstitutional," again quoting many authorities in a masterly manner. He ended with the contention that Harriss and the old Board of Aldermen still formed the legal government of Wilmington and would until their successors were elected and qualified.[38] Thus, Rountree's arguments closed the court contest over the mayoral election.

The public anxiously awaited the outcome. The *Messenger* notified them:

"Judge McIver Decides in Favor of Mayor Harriss." His ruling was stern and clear: The act of 1897 was unconstitutional, no valid election had been held, and the board known as the Harris Board was entitled to the offices of mayor and aldermen of the city of Wilmington.[39] His ruling ordered the defendant Silas P. WRight and his board of aldermen to vacate their offices and deliver the possession thereof to Harriss and his Board.

Naturally, the controversy was appealed to the state supreme court. By common consent, the four cases were again consolidated for the September term in 1897 in the Supreme Court of North Carolina before Chief Justice William T. Faircloth and associate justices Walter Clark, David M. Furches, Robert Douglas, and Walter A. Montgomery.[40] The issues and arguments were the same and need not be repeated here. Nevertheless, the logic leading to Justice Faircloth's decision is interesting.

"Under our system," Justice Faircloth began, "sovereign power resides with the people . . . [and] the sovereign people have established national and state constitutions, and these constitutions are the supreme law of the land."[41] Justice Faircloth was no states' righter. Like Daniel Webster in his historic debate with Robert Y. Hayne, he pointed out that in establishing governments, people divide and subdivide the powers of government, and that the legislative branch was invested with a vast range of powers. Directing his remarks to the plaintiffs, he emphasized that these great powers were exercised at "legislative discretion."

He reminded the plaintiffs that legislative bodies sometimes abuse the exercise of powers. But no people, he told the court, "have yet been able to establish a government capable of accomplishing its legitimate ends and also incapable of some inconvenience and mischief." To those lawyers who argued that the law assumed more power than authorized, he said: "How it exceeds the authority is not clearly pointed out. Constitutions are general in their provisions and do not enter into details. Certainly, our has not done so in this instance." To those who argued that the act infringed on the power and principle of local self-governmetn, he quoted the Latin phrase of jurisprudence, *lex ita scripta est* ("it is the law as written").

Justice Faircloth contended that the people had clearly invested their representatives in the legislature with the power in question, "to be exercised at their discretion, with which the Court cannot interfere." Accordingly, he reversed the superior court's decision with these words: "Our opinion is that defendant Wright and his board of aldermen are the rightful owners of the offices in the city government now occupied by them."[42]

Associate justices Montgomery and Clark concurred, the latter saying, "It was the duty of this Court to construe what has been enacted by constitutional conventions or, within their powers, by Legislative assemblies."[43]

With three chances in four, and with their most skillful attorneys, the Democrats bungled their case. The Republicans' triumph in the courts naturally angered the Democrats; but if they had failed in the municipal elections of 25 March 1897 and in the subsequent September state supreme court decision, they had to wait only eighteen months to unseat the Republicans by the ballot. The North Carolina Supreme Court had ruled the act of 1897 valid, and with Wilmington's black majority, surely the Republicans would be successful in the next city elections. Their political power would be maintained indefinitely—a grim prospect for the Democrats. They began to look around for alternatives, as the Democrats lined up politically and looked expectantly toward the campaign of 1898. Frustrated by the opinion of North Carolina Supreme Court, leading Democrats of Wilmington were implacably resolved to go the route of a coup d'état if necessary, and to take over the government by revolutionary methods.

2
The Ax Is Laid: The Wilmington Conspiracy

SOMETIMES the public is the last to know. The Wilmington Democrats were ostensibly attending to their day-to-day concerns, but beneath the placid surface some were spinning webs of intrigue. The details of historical conspiracies are hard to verify unless they have the characteristics of Crédit Mobilier, Teapot Dome, or Watergate. These contrived acts will take place, encompassing a series of diabolical plots. The sociopolitical conditions of Wilmington in the 1890s presented the Democrats with an opportunity to impose their style of thought upon the movements they led.

When the riot and coup were first conceived, and who was behind them, are both shrouded in mystery. Thomas W. Clawson, editor of the *Wilmington Messenger*, wrote years later that "for a period of six to twelve months prior to November 10, the white citizens of Wilmington prepared quietly but effectively for the day when action would be necessary."[1] Harry Hayden, whose papers are in the depository at the Duke University Library, has written that the idea originated with a "group of nine influential citizens": J. Alan Taylor, Hardy I. Fennell, W. A. Johnson, L. B. Sasser, William Gilchrist, P. B. Manning, E. S. Lathrop, Walter L. Parsley, and Hugh McRae. He dubbed this self-styled Committee of Democrats the "Secret Nine."[2]

Several nights after their initial gathering at McRae's home the Secret Nine held a second meeting at Parsley's home. At this time, they "mapped out a city-wide protective campaign that was to be conducted [and] co-ordinated with the state-wide 'White Supremacy' movement," which was to burgeon forth in the 1898 statewide election. They also proceeded to divide the city into sections, placing a "responsible" citizen in charge of each of the city's five wards and designating these men as ward captains, whose main responsibilities were to direct the activities of the block lieutenants and the citizenry of their respective wards. Lathrop and Manning acted as liaisons for the Secret Nine—the only two chosen by the revolutionaries to pass on

49

orders and suggestions to the ward captains. Hayden maintained that the "existence of this secret group was known to none, save to the nine members themselves."[3]

The web of conspiracy was widening. Hayden reports that another group of citizens, oblivious to the fact that a secret movement had already been organized, was directing a similar group, which assembled at William L. Smith's residence, across the street from the old Bellamy mansion at Fifth and Market streets. This second group, including Smith, was composed of John Berry, Henry G. Ferrell, Thomas D. Meares, and Walker Taylor.[4] Meanwhile, the Secret Nine continued to hold their meetings at Parsley's home on Market Street and planned to instigate the Wilmington race riot on the day after the statewide election on 10 November 1898.[5] The Secret Nine, contended Hayden, "did not discountenance this auxiliary group of revolutionaries, as they were also men of prominence and influence."

The men of both organizations were playing a difficult game. They did manage to maintain a cloak of mystery about their organizations, yet it is hard to ascertain the actual extent of this cloak. Some men, like Walker Taylor, were also members of the legitimate policymaking bodies, and the revolutionary groups were able to keep in close contact with each other.

Both groups contended that under the Fusionist administration the city government was paralyzed with incompetency, and that New Hanover County was equally demoralized in the administrative branch; Wilmington, in particular, was experiencing an epidemic of crime. The conspirators charged that blacks had control of the city government, not by virtue of election, but through the connivance of the legislature and the governor, who desired the humiliation of the decent people among whom he had lived prior to his elevation. They also held Governor Russell responsible for the special act of 1897, which amended the city charter and enabled him to appoint five members of the Board of Aldermen. The result of this act was that Silas P. Wright was elected mayor; in their opinion, he was not qualified for the position.

In reality, Mayor Wright was held in respect throughout most of the city—even in some Democratic quarters. Nevertheless, as an outsider (a carpetbagger, in fact), Wright became the focus of some resentment. His life-style infuriated some poorer Democrats. He maintained an office on the north side of the Fourth Street bridge, on the fringe of the black community of Brooklyn. The "dapper mayor" always wore a Prince Albert, white gloves, and a black felt hat, and was often seen driving a pair of prancing black horses through the city.[6]

According to the Secret Nine, the Populist chief of police, John R. Melton, was also not qualified for his position. Complaints against him included the charge that he owned no property and lived in a cheap, rented house. His police force, composed of whites and blacks of questionable character, was thoroughly demoralized and respected by no class of citizens, and the lawless defied it at will. Policemen were often scoffed at and resisted when trying to make an arrest, and if they succeeded in arresting a violater, the chief would always release the culprit on bond.[7] Finally, the New Hanover County government, so it was claimed, had passed into the control of the Populists and Republicans with the fall election of 1896, under the county system provided by the Fusion legislature.

G. Z. French, a former orderly in General Willim T. Sherman's army, was another special target of the conspirators.[8] He was chief deputy sheriff of New Hanover County. His political enemies claimed that it was French's wish to be elected sheriff, but Governor Russell wanted him in the General Assembly. An arrangement was made by which Elijah Hewlett would be sheriff and would receive a nominal salary from the office, and French, after coming back from the legislature, would administer the office and take the fees. French was therefore de facto sheriff, and the greater number of his deputies were Negro politicians of objectionable character. Hewlett was afterward indicted for farming out his office, and rather than face the indictment, he settled out of court.[9]

The sheriff of New Hanover County was allegedly surrounded by black deputies, and the criminal court was a travesty of the administration of the law. Critics charged that the room was packed with blacks who took possession of the criminal court, crowding the juries and intimidated their members—they frequented the courthouse only for that purpose. It was impossible to convict a Negro of any offense when the blacks did not want him convicted. Furthermore, the complaints charged that the court was run by a group of Negro lawyers, incompetent and insolent, and that Judge David B. Sutton seemed to encourage their presence.[10] In this Southern town, Negro lawyers had an opportunity to sass white men in the courts! This situation gave the Democrats an opportunity to discredit Wilmington's four black attorneys—L. A. Henderson, William A. Moore, Armond W. Scott, and L. P. White. Since this group of Negro lawyers made it difficult to convict a Negro, the white lawyers of the Wilmington bar practically withdrew their participation from the criminal court.[11]

Perhaps no other cause contributed more to the demoralization of the county and the city than the administration of the law in the criminal court. Judge Sutton was apparently indifferent to the alleged miscarriage of justice, and he did not command the respect of either race. The conspirators contended that, as the Negro's power behind these officials grew in strength, it grew equally in insolent self-assertion.

The Negro thus began to feel that he was in the saddle, the reins were in his hands, he was riding and he steered the white men when and where he pleased. Wilmington was being advertised as a town for blacks, and they were flocking to it from all sections.[12] In the judgment of the Secret Nine, conditions in Wilmington were going from bad to worse, until it became evident to them that the city had to be either turned over to the blacks or taken by the whites. Accordingly, the Secret Nine was resolved that whites should seize control of Wilmington and reestablish white supremacy.

2

As the groundwork was laid for the Wilmington conspiracy, blacks were depicted as the perpetrators of most crimes. Accounts of Negro felonies appeared more frequently in the local papers, with every crime committed by blacks playing right into the hands of the Democrats. The local papers were replete with the stereotype of the era that blacks were prone to criminality. For example, the *Messenger* reported a theft as follows: "Negro Man Boldly Stole a Cheese." Later the missing cheese was found at Panpe's store; there the "thief," after making a vain attempt to effect a sale, had abandoned it. Another time, the *Messenger* reported that "impudent Negroes would enter stores operated by white business men, take what they wanted and walk out without paying for what they had taken." Still another account declared that "a Negro burglar was detected by two ladies. Neighbors were called and the burglar secured. On the following morning, notwithstanding the frequent happening of these burglaries, the chief of police released the fellow on a straw bond and before night he was out of the city."[13]

Some of these news reports were circulated in both the South and the North. Under the title "Alleged Conditions in Wilmington under the Republicans," an Atlanta correspondent wrote: "One citizen captured a negro on the street carrying articles which had been stolen from the citizen's house several days before. The police had been given a description of the articles stolen, and the prisoner stated that he had passed five policemen with the plunder in his arms." An identical piece appeared in New York in the *Literary Digest.*[14]

During the Fusionist administration, blacks were supposed to have become more insolent, openly displaying malice and disrespect toward whites in public. Harry Hayden reported: "Hugh McRae . . . was standing in the intersection of Seventh and Market streets conversing with a friend one day. A dray, drawn by a fast stepping horse, was approaching. There was plenty of space for this two-wheeled vehicle to pass, but the Negro driver lashed his horse and snarled as he drove defiantly towards the white men, who had to step up on the sidewalk to keep from being run down."[15] Similarly, the *Messenger* reported that in Wilmington, white men, in order to avoid a collision and cause for a race fight, were shutting their eyes and stopping up their mouths. For instance, an elderly white man of character was seen being pushed into the street by two "raw-buck niggers" when there was plenty of room for all on the sidewalk.[16]

Whites complained of corruption and brutality on the part of Negro policemen. In an editorial, "A Sample Negro Policeman," one white said: "Monday night, about 10:30 o'clock on the beat on Front, between Dock and

Orange streets, a Negro policeman joined a mulatto woman who came out of a shop with a bottle of liquor. He put his arm around her, and the pair went down the alley in the direction of what is known as 'Hell's Half Acre,' and they did not return during the fifteen minutes I waited."[17] G. Fred Orsland, of Cambridge, Maryland, wrote: "While in Wilmington we were very comfortably located. We spent part of Saturday, August 13, at Ocean View, where the spectacle of a burly negro fighting a white policeman and defying everybody was witnessed."[18]

There were also reports of black police brutality. The *Literary Digest* reported, "Last winter . . . a negro policeman entered the store of a prominent merchant and beat him unmercifully. The policeman said that the merchant had insulted his little daughter. The merchant had waited on her during the morning, and not having what she wanted she went home. The negro policeman was never punished."[19]

The conspirators did not neglect Negro dealings with white women, a sensitive subject in Southern race relations. The Reverend Alexander J. McKelway wrote in *Outlook* that white women were slapped in the face on absolutely no provocation. Most of the testimony as to the language used to refined and gentle women was unprintable.[20]

The *New Bern Journal* reported: "One day last week a young lady of this city, returning home on one of New Bern's public streets, came to where three young negro men stood on the sidewalk in such a way as to obstruct the way. They made no effort to move so as to let her pass. She chose to leave the walk in order to pass around them. As she did so and reached a point opposite the three negroes, one of the brutes, seeing what he considered 'airs' in the young lady stretched out and slapped her in the face."[21]

The *Messenger* reported a similar occurrence: "The wife of a highly respected gentleman went down to the shore on Middle Sound, about 100 yards in the rear of her home, to gather some oysters. While there three negro soldiers came suddenly to her and extending their hands asked her to shake hands with them. This, of course, she declined to do and turned to run toward home, whereupon they offered the most insulting indignities."

On 19 September 1898, Joseph Gore signed an affidavit before Justice of the Peace George H. Bellamy:

Some days ago my daughter, aged 15 years, was returning from Sunday School, accompanied by her little brother aged 12 years, about 3 o'clock in the afternoon. When about a quarter of a mile from home, two negro boys, aged about 16 to 18 years, ran after my daughter, with their coats turned over their heads to conceal their identity, and attempted to take hold of her, and doubtless would have placed their unholy hands on her person, and had it not been for her screams, would have doubtless accomplished their purpose. This was done in Town Creek township, in broad daylight.[22]

Black women were also accused of insolence, especially toward white women. The *Wilmington Star* wrote: "black women insult white women in a disgraceful affair" by refusing to give the white women half the sidewalk. After forcing her off the sidewalk, the Negro woman struck the white woman over the shoulder with an umbrella. A Negro man standing nearby called approvingly, "That's right, give her hell."[23] Citing another case of such insolence, the *Wilmington Messenger* described a young white woman, dressed in white, who "stepped upon the Trent bridge to walk out a short distance to feel the cool breeze that usually passes up the river. Passing the negro woman she was startled by a woman walking close to her and thrusting the point of an umbrella into her side. She walked a little further, and turning to go home she again encountered the black wench, who again did the same thing, saying, 'Oh, you think you are fine.' "[24] Similarly, another incident occurred one Sunday afternoon: "Some colored women met some white youths on the street. One of the women insolently shoved one of the boys into the ditch and then turned loose upon him a filthy tirade of abuse. The same day a colored woman passing along the street insolently shoved her elbow into the face of a white man who was standing in his yard leaning over the fence.'"[25]

The conspirators did not exclude black children from the propaganda. White children were allegedly abused on their way to school and crowded off the widewalk by Negro children who taunted and insulted them.

In *Outlook,* the Reverend Mr. McKelway wrote that Negroes talked openly of "burning the town," of "killing the women as they ran into the street"; the nurses began to threaten the safety of their charges, and the cooks began to hint at poisoning. There was a great deal of talk of matches and kerosene and even dynamite. The black churches were said to be hotbeds of murderous ideas. The Negroes began to gather in mobs, blocking the streets, and the policemen were powerless. The streetcars were often stoned, and once or twice they were fired into. Another column bewailed: "In wanton deviltry the street cars in the remote section of the city were fired upon by lawless negroes. On one occasion a motorman of one of these street cars discovered a negro in the act of firing upon the car. He attempted to pursue him and was stopped by a mob of negroes, and, though a riot was threatened . . . neither the chief of police nor the mayor of the city could be found, and not until a number of citizens took the situation in hand was a riot prevented."[26]

One who fully understands Southern race relations in this era could hardly believe that most of the episodes described actually occurred; but these aspersions had a purpose. The Wilmington conspirators were creating an environment that would justify the white citizens' buying firearms for the protection of their homes, and that would also justify the organization of vigilance committees. The white citizens were organizing for the protection of life and property, to act in concert rather than individually against the enemy. The foe was not an outsider; he was in their very midst and was very discernible—he was black.

3

The Wilmington race riot might not have occurred without the fortuitous impact of the statewide white supremacy crusade in 1898, unparalleled in American history. This was not the year of a gubernatorial election, which gives an added dimension to this effervescence of racism. Although this was the year of the Spanish-American War, in North Carolina the war occupied a secondary place to the white supremacy campaign. It was relegated to that position particularly by the *Raleigh News and Observer* and by many leading Democrats. Perhaps former governor Jarvis expressed the majority sentiments when he said; "Imperialism, it will cut no figure whatsoever, we are too much interested in home affairs to discuss the fate of the Philippines."[27]

The Democratic leaders resolved that the political campaign of 1898 would be one of redemption. They called for the restoration of good government and white supremacy in North Carolina. This weighty task fell upon the shoulders of shrewd Furnifold M. Simmons, chairman of the state Democratic Executive Committee. One of his contemporaries spoke of him as the grandest statesman that North Carolina had produced in half a century. He was recognized as "a genius in putting everybody to work—men who could write, men who could speak, and men who could ride—the last by no means the least important."[28]

Chairman Simmons was fully aware that his party would face defeat in the upcoming elections unless the campaign were waged on some issue that would cut across party lines. Southern political history had long demonstrated that the question of Negro participation in politics was a smoldering flame which could easily be fanned into a full one. He decided, therefore, to make *Negro rule* or *white supremacy* the watchwords upon which to return the Democrats to power. Charges of corruption, scandals, and extravagance were to be leveled against the Republican-Populist regime, but these were to be given secondary consideration. The campaign was to be increasingly centered around the issue of blacks' sharing in government. The color line would be so sharply drawn that, ultimately, little else would be talked about. All the offenses charged against the Fusion rule were made dependent upon the Negro in politics.

Simmons also bypassed the old Democratic personalities and recruited a group of aggressive, colorful, and dynamic young supporters from each of the state's sections—the Piedmont, the Carolina highlands, and the coastal plain. Among them was Josephus Daniels, editor of the *Raleigh News and Observer,* the Democrats' voice and publicity organ, which was relied upon to carry their theme and was the militant voice of white supremacy. In the

Black Belt, the *Wilmington Messenger* would ultimately give hints of things to come: that "the Democrats intended to overthrow the present political conditions—peacefully if possible, but by revolution if necessary." But the rallying cries of "black domination" and "Negro rule" would come directly from the Democratic Executive Committee, from which the people of Wilmington, and of all of North Carolina, would hear intensifying appeals to reestablish white supremacy.

Immediately following a key meeting of the Democratic Executive Committee in Raleigh on 20 November 1897, the first statewide call for white unity was issued. It was an eloquent address, written by Francis D. Winston of Bertie County. It called upon all white to unite and "re-establish Anglo-Saxon rule and honest government in North Carolina." It reported that evil times had followed as a consequence of turning over local offices to blacks. And the outcome—"Homes have been invaded, and the sanctity of woman endangered. Business has been paralyzed and property rendered less valuable. The majesty of law has been disregarded and lawlessness encouraged." Such conditions were "wrought by a combination of Republican and Populist leaders." The Democratic party promised to correct these abuses and restore security once more to the "white women of the state." To accomplish these ends, a clarion call was sounded: "Let every patriot rally to the white man's party. To your tents: O Israel."[29] In the 1898 campaign, the Democrats were to be the heroes, the saviors, the new redeemers, who would rescue the state from the villains—Republican-Fusionist regime.

From the outset, the Democrats made it clear that Negro domination did not mean that the government in every part of the state was under the control of Negro influence. They pointed out that few Negroes lived in the western part of the state; only the counties and towns of the eastern part were under Negro rule. Supplying figures to document their charges, the Democrats maintained that there were forty Negro justices of the peace in New Hanover County; thirty-one in Edgecombe; ten in Bertie; twenty-seven in Craven; twenty-nine in Halifax; fifteen in Vance; seventeen in Granville; and seventy-one in Caswell. The other counties had numerous Negro magistrates, sheriffs, deputies, and collectors of deeds. Wilmington and New Hanover County were made special examples of Negro domination; it was said that in the fall of 1898, there were as many as ninety-three blacks holding offices in the city and county governments, including some six or seven Federal appointive offices.

Historians in general have neglected to analyze the real meaning of *black domination*. The term certainly meant more than the suggestion of a predominance of blacks holding public offices. During an era of pervasive racism, many encounters made whites' blood boil with indignation. For instance, a Negro justice of the peace might summon by warrant a white man or woman to appear before him. White men were not familiar with the prospect of being arrested by a Negro policeman or of a Negro officer in charge of a white and Negro prisoner chained together. White women surely objected to having their homes inspected by Negro sanitation officers. Black lawyers got most of the business in the criminal courts, where blacks were able to dispute the testimony of whites. In New Hanover County, the whites complained of injustices before Negro magistrates, that equality before the law was a misnomer. If the legal question was between a Negro and a white man, they felt that the Negro had his case won before it was ever heard. In most cases there were two school committees—one for the whites and another for the blacks. The Democrats distorted the question, however, by claiming that Negro school committee members had authority to inspect the schools where the sons and daughters of white men are taught.

The *Messenger* pointed out that in some counties, such as Richmond, "there are negro overseers of the public roads. The white men of those down-trodden communities [are] being obliged to go out and work the public roads under negro overseers." In criticizing this policy, the paper said: "We cannot express our abhorrence of all these things. Will the white men give it their countenance?"[30]

With regard to patronage positions, a black, John Campbell Dancy, held the prestigious position of collector of customs at the Port of Wilmington. A nonresident of the city who had been reappointed by President McKinley in the summer of 1897, he had replaced a prominent local Democrat, Captain William Rand Kenan. Other Democrats replaced by Republicans were V. S. Worth (special deputy collector) and Edgar G. Parmele (deputy collector and chief inspector).[31] These changes were sufficent to equip Kenan for the military role he would play during the riot.

Now and then, the *Messenger* depicted Fusion corruption and made attacks upon Governor Russell; but mostly, the Negro was pilloried in the most sinister manner, with ugly cartoons cunningly drawn to make their points. The state Democratic chairman, Simmons, had scattered a large amount of racist propaganda, which preceded every speaker throughout the state. The Populists were in no way deceived by the Democrats' strategy. They warned the people that the Democratic machine was crying "nigger" with the purpose of diverting attention from real issues. Earlier, the Populists' official organ, the *People's Paper,* had pointed out that the "Negro Scare Crow" appeared every two years; just before election time, the Democrats shout at the top of their voices, "Nigger! Nigger! Nigger! . . . ." After a good rest, the paper stated, "The 'old crow' will again apear in your papers. It seems that something should be done to drive the political scarecrow from the door of the poor white man." The editorial suggested that the scarecrow be placed by the Democrats' ballot box. "Niggers to Work, Poor Whites to Vote" was the headline prediction.[32]

In the wake of political oratory and literary and cartoon propaganda movements, there emerged another strategem of the Democrats—the White Government Union clubs. These grass-roots clubs were the brainchild of

Edgar G. Parmele (1854?–1911), Chief of Police. From *Collier's Weekly*, November 26, 1898 (Library of Congress).

Francis Winston.[33] Their constitution read: "The White Government Union club, known as White Supremacy Club, with the purpose to fully restore and make permanent in North Carolina the SUPREMACY OF THE WHITE RACE." Under bylaw[11], both women and boys under twenty years of age were admitted as members, but they could not vote.[34] The White Government Union clubs were designed to engender a patriotic loyalty to the gospel of white supremacy in every community. The Democratic newspapers carried notices of meetings, urging every white man, regardless of former party affiliations, to identify himself with the Union. Becoming Democratic cliques, they experienced accelerated growth in both the Piedmont and Black Belt.

4

Determined to defeat the Republican-Populist coalition, the Democrats left no avenues unexplored. In early August, Josephus Daniels, editor of the *Raleigh News and Observer,* sent for the talented cartoonist, Norman Jennett, who was called "Sampson Huckleberry" because he was a native of Sampson County, famous for its big berries. He had once worked on the *News and Observer* for six dollars a week.[35] He later studied in New York where his drawing had improved and he had begun to rise professionally. On 13 August Jennett launched his sensational cartoon campaign with front-page coverage in the *News and Observer*. It was to continue for the remainder of the campaign.

Public persuasion from rostrums and stumps was the major artillery of each party. Some of the Democrats' most effective speakers were Alfred M. Waddell, Robert B. Glenn, and former governors Thomas J. Jarvis and Cameron Morrison. The king of oratory, however, was Charles B. Aycock, the Democratic Moses, who would lead North Carolina out of the chaos and darkness of Negro domination. Early in the campaigns, his cohorts began introducing him as idol of the east and the next governor of North Carolina. Aycock's name became the magnet that attracted the immense crowds: at Leesville, he addressed one of the largest groups ever assembled in Wayne County, comprised of men, women, and children, twelve hundred strong, who came in buggies, in carts, in carriages, in wagons, on horseback and on foot." The Leesville performance was dwarfed by the Raleigh rally held in the Metropolitan House, where the people had early "filled all seats, the windows, and occupied every inch of standing room in the rear of the hall." Aycock spoke for one and one-quarter hours and swept the audience off its feet with his magnetism.[36] As he was to do in all future addresses, he closed with an earnest appeal for white supremacy and the protection of white womanhood. Drawing his audience gradually to the dramatic climax, and like a skilled evangelist entreating backsliders and sinners to come forward and be saved, he would ask the multitudes if they would come and rescue the state from "Russellism, Fusionism, and Black Domination." Rising and cheering, they shouted, "Yes, we will!" Since the days of "Fire-eater" William L. Yancey of Alabama, no other political orator had possessed such rustic appeal in North Carolina.

By the end of August, every available Democrat who could write was writing; every Democrat who could speak was on the stump; every Democrat who could ride was riding. They fanned out in all directions, riding the circuit day and night, summoning their listeners to go to the polls and vote the Democratic ticket for white supremacy. Through the news media, Chairman Simmons kept the public informed with such announcements as "Grand Political Rally!" "Great Parade and Rally!" and "Big Rally and Barbecue!"

Attention now focused on the white supremacy movement in Wilmington. George Rountree has already been introduced in this narrative; he was to play an increasingly significant role in the coup plot, and he appears on the scene at this time. "I came down to Wilmington," recollected Rountree, "and found that the Democratic party had the usual kind of Executive Committee, composed of what in those days we called 'Reformers' (there had been a contest between the 'regulars' and 'reformers' and the 'reformers' were in charge)." The executive committee concluded soon after Rountree's arrival that the "Democrats did not have a ghost of a chance to win the

election with the organization constituted as it was." Plans were immediately formulated for putting some pep into the campaign. After the
proper sentiment was generated within the white community, a campaign
committee of twenty men was organized. Four men—Frank Stedman, -
Edgar G. Parmele, Walker Taylor, and George Rountree—were appointed
to take charge of the campaign, with the last being drafted as a legal ad-
viser.[37]

Soon after the campaign committee was appointed, it became apparent
that a considerable amount of money was necessary to do all the things that
were anticipated. To meet this need, T. M. Emerson, Preston L. Bridgers,
and Rountree were appointed by the committee to raise money. They so-
licited most of the businesses in the city and raised $3,000 in a single morn-
ing. According to Rountree, "Every man approached contributed except
George O. Gaylor and the two Solomons—who declined. Old D. L. Gore at
first declined but subsequently sneaked up to my office and gave me $50; Sol
Bear at first declined but subsequently gave me money."[38]

White supremacy clubs had been founded in the city. As Rountree later
recalled, "Francis Winston came down and helped to organize these clubs
which by this time in October were spread over the state."[39] The white
supremacy clubs in Wilmington were called the White Government Union;
some members came from the Democratic Executive Committee, and they
were enthusiastically received. The *Messenger* joined with the organization
and printed a weekly notice of meeting places and times. Every white man,
regardless of former party affiliation, was urged to identify himself with the
union. In the meantime, prominent political personalities abetted the membership drive in all the wards. Attorneys William B. McKoy, Iredell Meares,
John D. Bellamy, and others permitted the union to use their offices for
meetings, and on occasion made lengthy addresses before its members.

Recalling his former tirade before one of the union's meetings, Rountree
said; "I started to endeavor to inflame the white men's sentiment, and discovered that they were already willing to kill all of the office holders and all
the Negroes, and so I immediately reacted and became a pacifist."[40]

More and more, the union was to play both a unique and significant role in
the affairs of Wilmington. One of its most militant members—the hotheaded
Irishman Mike Dowling—was destined to surface as leader of the Redshirts.
Under the leadership of aggressive committees, white supremacy clubs in
every ward demanded that every white man in the city join. "Many good
people," wrote Keith, "were marched from their homes, some by committees, and taken to headquarters, and told to sign. Those that did not were
notified that they must leave the city . . . as there was plenty of rope in the
city."[41] He was not a Populist, but an anti-Democat, who had successfully
led the revolt against the city bosses during the 1897 primaries. Special
pressure was exerted on him to join the union, but he refused.

The harassment continued for weeks. Eventually, a committee of three came to his office. Keith does not identify any of them, except to say that one was an elder in a prominent church of the city and the other two were also churchmen and had been prominent in the former administration. They told him that they were authorized to offer him a high public position in the next administration if he would join the white supremacy club. Then anonymous letters began to come to him in nearly every mail, with coffins, skulls, and the like drawn on them, advising him to join or to leave at once. He was courageous and refused to surrender to the intimidations. Finally, an anonymous article was published in a local paper, designed to ruin both his character and his business. The column accused him of, among other things, "advocating social equality between the races, and marriage of white women and black men." Keith, incensed, went immediately to the newspaper office and demanded the name of the author, but the editor refused to give it. He discovered later to his surprise that one of his neighbors was behind the hoax.[42] Again he confronted the editor, who replied, "You know that is politics." Writing privately to his friend, Senator Marion Butler, Keith said, "They can kill me if they want to and that is all they can do; they cannot force me to join."[43]

Meanwhile, a racist labor movement had surfaced. It appeared that the White Government Union of Wilmington was politically motivated and aimed at white political supremacy; but *white supremacy* also implied total employment of the white labor force, even at the expense of black workers. This union was able to line up the support of the *Messenger* in its antiblack labor movement.

Prior to the founding of the White Government Union, the foundation had already been laid for the white labor movement, and it had the endorsement of the local newspapers. On 7 September, for example, the *Messenger* ran an eye-catching editorial entitled "Plain Facts for People of Sense." The article instructed all contractors and employees to "Stop! Listen! Read!"

> There is a great injustice done to a highly respectable portion of the whites . . . White mechanics by the dozens have walked our streets without money and without work often, while negroes were given steady employment. There have been instances when six, ten, twenty or more negroes were employed to work upon houses, even public buildings—while genuine worthy white men had to stand around and look on hopeless and helpless.

The main cause of this labor discrimination was that in Wilmington, for the past thirty years, Negro laborers of all kinds had generally been given preference by the employers. Accordingly, blacks had fixed the price of labor in all branches; white men had to work at Negro wages, when they could find employment. The editorial said that white carpenters who were Democrats had complained of the treatment they received from other Democrats in the city and that they gave their work to the Negroes to the neglect of the whites, while Negroes vote invariably against the Democrats. The *Messenger* also reminded the Democratic employers that Republicans supplied less than 3 percent of the employment to the Negro wage earners, "which applies equally to domestic help." A vigorous resolution asked the Democrats not to employ Negro help or to patronize Negro enterprises that persisted in antagonizing their interests by voting against good and orderly government.[44]

By October, the Secret Nine was spinning its web of intrigue wider in order to ensnare prominent businessmen, and the Wilmington business interests found themselves gravitating toward a stand for white supremacy. On 6 October, the *Messenger* announced that "the Chamber of Commerce Delcares against Negro Domination." The president of that body was Postmaster James H. Chadbourn, Jr., a New Englander and a Republican. At three-thirty on the afternoon of Thursday, 5 October, he opened the organization's monthly meeting held in the McRae building on North Front Street.[45] The enthusiastic meeting was larger than usual, and some of the more prominent members present were George Rountree, Thomas W. Strange, William Rand Kenan, Thomas C. James, Walker Taylor, former mayor S. H. Fishblate, Frank H. Stedman, William E. Worth, Thomas W. Clawson, and three members of the Secret Nine—Walter L. Parsley, J. Alan Taylor, and Hugh McRae.

After Secretary John L. Cantwell read the minutes of the last meeting and old business was discussed, the new business was called for. Samuel Northrop arose and asked for the floor. "In view of the horrible condition of affairs here, politically, socially and otherwise," he told the group, "it has been deemed expedient for this body to take some action looking to better government." He then waved before them a copy of some resolutions, declaring that he had been "asked to present them to this body with the request that they be adopted . . . and that copies of the same be furnished to the daily newspapers." Northrop then read the resolution, which declared that the present government "extracts tribute in taxes" and that the political situation in Wilmington and the county was a menace to the "peace and order," and property had no protection and citizens no security. The verdict of the Chamber of Commerce was that the government was "in the hands of corrupt and incompetent men, whose authority had failed to inspire fear in the worse element of the population, command the respect of the best citizens and prevent the indignities to white women, which had culminated in instances of personal violence to them in the streets." The resolution concluded that incompetent public services were detrimental to every business interest, arrest enterprise, hamper commerce, and repel capital that might otherwise find investment in the city, and that the logical outcome was commercial stagnation.[46]

Two days after the Chamber of Commerce had come out against the city administration, the White Government Union's antiblack labor movement picked up momentum. In response to the call for a meeting of businessmen and employers, a mass meeting was held on the night of 7 October 1898, in the rooms of the Merchants' Association and the Seaboard Air Line buildings. All lines of business and the professions were well represented. The meeting was called to consider, as the *Messenger* put it, "White Labor for White Men." Several stirring addresses were delivered in favor of white preference in all employment. Then Northrop arose, came foward, and began reading some strong resolutions that accused many of the leading black leaders, "including bishops and preachers," of being behind a conspiracy to colonize Negroes in New Hanover County and other eastern counties in North Carolina. Another resolution called attention to recent incidences of disorder and violence on the part of Negroes. It was also noted that the country belongs by right to the white man, and his peaceful occupation and development of it was seriously threatened by a "conflict for race supremacy," which made it necessary for the white men to organize for immediate and "permanent deliverance from such conditions," and that the progressive and effective remedy "would be the substitution of white for Negro labor." Therefore, it was resolved "that the chair appoint a committee of five, whose duty it shall be to consider ways and means of organizing a permanent labor bureau for the purpose of procuring white labor for employers."

Hearty applause rang out when Northrop had finished. George Harriss, Jr., moved that the resolutions be adopted by a rising vote, and the motion was seconded by Thomas James. "Any remark on the question?" asked President Chadbourn. Some discussion followed as to portions of the resolutions, but they were allowed to stand as presented. The resolutions were then unanimously adopted, "every man rising to his feet without regards to political affiliations."[47]

No one knows how the colonization conspiracy got started, but it was circulated as far as Atlanta, and even appeared in New York in *Appleton's Annual Cyclopaedia*, which quoted staff correspondent Frank Weldon of the *Atlanta Constitution*, who had written in September 1898 that "it was the purpose of the negroes to colonize and control North Carolina; that it was the purpose of the blacks thus to solve the race problem, by the establishment of a commonwealth of their own."[48] Weldon responded, saying:

> It is no secret that colored leaders, ambitious for their race, have matured in their minds a plan by which they hope to obtain absolute control of the legislative, judicial, and executive machinery, and then to rapidly carry out a scheme of colonization by which this will become a thoroughly negro sovereign State, with that population in the majority and furnishing all officials in the public service, from United States Senators and Governors down through judges, legislators, and solicitors, to the last constable and janitor. . . . If their plan succeeds, North Carolina is to be the refuge of their people in America. Their brethren from all Southern States will be

A SERIOUS QUESTION---HOW LONG WILL THIS LAST?

Raleigh *News and Observer*, August 13, 1898. "A Serious Question—How Long Will This Last?" (file, University of North Carolina).

invited to come here, cast their lot among their fellows, and together to work out their destiny in whatsoever degree of prosperity and advancement they may be able to achieve for themselves.

With this auspicious inauguration, the movement for white supremacy progressed rapidly. Party divisions disappeared, and in subsequent weeks these resolutions were regular verbatim features in the newspapers.

With the Chamber of Commerce, the businessmen, and most employers having endorsed the White Government Union's antiblack labor movement, feelings were beginning to heat up in Wilmington. Some members of the Democratic campaign committee felt that the city needed quieting down rather than heating up, but others thought otherwise, and they prevailed. The Republicans were in for some surprises.

Chadbourn, as president of the Chamber of Commerce, now found himself in an embarrassing position. On 26 September, he had written a letter to Senator Jeter C. Pritchard (Republican), who along with Senator Marion Butler (Populist), were the chief leaders in Fusion politics. When Chadbourn's letter appeared in print, it created a sensation, since it contradicted the Democrats' allegation of Negro domination. Pressure from close quarters was exerted on Chadbourn to change his story; in fact, some of the conspirators hinted that his name was on a special list—those Republicans earmarked to be banished from the city. He was told to correct his letter by writing another one, but to make it appear as though it was voluntary.

First, Chadbourn contacted George Rountree and members of the Democratic Executive Committee and made it known that he was now determined to acquiesce, to put himself "right before the community and correct any mistaken impressions he might have made."[49] He asked them if they would like to have a letter from him giving an account of the political conditions in Wilmington, New Hanover County, and other eastern counties, and advising the white people of the state to vote for a return of the white people to office. They agreed to this gesture, and on 18 October, the *Messenger* flashed the headline "His Eyes Opened—Another Letter to Pritchard":

> Since writing you on September 26th, events have taken place in this community which necessitate some further explanation on my part . . . For the sake of any fancied political advantage, I cannot afford to make a one-sided presentation of the situation in this city and county, and by naming only the white officials and leaving out the colored, doubtless some advantage has been taken, and a false color given to the actual situation, to which the business people and taxpayers, regardless of party, have made serious objections.

Marshaling figures in support of his new position, Chadbourn now claimed that there were in New Hanover County thirty-six colored magistrates, a colored Register of Deeds, and various other minor officials besides some presidential appointees, and that the property owners, taxpayers, and businessmen seriously objected to this state of affairs. He maintained that there "now exists in Wilmington the most intense feeling against any sort of Negro domination [and] a greater feeling of unrest and uncertainty about the maintenance of law and order." In his opinion, a race conflict was imminent, and nothing could be more disastrous than to have a race riot of "arson and bloodshed." Chadbourn concluded his letter:

> I had thought at first that it was merely the usual political cry and the fight for the offices but I am now convinced the feeling is much deeper than this, as it pervades the whole community, and there seems to be a settled determination on the part of the property owners, business men and taxpayers that they will administer City and County Government.[50]

From Marshall, North Carolina, Senator Pritchard replied to Chadbourn's letter of 18 October. He maintained that the "whole thing [Chadbourn's letter] was a lie" and was designed to deceive the people of the west. He accused the Democrats of, among other things, making Wilmington and New Hanover County the principal points of attack when arguing for white supremacy against Negro domination and this was totally unwarrented. To controvert their arguments, he marshaled evidence to support his case by correctly pointing out that "in Wilmington the whites were in absolute control." "We have," Senator Pritchard noted, "a white Mayor, Chief of Police and Captain of Police, three white Sergeants out of four, twenty-two white Policemen out of thirty-two, a white Superintendent of Streets and one-half

"The New Slavery," Raleigh *News and Observer*, October 18, 1898 (file, University of North Carolina).

of the street laborers are white, a white City Clerk and Treasurer, and a white Deputy Clerk and Treasurer." Turning to the Board of Aldermen, he also noted that seven out of the ten were white. Considering the Board of Audit and Finance, appointed by the governor, to have absolute charge of all the finances of the city, he further noted that four of the five members were white, of which three were Democrats, making it in reality a white, Democratic board. This board had a clerk, and he was a white Democrat. Senator Pritchard contended that in the post office there was only one more Negro man than there was under the last Democratic administration, and he was a night watchman. Every clerk in the post office who came in contact with the public was white.

As for New Hanover County, the sheriff was white, his deputy was white, the jailer was white, the sheriff's clerks were white, the criminal court clerk was white, the circuit court clerk was white, his deputy was white, the county physician was white, the whole Board of Health was white, the board controlling the city and county hospitals was entirely white, the deputy U.S. marshal was white, the deputy Internal Revenue agent was white, the clerk of the U.S. court was white, and the jury commissioner was white. Concluding, the senator said, "It isn't Negro domination or white supremacy. It is Democratic office-holding."[51] And what angered the Democrats was that the whites in power were not Democrats.

The Democrats remained mum on Senator Pritchard's letter, which the major papers had refused to print. Like the Chamber of Commerce resolution, *Chadbourn's* letter became a regular feature in the papers, however. It was published throughout the state, and the *Messenger* ran a column on it almost every day prior to the election.

Meanwhile, the conspirators had agreed upon still another scheme. They concluded that there ought to be a follow-up letter from Colonel F. W. (Flavell) Foster, one of the most prominent Republicans and influential businessmen in eastern North Carolina and lately county chairman of the Board of County Commissioners of New Hanover County. They reasoned that his views ought to carry great weight in the coming election. One night, members of the campaign committee, including Rountree, descended upon Foster's home. After arguing far into the night, Foster finally agreed to sign the letter that Rountree wrote. Elated, Rountree later boasted, "You know what a wonderful triumph we had."[52] On 21 October, the city paper disclosed that "a reporter of the *Messenger* last evening called upon F. W. Foster." The paper praised him as the only Republican leader who had a business standing comparable to that of Postmaster Chadbourn. "Who Pays Taxes Should Control" was the theme of Foster's letter. Pointing out that whites paid 95 percent of taxes, "I think," he said, "that the representatives of 95 percent of taxes ought to control. They ought not be deprived of their privilege of controlling the administration of their affairs."

Masterful duplicity is the appropriate phrase for those leading and conservative citizens who organized and directed events destined to climax in a coup and in the banishment of leading white and black Republicans. On discovering the plot, the ministers of several denominations . . . [called] a meeting of the ministers to voice their protests. In defense of what had exactly been done and what the white leaders further proposed to do, J. Alan Taylor addressed the ministers. "But that is not legal," two clergymen protested. "Of course it is not legal," Taylor answered. "Nothing is legal just now."

When the clergymen discovered that rebellion was unavoidable, and that the movement was directed by substantial citizens, they withdrew their opposition and surrendered to the inevitable. Actually, the Secret Nine and the Democrats were not simply making history, but forcing it. With the defections of Chadbourn and Foster, the major Fusionist forces had been reduced to Mayor Silas P. Wright, Benjamin F. Keith, John R. Melton (the Populist chief of police), and G. Z. French (former postmaster of Wilimington and acting sheriff of New Hanover County). The Secret Nine and the members of the campaign committee marked time hoping that something would happen to arouse the whites to concerted action. This watch-and-wait policy was well calculated. The Democrats exploded an eleventh-hour bombshell with the now famous Manly editorial, which turned out to be the main source of fuel for white heat. Writing in 1969 in the introduction of Jack Thorne's book, *Hanover; or, The Persecution of the Lowly,* Professor Thomas R. Cripps of Morgan State University said: "In addition to the election, another event was used to justify the massing of white vigilantes against the Negroes. In August, three months before the off-year elections, Alex Manly (or Manley—the spelling varies), the editor of the local black press, had chided Mrs. Rebecca Felton, a long time defender of southern womanhood, for her essays on the theme of rape."[53]

In late August 1898, North Carolina newspapers, led by the flamboyant *Wilmington Messenger,* began flashing headlines: "Negro Editor Slanders White Women"; "Negro Defamer of White Women"; "A Horrid Slander of White Women"; and "Infamous Attack on White Women."[54] The whites of Wilmington alleged that the Manly editorial, more than anything else, was the catalyst that precipitated the race riot.

Flaming mutilations of the Manly editorial were published all through the South, and extracts of them appeared in Northern papers and elsewhere. Henry L. West wrote in the *Forum:* "A Negro editor published an editorial, defaming the virtue of poor White women in the South. This fanned the flame of Anglo-Saxon resentment to White heat." Reporting the Wilmington race riot in New York, the *Literary Digest* said, "The chief cause alleged was an editorial printed in a paper edited by a mulatto named Alex L. Manly."[55]

Who was Manly? Why did Manly write the editorial? What part of the editorial infuriated the whites? And how did the Democrats use the issue to promote the Wilmington conspiracy?

It is of more than historical interest to include a brief sketch of Manly's background. The roots of his family were imbedded in the peculiar problem of miscegenation growing out of slavery and now expressing itself in the American color line, which in this case was invisible. For anyone with whom he was not acquainted, he could have passed as a white man. With his unmistakable Anglo-Saxon features, Manly was suspended between two worlds—neither white nor black. He was, in the public's eye, as white as any Caucasian and more white than the numerous rustic rednecks.

His immediate family was unique and represented a marked phase of the American race problem. Millions of Americans, both white and black, have encountered these people—so aggressively white that they could have been mistakenly taken for Caucasians. Such were the Manlys, for there was absolutely not the slightest earmark of Negroid about them. His son, Milo Manly,

Alexander "Alex" L. Manly (1866–1944). From *Collier's Weekly*, November 26, 1898 (Library of Congress).

reflecting on his lineage, said, "My father's family looked so much like whites that sometimes I wondered myself."

The Manlys were the acknowledged offspring of Charles Manly, Whig governor of North Carolina from 1849 to 1851.[56] Governor Manly had two sets of children—those born to a slave woman and those born to his legal wife. There is a controversy about the slave family's being ordered to add on an *e* or drop an *e* in the surname in order to distinguish it from the legitimate family.

Milo Manly explained the relationship of Governor Manly to his family: "As for Charles Manly, the only thing I know about him is that he was governor of the state. He had several children by his slave girls, and of course . . . that's where my family comes from." After pausing momentarily to reflect, he continued. "I guess he was pretty benevolent, because he freed his slaves, as I understand the story. . . . What we call his white family . . . went off and inherited property."[57] Considering the illegitimate offspring, Manly said: "He then gathered up a bunch of the children he felt [were] his by his slave girls—they all looked like him—and freed them, and gave them a valley, somewhere up in North Carolina, and gave them enough farm equipment for them to go for themselves. That's what you call manumission. And from then on, they proceeded to prosper."

Milo Manly relates the following about his surname: "I have had fun with that *-ly,* as I've come across . . . people who are members of the legislature or contractors or something of that sort and proceeded to tell them they are related to me. Not actually, but in that concept."[58]

Although Manly's given name was Alexander, he was seldom called anything but Alex, even by his mother. He was of average stature, thin, and sported a mustache that matched his heavy black hair. Born 13 May 1866, in Wake County, about two miles from Raleigh, he attended Hampton Institute, mastering the painting trade. Finding few opportunities for work in his hometown, he migrated to Wilmington and went into the painting business. His brothers Frank, George, Grimes (named after his father), and Laurin (who later became head of the printing department at Tuskegee Institute) followed him. Manly was intelligent, civic-minded, and taught sunday school at the local Presbyterian Church.[59] He also became involved in politics, later serving as Register of Deeds. He felt the need for a black newspaper, since little or no news about blacks was being printed in white newspapers. But there was the problem of securing a press. Fortunately, Thomas Clawson, editor of the *Wilmington Messenger,* owned a second-hand but practically new Jonah Hoe press. It had originally belonged to a carpetbagger named John C. Abbott. Along with some other Wilmington Republicans, he had published an ill-fated daily. Afterward, Clawson purchased the press at an emergency sale. Having realized a handsome profit, Clawson said, "I unloaded it [in an installment deal] on the Negro publishers when the Negro paper was regarded as a worth-while publication."[60] The *Record*'s office was established over a saloon directly across the street from the *Star*'s office. The newspaper was set up first as a weekly; it prospered and developed into a daily, with Manly as its editor. Other members of the staff were John N. Goins, business manager; Laurin D. Manly, general traveling agent; and Frank G. Manly, general manager. J. (Jim) W. Telfair, who held a position of responsibility at the Sprunt Cotton Compress, was also involved with the paper. According to Clawson, the Manly brothers conducted "a very creditable colored paper." An examination of old issues of the *Record* shows that the white businessmen gave them encouragement through liberal advertising support. The paper achieved a wide circulation among blacks throughout the state.[61]

Being both civic-minded and race conscious, Manly used the *Record* to champion the causes of Wilmington's black citizens, including the promotion of progressive legislation. Like the black presses, in general, he used the paper to expound Negro opinions. The black writer David Bryant Fulton (writing under the name Jack Thorne) gives a fictional account of Manly's fight for civic improvement in the black community. He called the city officials' attention to the need for better roads and bicycle paths, which were secured. He also dramatized the need for reforms by writing exposés. The *Record* wrote of the unsanitary conditions of the colored wards in the city hospital. The paper "made such a glowing picture of the state of affairs, the

Board of County Commissioners [was] compelled to investigate and take action, which resulted [in] remodeling the old hospital to habitable shape."[62] Nevertheless, Manly's militant pen did not enhance his popularity with some whites who thought him too *high strung, bold and saucy,* while some black leaders were a bit shaky over his many tilts with editors of the white papers.

From the beginning of the 1898 campaign, the Democratic papers, led by the *Raleigh News and Observer,* had carried on a smear campaign against black men, claiming that rapes and other attacks on white women had increased under the Fusion administration. The Democrats used the charge of rape by blacks as propaganda against Negro candidates, as a means of upholding the doctrine of white supremacy. Such inflammatory news releases and cartoons understandably embarrassed and infuriated the black leaders; even more galling to them was the fact that the cartoons were accompanied by lurid captions and were featured on the front page, a practice that intensified as the campaign continued. Manly employed the *Record* to rebut the Democrats' defamation of Negro males.

In August 1898, the agricultural society held a meeting at the South Bend Hotel at Tybee, Georgia. The main feature of the session was an address by a distinguished white woman, Mrs. Rebecca Felton, wife of ex-Congressman W. H. Felton, of Bartow County. She discussed at length the need for protecting poor white girls on the secluded farms from the black rapists. She certainly struck a sensitive chord. "There was real fear, and in some districts, even terror, on the part of White women themselves," wrote W. J. Cash. "And there were neurotic old maids and wives, hysterical young girls, to react to all of this in a fashion well enough understood now, but understood by almost nobody then."[63]

Felton reminded her audience that the crying need of white women on "the farm was security in their lives and their homes." Emphasizing the point, she said that strong, able-bodied men had told her that they had stopped farming and had moved to town because their womenfolk were scared to death if left alone. As a solution, she instructed her listeners with these words: "When there is not enough religion in the pulpit to organize a crusade against sin, nor justice in the court house to promptly punish crime, . . . [and] if it needs lynching to protect woman's dearest possession from the ravening human beasts—then I say lynch, a thousand times a week if necessary."

According to Thorne's fictional account, Manly was "sitting in his office one evening in August reading a New York paper, when his eye fell upon a [column] from a Georgia paper from the pen of a famous Georgia white woman, whose loud cries for the lives of Negro rapists had been widely read and commented upon during the past year." The article referred to the exposure of and the protection of white girls in the isolated districts of the South and called for the lynching of "lustful black brutes." Manly meditated: "White girls in isolated districts exposed to lustful black brutes. Colored girls in isolated districts exposed to white brutes: what's the difference?" Infuriated over the calumniation of a "defenseless people," he took up his pen and wrote the "retort which shook the state from the mountains to the sea."[64]

Thus emerged the Manly editorial, one of the most famous in North Carolina's history. Through certain omissions, it was distorted from the beginning by the Democratic news media. Scholars have perpetuated the distortion by using the Democratic papers as their sources, and of the major works sampled (J. G. de R. Hamilton, *History of North Carolina Since 1860;* Helen G. Edmonds, *The Negro and Fusion Politics in North Carolina 1894–1901;* and Josephus Daniels, *Editor in Politics*), not one has seen fit to include the reasons Manly wrote the editorial.

Manly entitled his editorial "Mrs. Felton's Speech." "A Mrs. Felton from Georgia," he began, "makes a speech before the Agricultural Society, at Tybee, Georgia, in which she advocates lynching as an extreme measure. This woman makes a strong plea for womanhood, and if the alleged crimes of rape were . . . so frequent as is oftimes reported, her plea would be worthy of consideration." Like many "so-called Christians," Manly contended, she "loses sight of the basic principles of the religion of Christ in her plea for one class of people as against another. If a missionary spirit is essential for the uplifting of the poor white girls, why is it? The morals of the poor white people are on a par with their colored neighbors of like conditions, and if anyone doubts the statement let him visit among them." He went on to point out that papers were frequently filled with reports of rapes of white women and subsequent lynchings of the rapists. The editors "pour forth volleys of aspersions against all Negro males, because of the few who may be guilty. If the papers and speakers of the other race would condemn the commission of crime because it is crime, and not try to make it appear that the Negroes were the only criminals, they would find their strongest allies in the intelligent Negroes themselves, and together the whites and blacks would foot the evil out of both races."

This section of Manly's editorial was intentionally omitted by Democratic presses, which began their account of his article at this point. The *Raleigh News and Observer* reported that Manly had written:

We suggest that the whites guard their women more closely, as Mrs. Felton says, thus giving no opportunity for the human fiend, be he white or black. You leave your goods out of doors and then complain because they are taken away. Poor white men are careless in the matter of protecting their women, especially on the farms. They are careless of their conduct toward them and our experience among poor white people in the country teaches us that women of that race are not any more particular in the matter of clandestine meetings with colored men than the white men with colored women. Meetings of this kind go on for some time until the women's infatuation or the man's boldness brings attention to them, and the man is lynched for rape. Every negro lynched is called a Big Burly

Black Brute, when, in fact, many of those who have thus been dealt with had white men for their fathers, and were not only not black and burly, but were sufficiently attractive for white girls of culture and refinement to fall in love with them, as is very well known to all.

The Democratic presses terminated the article at this point. Manly, however, had more to say.

He recommended that "Mrs. Felton should start at the 'fountain head' if she wishes to 'purify the stream.'" Further on, he suggested: "Teach your men purity. Let virtue be something more than an excuse for them to intimidate and torture a helpless people. Tell your men that it is no worse for a black man to be intimate with a white woman then for a white man to be intimate with a colored woman." He wrote in conclusion: "You set yourselves down as a lot of carping hypocrites; in fact, you cry aloud for the virtue of your women while you seek to destroy the morality of ours. Don't think ever that your women will remain pure while you are debauching ours. You sow the seed—the harvest will come in due time."[65]

The indignation that this article aroused among whites of all classes can be easily understood. Threatening letters were sent to Manly's office: "Leave [town] on the pain of death"; "stop the publishing of that paper"; "apologize for that slander." The *Progressive Farmer* urged all blacks with a "scale of decency" to drive Manly from the states, "never to return."[66] The *Raleigh News and Observer,* the Democrats' major organ, could naturally be relied on to inform the people of North Carolina, and it did not fail. On 24 August 1898, it editoralized about the "vile and villainous" attack on white women by a Negro newspaper publisher in Wilmington.

What was the reaction of black leaders to the Manly editorial? As whites blazed their indignation, some leading blacks, including John E. Taylor, chief deputy at the customhouse, Elijah M. Green, city alderman, and John Dancy, collector of the customs at the Port of Wilmington, "urged Manly to suspend the paper and thereby quiet the bitterness growing out of his indiscreet and inflamable utterance."[67] Frank Denham, a member of a prominent black family of Raleigh, wrote in the *Raleigh News and Observer:* "Not a word of Manly's editorial expresses the sentiments of the colored people in North Carolina. I was never so shocked in my life. I shall not be surprised to hear that violence has been done Manly by either whites or negroes."[68] In contrast to these sentiments, many black spokesmen, some quite prominent in and out of the state, concurred with Manly's conclusion. One Negro minister braved ostracism by contending that there was no repugnance felt toward marriage between black and white persons of the "same financial, educational and social levels."[69] Among those who endorsed Manly was the city's leading lawyer, L. A. Henderson. In addition, a society of black women of Wilmington passed resolutions praising Manly for defending the race.

Meanwhile, Manly was having trouble finding a new location for his press, which was located downtown. The owners of that property refused to let him remain in the building. Even the Colored Odd Fellows refused to rent him a room in their large edifice. He would not give up, however, and took his problem to the Ministerial Union, composed of the black ministers of the city. The Reverend J. Allen Kirk, formerly of Boston, Massachusetts, and then pastor of the Central Baptist Church of Wilmington, was a person of influence in the union. He successfully secured an office for Manly, and the *Record* continued its publications. The union also passed a strong resolution making it clear that it was in sympathy with the efforts of the *Record* "in defending the rights of the race." Meeting at Lake Waccamaw, North Carolina, members of the Wilmington District Conference and Sunday School Convention also endorsed the Manly cause. As mentioned in the prologue, one person's recollection was that Manly was the editor of the "only Negro daily in the world."[70] Cognizant that the *Record* was the only Negro daily paper in the South, they asked their congregations to support it as an enterprise for racial pride, "without any thoughts of endorsing the much talked about article."[71]

Negro spokesmen and others have constantly and vociferously argued that no rape menace has ever existed in the South, and have concluded that the rape complex was a broad and hypocritical pretext. The black man was obviously the scapegoat and the need to protect the white woman was the excuse for Southerners to commit acts of violence. "The danger of Negroes' desire to rape a white woman" the eminent authority, Gunnar Myrdal wrote, "has acquired a special and strategic position in the defense of lynching practices." The 'rape complex' includes all sex relations between black men and white women. Myrdal maintained that the percent of victims accused of rape "has been inflated by the fact that a mob which makes the accusation of rape is secure against any further investigation."[72]

More to the point, the theme of Manly's editorial had been voiced earlier in the U.S. House of Representatives. Congressman Thomas E. Miller was the most distinguished of South Carolina's black political leaders, a graduate of Lincoln University, and an astute attorney and politician. He had fought courageously against Benjamin Tillman's effort to write a grandfather clause into South Carolina's constitution of 1895. While a member of Congress in the 1890s, he had become particularly incensed at a Georgia congressman, Alfred Colquitt, who charge that white men in the South must constantly worry about the chastity of their women. Miller responded with these words: "My God, is there no limit to the slander and malignant utterances of these self-constituted friends of a toiling . . . portion of the American people? . . . Stand up and indict a race of males as the invaders of the sanctity of Caucasian home ties, as the brutal destroyer of that in woman which is her very existence. The charge is groundless, mean, slanderous, and most damnably false." He informed Congress that there had been no proven cases of assault or rape by blacks against white women—those "walking emblems of American purity," as he called them—in his district since Emancipation. He maintained that the records of Southern courts would prove that such charges were usually untrue; generally, interracial sexual contact was a matter of mutual consent. "Whenever [a rape charge] is hurled at [the black man] the crime is laid in a locality where the numbers of the whites and the Negroes are nearly equal, where the whites and the Negroes are equal in morals; and, even after the poor unfortunate victim has been lynched and his spirit gone to the eternal world, letters or verbal admissions coming from the supposed victim of licentious brutality invariably absolve the innocent dead man from the crime charged."[73]

5

It would be enlightening to include here a discussion of the intense *sexism* expressed by both races, and the propensity of everyone (both black and white) to view women as they formerly had viewed slaves, i.e., as the possession of white men. To fully appreciate this section of the essay, some background is necessary.

In the United States, as in the rest of the world, men believed in the inferiority of women. In the ante-bellum South, particularly, there was a close parallel between the subordination of both women and blacks. For example, as blacks were awarded their "place" in society, so were women relegated to their "place."[74] "The Southern wife (a statement attributed to Dolly Madison) was 'the chief slave of the harem.'"[75]

Southern laws reflected attitudes about masculine superiority and woman's inferiority. Throughout the South, women were subjected to political, legal, educational, social and economic restrictions, "such as their inability to sue or be sued alone or to own property separate from their husbands or to dispose of property they owned before marriage without the permission of their husbands."[76]

At the same time, upper-class women were expected to reflect the model that Professor Anne Firor Scott dubbed "The Image." And from early childhood, young girls were trained to fulfill that image. "This marvelous creation was described as a submissive wife whose reason for being was to love, honor, obey, and occasionally amuse her husband, to bring up his children, and manage the household." Upper-class white men viewed her as innocent, timid, modest, beautiful and graceful—and dependent upon male protection.[77]

In the delineation of the image, Professor Scott neglects to discuss whiteness, which carried a special significance for white Southern men. White connoted purity, the color of "perfect human beauty, especially *female* beauty . . . no other color except white conveyed so much emotional impact."[78] The concept of racial purity rested on the proposition that the white women of the South was "supposed to be of the purest 'Nordic' stock in existence." Even the poorest white women were persons of pure "Nordic Ancestry," a popular theory that fastened itself upon the South during slavery days. Hence as a wife the Southern white woman's basic role was to perpetuate the Caucasian race, while "the cross between a white man and a Negro was a Negro."[79]

Historically, in the American South, any person with Negro ancestry has been considered a Negro, even if he has blue eyes, fair skin and sandy or blonde hair like Walter White, who for many years was head of the National Association for the Advancement of Colored People. White was considered a Negro simply because he acknowledged his ancestry. Similarly, Alexander L. Manly was considered Negro because he too acknowledged it. But in the South, there was no racial middle ground for gradation of color of the two races. Brazil offers an interesting and illuminating contrast with its *branco de terra,* the name throughout Brazil for a person with a small amount of Negro blood. Although these persons look white, everyone else recognizes that they have some Negro blood, but *brancos de terras* are always spoken of as white and receive from everyone the same treatment accorded whites.[80]

But the Southern definition of race goes considerably deeper. A popular belief among Southerners perpetuated by the "black baby myth" was that the slightest amount of Negro ancestry in an individual who does not show even a trace of Negro characteristics can cause a "throw back," and that this person—in mating with a white individual—can become the parent of a black baby.[81] Mixed offspring, the result of illicit sex relations between white men and black women, fortified the concept of the pure white woman, who was forced to accept a double standard of morality—which included miscegenation between white men and black women.

The white Southerner's double standard must have been extremely embarrassing for upper-class white women. As lord and master and by his own conduct, the slaveholder defined the role of black women, whose natural lot was slavery. Some existed for the sole purpose of gratifying the lust of their masters, who made concubines of them. By "the nocturnal visit—or, for that matter, the emboldened daytime visit—to the slave cabin," the slaveholder sired two sets of children.[82] The regular appearance of mulatto babies on the plantation was convincing evidence.

W. E. B. DuBois overstated the proposition when he wrote: "The rape which your gentlemen have done against helpless black women in defense of your own laws is written on the forehead of two millions of black mulattoes, and written in ineffaceable blood."[83] The one-half million mulattoes reported in 1860 by the United States Census is believed to be more accurate.[84]

Nevertheless, the mulatto class must not be attributed to slaveholders only. Often the adult sons of slaveholders fathered mulatto children after taking slave mistresses or raping women who resisted. At the same time, overseers behaved promiscuously with black women, and often kept mistresses with or without the consent of their employers. Finally, white laborers and local poor whites fathered an undetermined number of mulatto children.[85]

The mulatto woman possessed a somber beauty that was intriguing to white men and disturbing to white women. Everywhere she went, she attracted attention. "When Frederick Law Olmsted visited Richmond in the autumn of 1855," wrote historian John Hope Franklin, "he was surprised at the number of fine-looking mulattoes, or nearly-white persons that he saw." Many of the colored ladies were dressed not only expensively, but with good taste and effect, after the latest Parisian mode. About one-fourth of those whom Olmsted observed "seemed . . . tó have lost all distinguishing African peculiarity of feature, and to have acquired, in place of it, a good deal of that voluptuousness of expression which characterizes many of the women of the south."[86]

There is an irony here: It was through the hue of black women that the mulatto had its origin.

Whether mulatto or black, the woman was at the center of the tragedy of slavery. During the sexist-dominated ante-bellum era, indeed, her lot must have been most difficult. In slave society, sexual promiscuity occurred rather freely. If a woman tried to exercise the right of refusal, she could still be raped with impunity by both white and black males, for slave codes did not include negative sanctions against the rape or quasi-rape of slave women. To seduce attractive single girls, planters used a combination of flattery, bribes and the ever-present threat of force.[87] "When she was fourteen or fifteen," Professor Franklin wrote, "her owner, or his sons, or the overseer, or perhaps all of them, begin to bribe her with presents. If these fail to accomplish their purpose, she is whipped or starved into submission to their will."[88]

One could hypothesize that the all-powerful male image of the ante-bellum white man inevitably influenced the sexist attitudes of male slaves. Notwithstanding the degrees of nuance, slaveholders concluded that black males "were by nature tyrannical in their disposition."[89] Having "little sense of responsibility toward their families, slave men abused their women mercilessly." Court records, plantation papers, and ex-slave accounts reveal evidence of wife beating.[90] On the other hand, some black women, made physically strong by hard field work, were not about to be beaten. Thus, family life in the slave quarters, like lower-class life generally, sometimes exploded in violence. Promiscuity and illegitimacy were accepted mores, and many slaves became irresponsible husbands and indifferent fathers; women raised the children and maintained some order in the cabin. Enough men and women fell into this pattern to give rise to the legend of the matriarchy, the emasculated but brutal male, and the fatherless children."[91]

While the emancipation of slaves inevitably meant the breakdown of the concubinage system and the breeding of mulatto children, black women continued to be sex objects of white men. Enduring resolutely from slavery days to the present is that legend of lascivious black women which stimulated the common assumption that black women were especially passionate, an idea which offered the best possible justification for white men to lust after them.[92]

In contrast to the legend of racial purity, white women of the South of all classes had black lovers.[93] In the black oral tradition, it is not a legend but is accepted as truism from experience. When Alexander L. Manly wrote his editorial, one could hypothesize that he was writing from personal experience. If he had included only poor white women, his editorial might not have been sensational. But Manly included white women of the upper classes as well.

The Manly editorial was not unique in Southern history. Eleven years earlier, for example, both white and black citizens of Montgomery, Alabama, had to contend with a similar editorial that appeared in the Montgomery *Herald,* a black weekly, edited by Jessie C. Duke. Exactly like the Manly affair, Duke's article confronted the white women of that city; and, exactly like the Manly editorial, the major objective of the Duke article was to attack the lynching phenomena. It is significant to point out that Montgomery, a city in the deep South, certainly did not have Wilmington's liberal tradition in race relations. Hence, a comparison of the two articles and the outcomes should give a greater appreciation of the Manly dilemma.

Duke's editorial appeared in the *Herald* on August 13, 1887. He began by noting that daily the public read of the lynching of some Negro for raping a white woman. "If something is not done to stop these lynchings," the *Herald* told its readers, "it will be so after awhile that they will lynch every colored man that looks at a white woman with a twinkle in his eye." Then he raised a significant question: "Why is it that white women attract Negro men more than former days?" And he reminded his readers that "there was a time when such a thing was not heard of."[94]

The reader will recall that Manly had said in his editorial that many black men were sufficiently attractive for white girls of culture and refinement to fall in love with. Following a similar line, Duke wrote: "There is a secret to this thing, and we greatly suspect it is the growing appreciation of the white Juliet for the colored Romeo, as he becomes more and more intelligent and refined."[95]

The white reaction to the Duke editorial was predictable. But there was no talk of organizing a lynching bee. However, it did cause some consternation. The white leaders of Montgomery called a public meeting, attended by people from all walks of life. A series of resolutions were proposed and debated. Among them, all agreed that "Duke must go!" At the suggestion of Dr. I. L. Watkins, who presided, a committee of ten was appointed to call upon Duke and give him eight hours to leave town, coupled with the warning not to come back. Beyond this act, the committee had no authority; anything else was deemed "an authorized act."[96] Meanwhile, Duke had already left the city or put himself in hiding before he was warned to leave.

Next, the committee embarked upon a "witch hunt," starting by taking action against a black attorney named A. A. Garner whose office was in the same building as Duke's attorney. Garner made himself repugnant to some whites by suggesting that Duke be given a chance to explain. Perhaps they wanted to get rid of Garner. In some way, rumors were circulated that Garner was privy to the article in the *Herald,* if not the real author. The committee confronted him about it in an argumentative manner. Garner, a forceful debater and possessing a strong voice, disclaimed any connections with the article. When the whites pressed for further proof, hot words were exchanged. In Alabama it might have been all right for a black lawyer to sass a white lawyer in the courtroom, but not elsewhere. Hence, right there on the spot, the whites began passing the hat for a collection. With "a purse of $4 or $5 being raised, Garner was ordered to pay his railroad fare as far as it would take him . . . out of Montgomery in all possible haste and to stay out."[97]

News of the banishment of Attorney Garner quickly spread in the black community. Several prominent black citizens, fearful of an explosion, quickly disclaimed any connection with Duke and the *Herald.* Ironically, a few personally appeared before the justice of the peace and took an oath of innocence, and condemned what they were quick to call the incendiary utterances of Duke. On August 16, they met as a body and sent the office of the Montgomery *Advertizer* the following resolution:

Resolved, That the colored citizens of Montgomery have no sympathy whatever with the sentiments expressed by editor Duke in his issue of the 13th August.

Resolved, That the article in question is as much distasteful to us as it is to the white citizens of Montgomery.

Resolved, That we are disposed to cultivate friendly relations with the whites, and we deprecate anything that has a tendency to stir up strife and bad feeling.[98]

Meanwhile, unlike Manly, Duke retracted the "slander" and apologized. "Please let me say through the columns of your paper," he wrote the editors of the *Advertizer,* "that the article copied from the *Herald* and commented upon by the *Dispatch* on Sunday was unfortunate, and that when I published it, I had not the remotest idea of reflecting upon or offending any one, and that I am very sorry. . . ." He tried to assure the "good people of Montgomery" that he had no intention whatever to do wrong and was "sorry for what happened." He also wanted to return to the city. "Please publish this for me," he asked, while pointing out that he had a wife and four small children depending upon him for their bread.[99] But the whites of Montgomery remained adamant and were resolved that this black editor should stay away permanently from Montgomery. Duke later settled his family in Pine Bluff, Arkansas.

On August 18, three days after the Duke affair burst upon the people of Montgomery, the *Advertizer* announced, "The Excitement Over." On this date the paper also announced the return of Attorney Garner, who made "no concealment of his presence."[100] Hence, the Duke editorial, so much similar to the Manly controversy, was to go into oblivion. And while Duke was given his walking papers and would not ever be allowed to return home, Montgomery settled back to its normal conditions. This conclusion was in great contrast to the Manly affair in Wilmington.

It is important to remember that the Manly editorial first appeared in late August of 1898. And like a tidal wave, white indignation against Manly grew from one end of the city to the other. He and his editorial were discussed in the streets, bars, and offices by white men. No doubt one voiced the sentiments of many when he groaned, "The impudent nigger ought to be horse-whipped and run out of town." Some suggested, "Break up the press!" Others spoke of organizing a lynching party, but the talk of violence subsided almost as quickly as it had begun.

As Walker Taylor recalled in 1905:

> I may state right here that when that article appeared, it required the best efforts we could put forth [to] prevent the people from lynching him. The office was right over a saloon across the street from the *Star*'s office. Senator Simmons, who was here at the time told us that that article would make it an easy victory for us and urged us to try and prevent any riot until after the election.[101]

Thus the Manly editorial was pigeonholed until it could be used as a more effective campaign issue. *Collier's Weekly* reported, "Cooler heads persuaded the hot young bloods to wait. The older men had planned to combine revolution with profit."[102] And while there were to be more plots and subplots, the name of Manly continued to weave in and out of the web of intrigue.

3
The Foreboding Clouds: Final Days and Things

1

Wᴵᵀʜ the campaign moving into high gear, the Democrats intensified their strategy of mudslinging and the "waving of the bloody shirt," particularly against black leaders, Republicans, and Populists. In mid-October, led by the *Raleigh News and Observer,* they exploded an eleventh-hour bombshell with the Manly editorial. The editorial was published in the *Record* in August; its resurrection was a classic example of stirring up racial hatred for partisan purposes. The Manly editorial reappeared in the *Morning Star* on 18 October and again two days later, the "most horrid slander" and the "most infamous assault upon the white women of the state."[1] "Every white man in the state," wrote the *Fayetteville Observer,* "having any regard for the purity of his mother, sisters and daughters, must take this matter into consideration." Doubters were invited to the office of the paper "to see the original copy of the slanderous sheet."[2] Meanwhile, the article was circulated inside the state and beyond, and went like wildfire from house to house, especially in the rural communities, while the Democratic orators added it to their theme song.

It was up to the Wilmington papers, especially the *Messenger* to keep the issue alive, and they did. There were demands for copies of the *Record;* the *Wilmington Star* advertised to pay twenty-five cents per copy for the issue that contained the article, and in the meantime 100,000 copies were printed.[3] Clawson announced in the *Messenger,* "We have received so many requests for copies of the *Record* containing this article that we herewith reproduce it in full." The paper emphasized that "Manly was not regarded as a simpleton or a nobody before he startled the Republican bosses by the publication of that awful article."

Some Republicans and Populists repudating the article charged that it was a Democratic trick. Hill E. King, chief clerk of the agricultural department at

Raleigh, said: "I believe the Democrats either dictated or wrote the editorial in Manly's paper, *The Record*. It looks to me like a Democratic trick for campaign purposes." The Democrats responded with an original copy of the editorial and an affidavit, validated by John D. Taylor, clerk of the Superior Court of New Hanover County, that the article was "an accurate and true copy of an editorial in the *Daily Record*, a paper published in the city of Wilmington." It also declared that its editor "is well known as a Republican and has before this held the office of Deputy Register of Deeds of New Hanover County, by appointment from Charles W. Norwood, Republican Register of Deeds of New Hanover County." Further, the document identified John N. Goins as business manager, Laurin D. Manly as foreman, and Frank G. Manly as general manager, "all black and known as Republicans," along with John T. Howe, traveling agent of the *Record* and "a Republican Representative from New Hanover County in the Legislature of 1897."[4] Finally, some leading businessmen of Wilmington (B. G. Worth of the Worth Company; R. W. Hicks, wholesale grocer; C. E. Borden, president of Navassa Guano Company; W. L. DeRossett, commander of the North Carolina Division of Confederate Veterans, and John L. Springer, of the firm of W. E. Springer and Company) signed the affidavit and sent it all over the state.

Some of the Democratic campaigners carried copies of the editorial with them. One was Robert B. Glenn, a future governor (1904–08). His contemporaries described him as a gully washer and give 'em hell type of speaker, who used every muscle in his body with dramatic emotion. Truly a crowd pleaser, he was a political revivalist whose speeches contained little or no logic. Rarely speaking for less than two hours, he often began slowly with a deliberate cadence, and gradually his words accelerated. One of his favorite antics was to take off his coat and collar and when he would get half through, if he hadn't taken off his coat, the people having heard that at some other place he had done so, would cry out: 'Bob, take off your coat and give 'em hell,' which he proceeded to do to the cheers and hurrahs of the great body of people. According to Josephus Daniels, Glenn "could tell a story of Fusion outrage in a way to excite his hearers, so if any Fusion office holders had been present he would have feared for his life." He would dramatically raise a copy of the Manly editorial, shaking it several times in the direction of the crowd. To hear him read and interpret it, with tribute to rural white women, "which he delivered in a voice that could almost be heard in the next county, was terrible and terrifying."[5]

2

On the morning of 20 October, at eight-thirty, a buoyant delegation of eighty-two Wilmingtonians boarded the Fayetteville-bound train on the Cape Fear and Yadkin Valley Railway. In the party were members of the

White Government Union, a detachment of Cape Fear Militia under the command of Captain James I. Metts, and the Fifth Ward Cornet Band. At every station along the railroad line, high-spirited men and women boarded the train, and the band played at all stops to generate a greater enthusiasm. They arrived in Fayetteville at 11:40 A.M. With the band playing and banners fluttering, the groups left the railroad station. Turning from Maxwell into Hay Street, the procession assembled in front of the Hotel Lafayette, where they were "greeted with cheers, shouts of greeting and waving of hats and handkerchiefs."[6]

The Wilmington delegation was among the thousands of people attending the giant Fayetteville rally, the largest ever staged by the Democrats. Early in the morning people began to pour into the city, despite the fact that a heavy rain had fallen during the night and frequent showers continued until noon. The rain did little to dampen the enthusiasm or diminish the crowd pouring into the city from all directions—they had been gathering since sunrise. All the trains arriving were crowded; people came into Cumberland and surrounding counties in buggies, carriages, and wagons. The long lines of "vehicles filling all the streets and thoroughfares gave evidence that the white people of upper Cape Fear had left the plow, the machine shops, the kitchen, nay, the very neighborhood school-room."[7]

Benito Mussolini had his Blackshirts, Adolf Hitler had his Brownshirts, and the North Carolina Democrats had their Redshirts. The Redshirts were a sinister Klan-like organization. Wearing the "red-shirt badge of Southern terrorism" as a new attraction for the Democrats' great rallies and parades, they made their first appearance at Fayetteville, accompanied by fiery "Pitchfork" Benjamin Tillman, the one-eyed, grim figure from Edgefield, South Carolina. It is not known who sent the Macedonian Cry over the South Carolina borders and identified Tillman with the North Carolina white supremacy movement.

At approximately half past noon, the procession began to move from its starting point. It was led by the Wilmington band; immediately behind was the imposing scarlet brigade of three hundred Redshirts riding in columns. They were followed by a float of ornate decorations drawn by four fine horses and occupied by twenty-two beautiful young ladies in white, representing the twenty-two precincts of Cumberland County. Then came the carriage containing the mayor and chairman of the Democratic committee of the city, the editor of the *Fayetteville Observer,* and Senator Tillman. This was followed by a long line of carriages and other vehicles. On either side marched the White Government Union clubs escorting their guests, the visiting delegations from Wilmington and other cities. Bringing up the rear was a large crowd of people riding and on foot—all pressing onward to the fairgrounds. Arriving there amid the boom of cannons, the great throng assembled and gathered around the speakers' stand, while the Wilmington brass band furnished the music.[8]

The main attraction was Senator Tillman, invited especially to speak in behalf of white supremacy. He was introduced by the editor of the *Fayetteville Observer* as the "liberator of South Carolina." A tremendous ovation greeted Tillman. He thanked the audience for its great heartiness, the complimentary way in which it received him, and for the thousands who had come out on this "inauspicious day."[9]

He inveighed against President Grover Cleveland, Alex Manly, blacks, Republicans, and Fusion politics, throwing them all together. In noting the Redshirts in the audience, he said they carried his memory back twenty-two years when the people of South Carolina rose up in their wrath and overthrew Negro domination and put it under foot forever. He had seen in South Carolina five thousand red shirts in one audience, and the red shirt had become the emblem by which a white man was known.

It did him good to see that the people of North Carolina had caught the inspiration. He denounced President Cleveland as the cause of Populism. "The result of Fusion in North Carolina," Tillman said, was that the "Democrats were turned out and a worse rule was reinstated in its place."[10] Pointing a finger at his audience, he said, "You are now consequently reaping the fruits of your own idiocy."

His address included an attack on the Manly editorial. Noting the "very beautiful girls" in the audience, he said that they reminded him to say that such articles as that written by the Negro editor in Wilmington were an insult to the women of North Carolina. He then shouted, "Why didn't you kill that damn nigger editor who wrote that?"[11] Continuing, Tillman said, "Send him to South Carolina and let him publish any such offensive stuff, and he will be killed."

Several times during the hour-and-a-half-long address, he attempted to conclude it, but the audience urged him on, enthralled by his ringing voice and imperious gestures. His sentences were well constructed with picturesque illustrations and bearing the "flavor of wholesome country life . . . [and] running into great rapidity of utterance at the climaxes, but hitting the mark every time." His main theme was how the whites of South Carolina, where blacks outnumbered them three to one, had risen up against Negro rule, and now blacks were denied the ballot by constitutional amendment. Referring to his fellow South Carolinians, he said: "When we were under bayonets we never did submit to negro rule and what are you here for? Your right arm is off. You must get it back."[12]

Largely as a result of Tillman's visit to North Carolina, the Redshirt idea picked up momentum, spreading like wildfire throughout the Black Belt counties. These men rode horses and carried Winchesters, shotguns, and even pistols. While the organization was tainted with hoodlumism, it also included wealthy farmers, schoolteachers, and bankers—young and old men. With pants tucked into their boots, they were cloaked in "red shirts of calico, flannel or silk, according to the taste of the owner and the enthusiasm of his womankind.''[13] Contemporaries have left us a keen insight into the Redshirts and have described them as a terrifying spectacle. Just before sunset, to see three hundred red-shirt men riding towards the sunset with the sky red and red shirts seemingly to blend with the sky . . . it looked like the whole world was carmine. Another reported, They rode out of the dawn and into the light of sunsets as red as their shirts into the Negro sections, and by the houses of Negro farmers . . . leaving terror in their wake. The more militant members of the party rode the county by day and by night, "a yelling file of horsemen, galloping wildly. They were men who meant violence if fear was not enough.''[14]

Some of the South Carolina Redshirts continued on the tour with Tillman; others fanned out over the Black Belt to help organize other such groups. In Wilmington, the unemployed Mike Dowling, already associated with the white labor movement, was the organizer and leader of the Redshirts.[15]

On 21 October 1898, the day after the Fayetteville rally, Senator Jeter C. Pritchard wrote two confidential letters—one to President McKinley and one to Joseph Weeks Babcock, chairman of the Republican Congressional Committee—and both were of similar tenor and purport. In the letter to President McKinley, which formed the subject of a special cabinet meeting on 24 October, Senator Pritchard briefed him on the threatening conditions in North Carolina. He expressed grave anxiety over the intense racial feelings instigated by the Democrats. Whites were arming and blacks were buying weapons wherever they could, and the most serious trouble could be expected "in counties where colored people predominate." Among other allegations, he contended that a race war was imminent; that "six prominent Republicans" were marked for slaughter at Wilmington, as indicated by the "Big 6" displayed in the papers; that Chadbourn's letter was written through fear, either with a pistol at head or with threats of assassination; that the Democrats were ready to commit all kinds of crimes in order to carry the election; and that in their supreme effort to control political affairs, any kind of crime would be considered justifiable.[16] Senator Pritchard asked the president, "Will you send deputy United States Marshalls to preserve the peace?"[17]

"To Invoke Bayonet Rule," exclaimed the *Raleigh News and Observer.* Its editor, Josephus Daniels, knew through reliable sources of the contents of Pritchard's letter and of its discussion in the cabinet.

To allay the Democrats' fears of federal intervention, the *News and Observer* quickly provided the answers. "Of course, the President has no power to send Federal troops into the State until the Governor has made requisition for them and shows that he is unable to handle the situation with the forces at his command." Further, Governor Russell could not call for federal troops until the anticipated rioting had actually occurred and he was able to show that he had exhausted all the efforts of the state to suppress it. In addition, the president could not send in troops unless the United States mails were

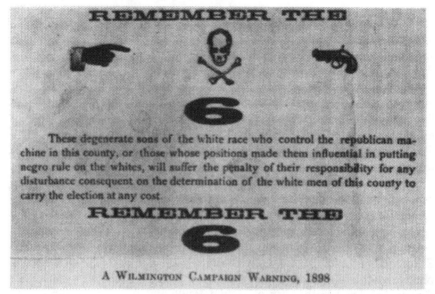

interfered with.[18] Daniels branded Pritchard's letter a ghost story, which soon threw Pritchard on the defensive.

3

Both before and after the Fayetteville rally, the Democrats of Wilmington were agitated over the movement of the Republicans to field a county ticket—a move that the Democrats were determined to block. The offices at stake were sheriff, Register of deeds, coroner, treasurer, clerk of the superior court, and members of the General Assembly. With the exception of the Register of deeds—a black man who had held that office for two years—the proposed ticket was composed of white men. Nevertheless, the Democrats of Wilmington began pressing the Fusionist forces to make no nominations in New Hanover County. Members of the Democratic Executive Committee argued that a race riot would occur at the election since the whites were so thoroughly aroused; but the real reason was that the Democrats knew that they would have a difficult time defeating the Republicans, who were supported by the black majority.

G. Z. French, the deputy sheriff, who had plenty of grit, was determined to nominate a Republican ticket, and his party so notified Governor Russell. A faction associated with Keith was also insistent about fielding a ticket in New Hanover County, and Governor Russell agreed to support that endeavor. Keith wrote his friend Senator Butler "to come down . . . [and] make a speech and please do not fail. We need you." He also invited him to be his houseguest. "I hear the Democrats," Keith continued, "will carry this part of the state. I look for a lot of innocent people to be killed here if things continue as they are." He cautioned Butler with these words: "You will keep what I have written to yourself."[19]

Some days later, the local papers announced that Governor Russell and senators Pritchard and Butler were scheduled to speak in Wilmington. Again the Democrats were thrown into a quandary. On the day of the announcement, George Rountree remembered going to lunch and being accosted on the street by Edgar G. Parmele, who said, "Those people were going to speak and we must not let them speak." Rountree replied he "did not see how in the H—— we could help it."[20] But Parmele was adament that the trio not be allowed to speak. Rountree told him to contact Frank Stedman and Walker Taylor, and they would talk it over at three o'clock. They met as agreed, debated the problem, and decided to call together representative businessmen of Wilmington, including members of the campaign committee.

When the group met, Taylor asked Rountree to state the objectives of the meeting. This he did, emphasizing that for Russell, Pritchard, and Butler's appearance, the blacks had arranged to have a brass band and a torch light procession and that this would influence the whites and there certainly would be a riot. A heated discussion followed, which included harsh and peremptory language, to the extent that Rountree was forced to protest. A committee was appointed to interview the governor and the two senators and to point out to them the extreme danger of a race riot that would follow an attempt on their part to speak.

During this controversy, the enigmatic attorney, Alfred M. Waddell, appeared on the scene. Where he had been all along is somewhat of a mystery; even his memoirs and his private papers are silent on this subject.

Waddell was noted for his superior eloquence. In some circles he was dubbed the silver-tongued orator of the East. At the apex of his political career, his appearance in any town or hamlet was greeted with the greatest enthusiasm. He was born on 16 September 1834, of slaveholding parents on a plantation that still bears the name Moorefield and is located three miles from the town of Hillsborough. He studied law and was admitted to the bar in 1855, but he apparently did not want to pursue this profession. In May 1860, he purchased the *Daily Herald*, abandoned the law practice, and devoted his full time to publishing until the outbreak of the Civil War. He served in the Confederate Army as a lieutenant colonel of the cavalry. After the war he went into politics and was elected to Congress, serving three terms (1871–77). He lost his congressional seat to Rupublican Daniel L. Russell in 1878, and his political career was permanently eclipsed.[21] For this reason, he viewed the governor with abhorrence.

Waddell was typical of the Southerners' definition of the term gentleman . . . [and] a descendant of the genuine aristocracy, the embodiment of arrogance. He was of average height, thin, and always immaculately dressed. He

Ex-Congressman (Colonel) Alfred M. Waddell (1834–1912). From *Collier's Weekly,* **November 26, 1898 (Library of Congress).**

sported a full and well-kept beard of gray that reflected a silver glow when the light touched it. In 1898, he looked fifty years of age, but confessed to being sixty-five.[22]

Beneath his shaggy eyebrows were a pair of cold gray eyes. He appeared on the surface to be conservative, calm in temper, and mild mannered; but his speeches contained some of the most violent tirades ever uttered from the rostrum. Among his racist views, he did not believe that any full-blooded Negro could ever attain greatness.[23] His philosophy was appropriate for the role he was about to play: the central role in the coup plot.

The evidence strongly suggests that, on the eve of the Wilmington race riot, Waddell was experiencing hard times. Keith confided to Senator Butler that "Waddell, Parmele and Walker Taylor did not have jobs."[24] The political struggle in Wilmington may have provided the occasion for political opportunism; it was indeed fortuitous for Waddell and others.

It occurred to Rountree that it might be a good plan to have Waddell make a red hot speech during the visit of the governor and the senators, in order to test the feelings of the community as to whether the whites would stand any more nonsense from the Republicans and the blacks. Waddell agreed on the condition that the campaign committee formally ask him. It seems that Waddell had previously offered his services to some of the key Democrats and had been turned down. Meeting Rountree on the street, he said that the body did not seem to want him to help. They questioned, in fact, whether he would be of any value. Soon after this conversation, Rountree was to discover that for some time a keen rivalry had prevailed between Waddell and

Stedman.[25] Perhaps Stedman had aspirations to be installed as mayor after the coup.

In talking the problem over with Parmele, who was a friend of Waddell, it was suggested that there be two speeches—one by Stedman and one by Waddell—and the campaign committee delegated Rountree to ask Waddell and Stedman about this arrangement. Waddell agreed, and it was advertised that he would speak in the Opera House on 24 October 1898. Then came the news that Governor Russell and senators Pritchard and Butler had called off their speaking engagement in Wilmington; the Democratic campaign committee now insisted that Waddell also should not speak. Certain Democrats were determined, however, that he fulfill his speaking promise; they informed Rountree that the committee had no authority over Waddell's speaking.

It was also time for another protagonist to enter: the unemployed and hotheaded Irishman, Mike Dowling, who was both the organizer and the leader of the Redshirts.[26] At dusk on 24 October, curious onlookers saw some sixty Redshirts assembled at Sixth and Castle. In a sergeantlike manner, Dowling called them to order, and they all marched down Castle to Front Street, then up Front to Princess, and from Princess to the Opera House.

The announcement that the "silver-tongued orator of the East" would address the white men of Wilmington was sufficient to pack the house floors and galleries. On the stage with him were Thomas W. Strange, chairman of the Democratic Executive Commiteee of New Hanover County, and about fifty of the city's most prominent citizens. At 8:15 P.M., Strange arose amid applause and introduced Waddell. The audience responded with a deafening ovation.

Sometimes dubbed an American Robespierre, with his silver voice and resourceful vocabulary, Waddell had mastered every oratory technique. His audience on this night listened to his lengthy address, sometimes as if hypnotized. At one point he said, "We are reduced to the pitiful necessity of choosing whether we will live under the domination of negroes led by a few unprincipled white men, and see the ruin of all that we hold dear, or prove ourselves worthy of the respect of mankind by restoring good government at all hazards and at every cost." This was the only issue in the impending election. In inveighing against Governor Russell, he said: "I do not hesitate to say this publicly that if a race conflict occurs in North Carolina, the very first men that ought to be held to account are the white leaders of the negroes who will be chiefly responsible for it. To begin at the top of the list. I scorn to leave any doubt as to whom I mean . . . I mean the Governor of this state who is the engineer of all the deviltry."[27]

He closed with the resolution that "we will never surrender to a ragged raffle of negroes, even if we have to choke the Cape Fear River with [black] carcasses."[28] A "Sizzling Talk," the *Messenger* complimented Waddell's address the next morning.

The Democrats felt somewhat elated over their triumph in getting the Republicans not to speak in Wilmington, but they were not through yet. Their next objective was to suppress completely the Republican ticket in New Hanover County. They now argued that such a ticket would surely result in a race riot. They soon convinced the business community of the danger, and the business interests, predominantly Democrats, now contended that their major concern was for the peace and welfare of the Wilmington community, and that there would be a revolution if a Fusionist ticket was put up. James Sprunt wrote to Governor Russell that the approaching election "threatens to provoke a war between the black and white races . . . The white people and taxpayers generally protest that they have been driven to desperation, and we have no hesitation in saying that, even the usual indiscretion of political partisans on the next election day, will precipitate a conflict which may cost hundreds, and perhaps thousands, of lives, and the partial or entire destruction of the city." Stressing his main point, Sprunt said, "We declare to you our conviction that we are on the brink of a revolution which can only be averted by the suppression of a Republican ticket."[29]

As an initial move toward their objective, the Democratic Executive Committee called a caucus. After some discussion, they delegated George Rountree to talk to E. K. Bryan, a former law partner of Governor Russell. Bryan agreed to go to Raleigh to persuade the governor to use his influence to prevent the Republicans from putting up a ticket in New Hanover County. Later it was decided that James Sprunt and James Chadbourn should accompany Bryan. The three men went to Raleigh quietly and received favorable consideration from Governor Russell; however, the governor hesitated on the idea of not fielding a Fusionist ticket in New Hanover County. The governor saw clearly through the Democrats' scheme. Among other things, the suppression of the Republican ticket would not only deny the Republicans of New Hanover County the privilege of exercising their constitutional rights to vote for members of the legislature and for county officers, but would also deny them their right to vote for members of Congress. They would thus be deprived not only of their rights under the state constitution, but of those secured to them under the United States Constitution as well. Finally, what the Democrats were advocating violated the one man–one vote concept and was contrary to the two-party tradition.

Important to note at this point is the keen rivalry that existed between the Democratic Executive Committee and the business interests to control Wilmington politics. James Sprunt, owner of the largest cotton press, concluded that candidates representative of the business interests would bring about feelings and would result in a peaceable and orderly election for county, state, senatorial, and congressional offices. He informed the governor accordingly, supplying him with a list of people the business interests of the city and county would support for the General Assembly.

The Democrats had put two anti-Russell candidates in the race for the General Assembly—George L. Peschau and J. T. Kerr. The former was a vigorous young attorney, who was canvassing the eastern Carolina district for nomination and election to the North Carolina House of Representatives on a platform calling for the impeachment of Governor Russell.

Aware of the move to impeach the governor, the Democrats were resolved to capitalize on it. They sent to Raleigh a committee composed of Sprunt, Bryan, Chadbourn, and Peyton H. Hoge, pastor of the First Presbyterian Church. These Wilmingtonians were delegated to enter into a political agreement with the governor. They pledged the withdrawal of the two anti-Russell candidates, Peschau and Kerr, on the condition that Governor Russell and G. Z. French would agree to use their influence in preventing the nomination of a Republican slate in New Hanover County.

Immediately after the delegation returned to Wilmington, the Democrats called a meeting for the purpose of nominating two candidates for the General Assembly in place of Peschau and Kerr; Rountree and Martin S. Willard were nominated.[30] The selection of Rountree was another trump card the Democrats were later to play. If the businessmen had desired a candidate representative of their interests, they had failed. "I regret," the Republican F. W. Foster noted, "to see by the morning papers that the business men's meeting did not select the two legislative candidates, but that it practically turned it over to the political machine."[31] The candidates, representative of the business interests or of the political machine, were Democrats, nominated to eliminate any possible race war, and the die had been cast in a greater mold in Wilmington.

The Redshirts were not quiescent. As long as they were under the guidance of respectable leaders, some control prevailed; but once left to their own devices, they degenerated into numerous small gangs, growing ruder and bolder as their numbers increased. The civil forces were too timid to challenge the Redshirts and their cohorts. Governor Russell called the public's attention to the fact that it has been made known to him in such a reliable way that he could not doubt its truthfulness, that certain North Carolina counties lying along the southern borders have been actually invaded by certain armed and lawless men from another State; that several political meetings in Richmond and Halifax counties have been broken up and dispersed by armed men, using threats, intimidation, and in some cases, actual violence. Continuing, the governor said "that in other cases property had been actually destroyed and citizens fired on from ambush; that several citizens have been taken from their homes at night and whipped; that in several counties peaceful citizens have been intimidated and terrorized by threats of violence to their persons and their property, until they were afraid to register themselves, preparatory to exercising that highest duty of a free man, the casting of one free vote at the ballot box for the men of their own choice in the coming election."[32]

Governor Russell issued a proclamation on 26 October 1898 against the activities of the Redshirts and other groups with a predeliction toward violence. It commanded "all illdisposed persons, whether of this or that political party, or of no political party, to immediately desist from all unlawful practices and all turbulent conduct, and to preserve the peace." In another part of this proclamation, the governor counseled all good citizens "not to allow themselves to become excited by any appeals that may be made to their passions and prejudices by the representatives of any political party . . . and to keep cool heads, and use their good offices to preserve the public peace," and to protect every "citizen in all his rights, political and personal."[33]

"A Proclamation by Russell," announced the *Wilmington Messenger,* calling it the Republicans' "last card." The next day the paper carried the headline, "Federal Bayonets to Be Used by Republicans in Carrying the Election in North Carolina."[34] The *Messenger* reported on 29 October, "Russell Working for the Destruction of Wilmington." It reported that the "war cloud thickens as the Governor had put on his war paint and was busily grinding his axe, while putting fresh ammunition in his guns and increasing his armament." "Dan is a terror," continued the editorial, and "his great eyes rolled now in anger and shoot forth with consuming fire. He means to have an election here if it lays the city in ruins and depopulates it." Russell was also accused of being willing to cause a race war, using the "warlike arm" of the federal government in his "vile and diabolican plans," for he expected the "United States Army to come down upon Wilmington, like a wolf upon the fold"; however, the editorial was quick to warn that Russell would be disappointed by the results.[35] At the same time, some Democratic leaders charged that the proclamation was a conspiracy hatched out in order to furnish a pretext for bringing Federal troops into the State.

As October was fading, final preparations were being made for the gigantic rallies and Redshirt parades, soon to mushroom in many cities. A cry for deliverance from Negro domination had gone up from the east. Heeding the desires of the Wilmington Democrats, Furnifold M. Simmons, chairman of the state Democratic Executive Committee, staged another giant political rally at Goldsboro on 28 October. It was the largest one yet, and he called it the "White Man's Convention."[36] The meeting was given wide coverage by the Democratic press, which included the *Raleigh News and Observer, Raleigh Morning Post, Wilmington Messenger, New Bern Journal, Winston Journal,* and *Goldsboro Argus.* "Special Trains from Wilmington," announced the *Messenger,* and noted that the "Atlantic Coastline's rate will be one first-class fare for the trip." The Seaboard and the Southern railroads did the same for Greensboro and other cities.[37] Some eight thousand white supremists were in attendance, representing nearly every county in the east and some parts of the west. Among the prominent speakers were Simmons, Aycock, Waddell and William A. Guthrie, the mayor of Durham. The last had run the gamut, from former Republican candidate for governor on the Populist ticket in 1896 to now being temporary Democratic chairman.

Simmons opened the conference and soon surrendered the chair to Guthrie, who was met with thunderous applause from the vast crowds. He immediately called upon Methodist minister N. M. Jurney, who prayed briefly but fervently. "Let us feel this day," he entreated, "the vibrations of our coming redemption from all wicked rule and the supremacy of the race destined . . . to rule this country."

Afterward, Guthrie said to his audience, "We have met, by common consent, to lay aside our former partisan differences and come together, breast to breast, and man to man, as patriotic white men [to] settle for ourselves, for our state and for posterity knotty questions." He then alluded to the conditions in the eastern part of the state under Fusion rule and Negro domination and asked, "Is there a good white man in North Carolina who loves his state and his race?" He then censured the Democratic apostates, calling them "bolters," whom he accused of having sold the party's flag. He asked, "What have they received for it?" Answering his own question, he said: "Negro magistrates! Negro legislators! Negro postmasters! Negro deputy marshals! And Negro revenue officers all over eastern North Carolina, and in some counties in western North Carolina."

In the tone of a zealot, he continued: "The Anglo-Saxon planted civilization on this continent and where ever this race has been in conflict with another race, it has asserted its supremacy and either conquered or exterminated the foe. This great race has carried the Bible in one hand and the sword [in the other]." In a stentorian voice, he warned the blacks, "Resist our march of progress and civilization and we will wipe you off the face of the earth."[38]

It was the fiery Waddell, however, whose speech electrified the convention. He spoke with fervor as he renewed and amplified his statement made four days earlier. He spoke of the insolence and arrogance of blacks and of increased burglaries and other crimes. He told of the insults to white women and of blacks' obscene language in the presence of white ladies, and he told of the white leaders who were "responsible for the evils of negro rule." After describing with vivid words the conditions in his city, he declared, "We are going to protect our firesides and our loved ones or die in the attempt." He concluded thunderously with the defiant promise that the white people of Wilmington would drive out the Manlys and Russells and the hordes of corruptionists if they had to throw enough Negro dead bodies into Cape Fear to choke up its passage to the sea.[39]

Eight militant resolutions were enthusiastically adopted; this best explains the purpose of the Goldsboro rally. In summary, the resolutions recognized that the eastern section of the state was "divided into two distinct races—the

Anglo-Saxon and the African." In the Black Belt where Negroes constituted a substantial portion of the population (and in some counties exceeded the numbers of whites), the problem had always been the maintenance of political control by the white minority. Now there was a call to close the ranks of the whites. The eight resolutions mandated that the purpose of the Goldsboro convention be published in every newspaper, notifying all "North Carolinians to know what the fusion of the Republicans and Populists had done to Eastern North Carolina."

After the Goldsboro convention, the political rallies picked up momentum, exploding throughout the Black Belt counties. Conditions in Wilmington, meanwhile, were already bordering on anarchy; the city was sitting on a racial powder keg. As correspondent Henry L. West of the *Forum* observed, the fear of a Negro uprising in defense of his right to vote, with a forcible and revengeful retaliation, offered the whites an excuse for the display of arms. White supremacy was the goal; the wholesale armament was intended to convey this to the blacks. There would thus be rapid-fire guns and Winchesters if "every church had held a silent pulpit, and every lodge-room where the Negroes met had been empty."[40]

4

Focusing on the days prior to the 1898 election, one finds Wilmington preparing for its 2 November Redshirt parade and rally. The city dubbed it, appropriately, the "White Man's Rally" and for an added incentive advertised "Barbecue and Rally" at Hilton Park along Front and Market streets. At dusk, barrels of tar were lit all over the city, and from them rolled upward a maze of varied colored smoke printed in gorgeous hues by the consuming fires that lit the landscape and silhouetted the heads of the passing throng against the surrounding darkness. These barrels of blazing tar gave a glow to the occasion and advertised the meetings at several places. The New Hanover County horsemen met the Wilmington Redshirts and Rough Riders and a delegation of Croatans, wearing White Government Union buttons.

Dowling was in his glory at the head of the Redshirts, who lead the parade. At approximately seven-thirty in the evening, the procession began to move down Market to Front, then up Front to the Democratic headquarters in the old First National Bank building, where the speakers, Fishblate, Rountree, Iredell Meares, and others joined it. The parade created enthusiasm among the whites and consternation among the blacks, while cheering white women waved flags and handkerchiefs as the long column of armed and menacing horsemen rode by. For this occasion, Dowling also performed the role of master of ceremonies. During the long speeches, the crowd often applauded and yelled itself hoarse. Afterward, the Redshirts and others whooped it up far into the night.

Three days later, Waddell made another "sizzling talk" at the Opera

House. After a brief introduction, he arose amid deafening applause and cheers; in a typical white supremacy speech, he devoted a sizable part of his address to the Manly editorial. "I understand [Manly] is still here," he said, "and is educating his race" to exercise their natural rights as electors. Waddell hinted that Manly should have been lynched.[41]

Conditions were beginning to look more serious in Wilmington as the frenzy mounted. Headlines in all the papers gave daily notice of meetings, which were held nightly in public buildings and daily on street corners, and were apt to be near some bar, whose owner was one of the leading Democrats. Food and special spirits (moonshine) were free on almost any corner as the dispensers of the liquor, like any special-interest group (saloon owners such as Charles Schnibben, Bernhard Balzois, Gieschen Bros., J. D. Steljes and Frank B. Brown could always be expected to be on the winning side. They offered an opportunity for agitators and fiery orators to attempt to impose their ideas on the audience. "One pompous, beaver-diked specimen of their number," wrote Keith, "got up and made one of the bitterest talks, urging the boys on." He was one of their first recruits, and his name always garnered big headlines in the papers. He often boasted that "he had been in one riot before he came here, where they killed nine, and was itching to be in another one." Keith was describing the Reverend Peyton H. Hoge, pastor of the Presbyterian Church in Wilmington, who looked "like a character out of Charles Dickens' works." The "heavy bearded" preacher wore a "high-hat" and a "spike-tailed coat and a gun on his shoulders . . . [and] went out hunting blackbirds."[42]

As the atmosphere of Wilmington became charged with passions that a mere spark could ignite, both the Democrat's chief executive, Furnifold Simmons, and Governor Russell became alarmed. Simmons dispatched Colonel Wilson G. Lamb to determine with certainty what was actually going on in the city. Lamb informed the Wilmington Democrats that they were doing things that might not meet approval, and he received a strong rebuff for trying to intervene in the city's political affairs. Rountree later recalled, "I remember I told Colonel Lamb that Simmons might go to H——, as we were going to run the campaign to suit ourselves down here."[43]

Governor Russell with each passing day became more nervous over the Wilmington crisis. Because of the volatile state of affairs, he made an unexpected visit; prior to this time, the governor had avoided Wilmington by proceeding to his country estate on the left bank of the Cape Fear river, down in Brunswick County, without even passing through the city. He had heard of the movement of the blacks to place a county ticket in the field and had come down to suppress it if possible. Then there were other theories in regard to the purposes of his visit.[44] For instance, some thought that to insure a smooth election, he wanted to give instructions to the black leaders on how to conduct themselves on Election Day. He held a parley with the Democrats and reached an accord by which the Democrats accepted the resignation of both of their nominees for the state house of representatives and agreed to support George Rountree and Martin S. Willard, who were also named by the business interests.

The governor also held a conference with the black Republicans, stressing that they should vote the Fusion state, congressional, and senatorial tickets. As a follow-up, the governor, Senator Pritchard, and A. E. Holton, chairman of the Republican state committee, issued a circular to the blacks: "Do not hang around the polls on Election Day. Vote and go to your homes." Leading persons believed, or at least hoped, that there would be no disturbances if the blacks did as the Negro lawyer Henderson advised them: "Go to the polls and cast [your] ballots quietly and go home."[45]

While the majority of black voters would voluntarily stay home, hoping that bloodshed might be avoided, some of the more militant blacks were going to insist upon exercising their constitutional rights. It was common knowledge that racial conflict was inevitable.

By this time, another illegal organization—the Rough Riders—had surfaced as a self-appointed vigilante committee. This was a much larger organization than the Redshirts. Some members were poor whites, who rode bareback on mules and mares. Rumors ran rampant through Wilmington, and no one knew how they got started; one was of the movement to hang Deputy Sheriff French from the limb of an old tree on Church Street near the Cape Fear River. Perhaps influenced by the recent speech by Waddell, the idea to lynch Manly was rekindled. Hugh McRae maintained that he was sitting on his porch on Market Street that afternoon and saw a band of Redshirts, fifty in number, with blood in their eyes, mounted upon their steeds, and led by Mike Dowling. They came to a quick halt in front of his home. Before the dust had settled he had gone out to find what their purpose was in coming. Dowling dismounted and told McRae that they were headed for the *Record* building to lynch Manly and burn the structure. This would never do, for it would upset the Secret Nine's scheme to overthrow the city government; McRae had to persuade them (perhaps with threats of arrest) to desist from their plans.

Some members of the Secret Nine enlisted the support of the Reverend Christopher C. Dennen, pastor of Saint Thomas Catholic Church, to restrain Dowling and exacted a promise that he would not lead his hotheaded Redshirts through the city, wantonly killing blacks.[46] In fact, the Redshirts were not under the direction of any of the other cabals, and lynchings were only prevented by the determined effort of a few men.

5

Alex Manly's escape from Wilmington is a fascinating episode in itself. For fear of being injured or murdered, Manly had ceased publishing the *Record* and was waiting for an opportunity to leave the city. The exact time he left will never be known, and there are several versions. Manly did not like to talk about his escape.

One version of Manly's escape was given by Thomas Clawson, editor of the *Messenger,* who stated that it happened on the night of the election. The date is in question, but not the event. Blacks were staying off the streets, even in their own community. One night, Clawson and a friend went into Brooklyn and did not meet a single Negro in the streets. They moved from Front Street to seventh on Nun, and at the corner of Seventh and Nun streets, an old-fashioned incandescent light was sputtering overhead. It was shedding a faint light in the street, darkened by shade trees along the pavement. The figure of a lone black man showed up under the light. He raised both hands and said, "For God's sake, Mr. Clawson, what are you doing over here?" The man was Alderman Andrew Walker. Clawson told Walker that he wanted to speak to the Manly brothers to advise them to get out of Wilmington as quickly as possible. He also wanted to assure the return of his Hoe press, on which the Manlys had made a small payment when they were publishing the paper at Princess and Water streets. Clawson demanded the return of the press and a signed statement from the owners that the real ownership rested in him.[47]

It is safe to assume that Manly had already left town before this incident, based on information passed down by members of his family. A letter written in 1954 by his wife, Carrie Manly, to her sons sheds the most authentic light on her husband's escape. She wrote that a prominent white man and friend of the family sent for Manly and "told him that they were going to lynch him, and he must get out of town that very night." The friend gave him twenty-five dollars and said, "Now, this is the pass word, and may God be with you—boy, you are too fine to be strung up to a tree."

Manly immediately prepared for his departure. After the sad farewell to his family, he left with no baggage; he rode with his brother Frank in one buggy and J. W. (Jim) Telfair and Owen Bailey in another. According to Manly, the river banks, railroads, and steamboats were all patrolled by Redshirts on horseback holding Winchesters.[48] The blacks moved along the road, and the horses' hindquarters bounced up and down at a sharp trot. Several Redshirts were sighted in the distance near a wooded area. The men used the "pass word and escaped in the woods over Fulton Bridge." Now Redshirts could be seen everywhere, in front and to the right and left. Someone shouted, "Halt!"

They all gazed with some apprehension at the crowd of horsemen assembled, and especially at the inquiring expression of their apparent leader. Then they gave the password, and the leader said, "We are having a necktie party in Wilmington. Where are you gentlemen going?"

"We are going after that scoundrel Manly."

"What! With no guns?"

The entire conversation is not available; however, Mrs. Manly wrote that

Congressman George Henry White (1852–1918). From Josephus Daniels, *Editor in Politics* **(copyright 1941, The University of North Carolina Press). Reprinted by permission of the publisher.**

the horsemen "filled the buggy with guns," with the instructions, "If you see that smart nigger—shoot him!"[49]

Manly's party was no doubt instructed where to return the weapons; then they commanded the horses to start, turned sharply up the road, and galloped off, losing sight of the horsemen. The would-be lynchers were on the lookout for a male with negroid features; all four men in the buggies looked like white men, and the Redshirts did not know the difference. That is how Manly was able to escape from Wilmington.

He migrated to Asbury Park, New Jersey, and resided with his brother-in-law, the Reverend I. N. Giles.[50] Soon afterward, he migrated to Washington, D.C., and found employment as a secretary to Congressman George H. White, the last black congressman of the post-reconstruction era.

6

Although armed Redshirts stalked the streets and racist rhetoric increased, it would be a mistake to assume governmental paralysis during the weeks immediately preceding the coup. All this went on without any public event to disturb the town's tranquility, for the Democratic coterie kept its devious schemes well hidden from the public. It provided the stump orators with the propaganda themes, while at all times controlling the poor whites and the Redshirts. Hugh McRae, for example, had vetoed Dowling and his Redshirts' desire to lynch Manly. To the spectators, the Redshirts' and Rough Riders' activity looked ominous, but it often was nothing more than intense ribaldry, while the police looked the other way for various reasons.

In certain respects the Wilmington event of 1898 had some of the ingredients of the early French Revolution. In regard to the latter, historians know that a cabal of politicans generated the "Great Fear." They made the public believe that the aristocrats were secretly recruiting brigands to terrorize the Third Estate. All elements of the Third Estate, which included persons ranging from the wealthiest business and professional classes to urban workers and the poorest peasantry, began to arm in self-defense. Crowds turned into mobs and assaulted everything that symbolized the aristocrats. The French conspirators thus used class hatred for their purposes. In the Wilmington coup, conspirators used the Negro for their purposes, with bigotry and economics as motivation. They generated the bugaboo of the Negro and the impression that whites must arm for a defense against it. By the same token, the blacks deemed it necessary to arm for defense against the whites. White people withdrew to themselves, as did the blacks; each race closed its ranks and drew away from the other. By this time the white demagogues had Wilmington taut with both excitement and activity. They spread the word that the blacks had planned to burn the town. Hearsay had it that blacks were buying guns and ammunition and, being well armed, were conducting secret military drills and preparing to fight. There were also reports that black ministers and spokesmen were using "churches to deliver incendiary speeches and impassioned appeals to blacks to use the bullet that had no respect for color and the kerosene and torch that would play havoc with the white man's cotton bale and warehouse."[51]

These rumors flowed to the campaign committee. Four men met, and at the suggestion of John R. Kenly, president of the Atlantic Coastline Railroad, they employed a Negro detective to move among the blacks and let them know what they were doing. The detective reported that the blacks "were doing practically nothing."[52] In contrast to the findings of the black investigator, two white Pinkerton detectives reported to their employer, through Walker Taylor, that the Negro women servants in the homes of the white citizens had agreed to set fire to the dwellings of their employers; and the Negro men had openly threated to 'burn the town down,' if the white supremacy issue prevailed in the political contest.

The Wilmington situation could not pass unnoticed, and it stimulated much interest outside the state. There were a number of both Northern and Southern correspondents in the city, and they reported the large sales of weapons. Frank Weldon, staff correspondent of the *Atlanta Constitution* reported that "carloads of guns have been secured for use." He also warned that a "revolution was impending, which will be wrought by ballot or the French variety of a century ago, and enough arms had been imported in the last sixty days to equip an entire division of the United States Army."[53] From another souce came the statement that it was doubted if there ever was a community in the United States that had as many weapons per capita as here in Wilmington.

When Henry L. West arrived in Wilmington, he was appalled at its military preparation, so extensive as to suggest "assault, and besieged from some foreign foe, or that the city had been preparing for a siege instead of an election." He asked for an explanation of the situation; the answer was given in four words: "The Whites must rule."[54]

With the statewide supremacy election some distance off, the Democratic cabal, along with some wealthy citizens of Wilmington, accepted the premise that violence was inevitable to restore the government to those to whom it rightfully belonged. More and more, it became common knowledge that the right of suffrage would be denied the blacks. The Redshirts were terrifying everybody they could; hence, most blacks were lying low, and most had already made up their minds that they were not going near the polls on election day. The demogogues spread the word, however, that the intrepid ones would insist on exercising their constitutional rights and would in the process ignite a race riot.

This potentially explosive situation was the ostensible justification for whites securing arms for their defense, but in the background lurked the devious purpose. Already carefully listed were names of white Republicans and blacks who were scheduled to be banished. As was pointed out above, many merchants had supported the movement to raise a special fund (see p. 60). According to a contemporary, more than $30,000 was subscribed to buy weapons and ammunition to equip the poor whites in the city and the county to carry out the plot.

In anticipating the rebellion, the white leaders had taken extensive precautionary measures for the protection of their lives and property. A vigilance committee separate from any campaign organization was formed so that the whites could act in concert.[55] This body had its own tactics and signals.

After the inception of the plan placing the city under a military department, a conference was held among the leading white citizens. Colonel Roger Moore, "veteran of the Southern Confederacy," was selected commander-in-chief and placed in full charge. Next, a protective scheme was designed dividing the city into sections that, in turn, were divided into wards and then into blocks. The wards were placed under the command of a captain and the blocks under a lieutenant. Onlookers could observe each lieutenant meeting his captain "almost nightly," reporting that "each lieutenant, when called upon for a report, announced the number of able-bodied men in his block willing to bear arms; while the aggregate number of rifles, shot-guns, and revolvers was also made known. The number of women, children, and sick men requiring protection was also given; and the data thus presented were carefully noted down."[56] If a riot were to occur, all women and children in each ward were to assemble at a designated building. Each block in the city was guarded by armed citizens taking turns at patrol duty. Special sentries were placed around certain properties belonging to leading men active in the movement. Finally, mounted Redshirts patrolled all roads leading in and out of the city.

To give more meaning to the situation, the white citizens had equipped and manned a new Gatling gun, sometimes in the post office building and sometimes in the local armory. This awesome and destructive device had been purchased at a cost of $1,200.[57] Lieutenant Charles H. White later related his first experiences with the new gun. "The gun," he said, "was a great mystery to me and always will be and I did not know what kind of a gun it was, whose gun it was or anything about it." He saw it for the first time on Sunday at the armory, and he asked what it was. Someone replied that it was a rapid-fire gun. Next, he was asked to assemble it and admitted that he had little experience with big guns. Nevertheless, with Sergeant George Harris, Jr., they "got it in order, put it on a boat, and went down the river to try it out." Locating the right spot, White said, "When I took my seat on the gun I could not tell whether it would shoot front or back, but just closed my eyes, pulled the trigger and let her go and all I knew was I heard a loud explosion and that is the first time and last time we ever worked that gun. As far as I know, it went everywhere the Wilmington Light Infantry went."[58]

Against the background of this heavily garrisoned white community and Redshirt intimidation, what preparations were the blacks making to meet this obvious threat?

With each day moving toward 10 November, blacks became more tense and apprehensive. A number of men attempted to purchase weapons. Since all merchants who stocked this type of merchandise were white and knew what was in the wind, they refused to sell blacks arms or an ounce of powder. Then the blacks sought to order arms from a Northern manufacturing establishment. Here again they were frustrated, for the local agent of the express company rejected the consignment.[59] Now they were cut off from all means of defense, except for a few blacks who owned some old army muskets or pistols.

7

On the eve of the election, trains were observed going north, south, and west from Wilmington, crowded with people. The apprehension of impending trouble had caused many white men to send their families away.

In Raleigh, there were rumors of threats to assassinate Governor Russell. Living in constant fear of assassination as he walked the halls of the state capitol, the governor maintained a personal bodyguard and kept a loaded shotgun and a pistol near him at all times.[60] Concurrently . . . there came from many quarters demands for the impeachment of Governor Russell.

At this time, Wilmington went temporarily dry, at least in the statute books. On 5 November, the Board of Aldermen had called a special meeting and had appointed extra policemen. The board passed an ordinance making it unlawful for any person in the city of Wilmington to sell or give away any whiskey, wine, beer, ale, or any other intoxicating drinks between the hours of 11:30 P.M., 5 November, and 6:00 P.M., 10 November, 1898. Violators were subject to a fine not to exceed fifty dollars or imprisonment not to exceed thirty days. The city already had ordinances against the carrying of firearms.[61] As in frontier days, many men carried pistols, rifles, and shotguns anyway, and the streets were filled with citizens, peacefully disposed, but whose pistol pockets bulged out ominously. As a backdrop for this, the fiery and passionate writings of the newspaper editors, the inflammatory oratory flowing lava-like from the stump and from the pulpits, and the doctrine of white supremacy being preached in the same breath with the story of Christ had galvanized many people toward anticipation of violence.

The Redshirts and Rough Riders continued to reign supreme. With the actual coming of the election, an uglier mood pervaded their ranks, and some degenerated into drunks. So far, however, everything had been done without violence. Then, on the day before the election, Governor Russell issued a circular informing blacks that they would be allowed to vote for a state senator, the only Republican candidate running. When some of the Redshirts and Rough Riders heard of this, they "growled angrily," and about three-thirty in the afternoon, "they started down to the polls with rifles and Hotchkiss guns to mow them down . . . but Mr. Eliott and some other sharp lawyers scurried down and told them it would be the worse [sic] possible policy, that the Republican leaders would plead intimidation at the polls and so have the whole vote thrown out, and we would loose our congressman."[62]

Waddell continued to be a pivotal figure. On the night before the election, for example, he told a madly cheering horde in the Opera House: "You are Anglo-Saxons. You are armed and prepared, and you will do your duty. Be ready at a moment's notice. Go to the polls tomorrow, and if you find the Negro out voting, tell him to leave the polls and if he refuses kill him, shoot him down in his tracks. We shall win tomorrow if we have to do it with guns."[63]

Election day, 8 November, finally dawned, with Redshirts milling around many precincts, armed with Winchesters and shotguns. Many persons in Wilmington and throughout the state apprehensively pondered the question, Will the election pass off peacefully? In New Hanover County, as well as in other counties, mounted Redshirts paraded, displaying their Winchesters, while intermittently firing in the air as if testing their efficiency. These demonstrations persisted throughout the course of the polling and had a purpose:

Governor Daniel L. Russell (1845–1908). From *New York Herald,* **November 20, 1898 (file, New York Public Library).**

to convince the black man not to attempt to exercise his constitutional right as a voter.

But Governor Russell was determined to exercise his constitutional rights and vote, and he encountered men of violence who had no respect for the status of the state's chief executive. Russell barely escaped death at the hands of the mob that was infiltrated with Redshirts, although the event managed to escape being reported in the major Southern papers, even those of North Carolina. The *New York Herald* reported it, however: "The Governor of South Carolina, said to the Governor of North Carolina, 'It's a long time between lynchings,' and the Governor of North Carolina, said to the Governor of South Carolina, 'Sh-h! Don't talk to me about lynching. Golly! Don't you know they came near lynching me the other night?' "[64]

Governor Russell had gone to Wilmington to vote. He had first intended to return to Raleigh by way of Goldsboro, but upon learning that there was a mob of several hundred men at Goldsboro waiting to give him a reception, and aware that he was a marked man, he changed his route and went via Maxton. Word got to Maxton ahead of the governor, and when the train arrived at Laurinburg, a swearing, howling mob of heavily armed Redshirts was awaiting him. The train was surrounded and boarded by Redshirts shouting, "Where is Russell?" "Where is the governor?" "Bring him out!" "Lynch him!" "Lynch the governor!" These outbursts were accompanied by

Mob attacking Governor Russell's train. From *New York Herald*, November 20, 1898 (file, New York Public Library).

vulgar language; it could be surmised that this included the expression, "Lynch the fat son of a bitch!" The governor weighed more than three hundred pounds, and his frustrated enemies . . . [were] speculating as to the figure he would have cut at the end of a rope. Anticipating that some violence would be inflicted on the governor, one of his friends moved fast and hustled him out of the coach and into a boxcar, which was locked behind him, and the conductor and his friends stood guard until the train pulled out. Governor Russell reached his home in Raleigh, over the Seaboard Air Line, very badly frightened. The friend who had guarded him did not have a "button on his coat and his clothing were in tatters."[65]

When the Redshirts and the Rough Riders all came together, there was no police force to restrain them. They raced their horses through the main streets. According to an eyewitness, they rode the "mares . . . so successfully that they kept up the enjoyment even to planning and having carried into execution the killing of negroes, the driving them out of town into the woods and cemeteries, the arresting of the leaders—that is, all men who had property (who might be presumed . . . to be leaders, for really they had no leaders) whose lynching was only prevented by the determined efforts of a few men."[66]

Election day came to an end; it had passed off without much racket. The greater number of blacks had avoided the polls in the hope that the bloodshed which the hot-headed Democrats had been clamoring for as the only means of carrying the election might be averted. Nevertheless, the militant ones displayed a rugged front; not only did they vote, but they loitered about the polls all election day. A number of incidents occurred under the cover of darkness, and were reported at some precinct boxes. Rifle shots from ambush rang out as the votes were being counted; ceiling kerosene lamps were extinguished and table lamps were bowled over and blown out by gunfire. The Reverend J. Allen Kirk, a black minister, described one incident: "Pistols were held in the faces of Negro poll holders who had to leave to save their lives, for the light was extinguished and they knew not what moment they would be killed."[67]

Afterward, the night was quiet until about ten o'clock, when Captain N. B. Rankin of Block N rushed in, and in a very excited manner called the military out to patrol the sidewalk for fear that the Negroes, disappointed in having been cheated out of the election, might set fire to somebody's property. Later he

> took his gun and went out in spite of his family's protestations. After being out in the cold and damp for three hours, he came in a moment, and four women took hold of him so vigorously that they made him promise to come in before very long, threatening to go out with him if he did not. He knew what a perfect farce it was to be out there in the damp and cold, watching for poor cowed disarmed negroes, frightened to death by the threats that had been made against them and too glad to huddle in their homes and keep quiet. So after a time he came home and went to bed.[68]

Meanwhile, sentinels appointed by citizens walked their beats through the night, some until early morning, "without going to supper, though the ladies of the town brought baskets of food . . . until after eleven o'clock." On duty that night also were members of the Wilmington Light Infantry and the naval reserves, who were on alert and billeted in the homes of private citizens or in the local armory, where men were sleeping on the floor, using their overcoats for pillows. Sergeant J. Van B. Metts remembers looking for Sergeant Harris, and pointed out that there were "so many men asleep on the floor that he could not walk [and] so had to wake them up to find him." Toward morning, he said, "I was tired and tried to find a place to sleep and the only place I could find was the steps leading upstairs and had hardly closed my eyes when I received orders to take a squad to Kidder's Hill."[69]

The next morning, the *Messenger* announced "The Great Victory" and "Negroism Defunct." The Democratic triumph included New Hanover County.[70] The political conquest was not the result of a free and untrammeled election—there were irregularities in Wilmington and elsewhere. In many precincts the ballot boxes had been stuffed with white supremacy votes. The law specifically required that the ballots be printed on white paper; Populists ballots, which had been printed on yellow paper, were thrown out. The Republican tickets had been suppressed in New Hanover County, and evidence strongly suggests the manipulation of votes to nullify

Wilmington's black majority. As reported by a Northern correspondent in Wilmington, a Republican majority of 5,000 in 1896 gave place to a Democratic majority of 6,000 in 1898—a gain for the Democrats of 11,000.[71] In their determination to win the election, the leading Democrats had said that they would win by hook or crook, peacefully if possible, by revolution if necessary. There was no faltering in this resolve at any stage of the proceedings.

All peaceful white and black citizens were relieved that with the dawn of 9 November the foreboding clouds had passed without a violent racial storm. Jane Murphy Cronly expressed the majority sentiment when she wrote: "I awoke that morning with thankful heart that the election had passed without the shedding of the blood of either the innocent or the guilty. I heard the colored people going by to their work talking cheerfully together as had not been the case for many days."[72] Some hours later this situation would change, for sinister forces were at work.

4

Act 1—The Storm Breaks: "Inhabitants of the Land Tremble"

1

ON election day, 8 November 1898, Hugh McRae of the Secret Nine had telephoned the *Messenger* and dictated the call for a mass meeting. The next morning the *Wilmington Messenger* ran an eye-catching announcement: "Attention White Men." As if a crisis actually prevailed, it asked all white men to meet at the courthouse at 10:00 A.M. and urged "full attendance as business of marked importance would be transacted."

The early morning sun of 9 November hovered over the white-columned county courthouse. At about half-past nine, a steady flow of men, representing people of all walks of life, could be seen entering the building—merchants, bankers, lawyers, physicians, clergymen, clerks, mechanics, and laborers. "The business men are at present," wrote a member of the Wilmington Light Infantry, "holding a big meeting to take steps to run the mayor and some prominent Negroes out of town."[1] Yet the evidence suggests that the cloakness of the Secret Nine's agenda for this day had eluded the attention of most prominent citizens. George Rountree, for example, stated that he had no previous knowledge of the meeting. He explained:

I remained at the Cape Fear Club on election night and received telegrams from many places in North Carolina until very late, probably going home about three o'clock. The next morning I was sleeping the sleep of the just when my wife came in about nine o'clock and showed me an advertisement in the paper that stated that there would be a public meeting at the court house that morning at 10 o'clock of great importance, and asked all the white people to be present . . . I dressed as rapidly as I could and ran down town . . . At ten o'clock I went there and I had never seen more people in the courthouse in Wilmington.[2]

"Between 800 and 1,000 men had packed the courtroom to suffocation"

107

and overflowed into the corridor. On the rostrum sat McRae, former mayor Fishblate, leader of the Dry Ponders, and other prominent whites. Thomas C. Clawson, editor of the *Wilmington Messenger,* and the visiting correspondents were asked to serve as secretaries. When Fishblate, chairman of the meeting, rose to address the assemblage, "the drop of a pin could have been heard."[3]

On motion, the chairman called Waddell to the chair. Waddell was now the star; as he calmly made his way down the center aisle, the entire audience broke into sustained applause. After he had mounted the rostrum, the meeting was called to order. Waddell faced his audience and said that he had come to the meeting "entirely ignorant of its objective, but it was always a pleasure, as well as a duty, to accept the call of the people of Wilmington."[4]

The Secret Nine had drawn up a document entitled the "Wilmington Declaration of Independence." McRae handed the document to Waddell, who proceeded to read it. Its preamble began by declaring that "the Constitution of the United States contemplated a government to be carried on by an enlightened people . . . and its framers did not anticipate the enfranchisement of an ignorant population of African origin, and . . . that the men of the state of North Carolina who joined in forming the Union did not contemplate for their descendants a subjection to an inferior race."[5] Accepting the premise of the incapability of blacks to participate in government, because of their limited education and their alleged mental inferiority to the white race, it was also declared that the citizens of Wilmington and of New Hanover County would never again be ruled by men of African origin.

At the conclusion of the preamble, with a great burst of hand clapping, the large audience sprang to its feet and yelled madly. When this enthusiasm had died down, Waddell began reading the resolutions, with powerful effect, contrasting their main points as he went along.

The first of the eight resolutions pointed out that whites owned more than 90 percent of the property and paid a "like proportion" in taxes. Another contended that business was stagnated and progress was "out of the question," because the city was controlled by venal politicians who, in affiliation with blacks, were able to maintain their ascendancy. It reaffirmed the necessity of terminating the white/black coalition.

Bent upon ending the economic competition between white and black labor, the fourth and fifth resolutions declared "that the giving of nearly all of the employment" to blacks "has been against the best interest" of the city of Wilmington and of New Hanover County, and consequently, "white families cannot thrive here unless there are more opportunities for employment." It was thus mandated that employers in the future must "give to white men a large part of the employment heretofore" given to blacks.

The last two resolutions were concerned with the Manly editorial. The seventh resolution explained that a crisis was precipitated in the city by the publication of "an article so vile and slanderous that it would in most communities result in the lynching of the editor." Then it was ordered that "the paper known as the 'Record' cease to be published, and that its editor be banished from this community." The final resolution mandated that Manly leave town and that his press be "packed and shipped from the city without delay."

A twelve-hour deadline was set, with the following warning, "If the demand is refused, or if no answer is given within the time mentioned, then the editor, Manly, will be expelled by force."[6]

The last resolution brought a spontaneous demonstration with the assemblage rising to its feet and cheering: "Right! Right! Right!" There were cries of "Fumigate the city with 'The Record!'" and "Lynch Manly!" But Manly had left the city long before; many whites and blacks knew it, including members of the Secret Nine. This information was kept a secret to avoid cooling off the boiling caldron. "They seemed to have forgotten," Keith later wrote, "that it was printed in the leading paper of the city, eleven days before, that this . . . Negro editor was then in Asbury Park, New Jersey, having fled from town for fear of being lynched or killed."[7]

Fishblate arose when the cheers for Waddell abated, and he moved for additional resolutions demanding the expulsion of the major and the Board of Aldermen. Meanwhile, George Rountree had maneuvered himself into a position to catch the chairman's eye. Upon recognition, he moved that a committee of five be appointed to take into consideration the resolutions and to report as soon as possible on the action to be taken. The resolution was unanimously passed, and a committee of five was appointed.[8] The committee was composed of Rountree, Fishblate, McRae, Walker Taylor, and Iredell Meares.

While the committee was in caucus, there were calls, "Bellamy! Bellamy!" John D. Bellamy, Jr., a recent Democratic congressman for the district and the only native Wilmingtonian ever to be nominated and elected to Congress, mounted the rostrum and told the audience that it was proper for the meeting to take some action about the vile and slanderous defamer of white women, and that he was heart and soul in favor of whatever it was necessary to do. He voiced the hope that there would be no violence, but that notice should be given the scoundrel, Alex Manly, to leave the city immediately. Someone in the audience shouted, "He's gone now!" "Well then," Bellamy replied, "Wilmington has been rid of the vilest slander in North Carolina." "I counsel moderation," he said in conclusion.[9] Short speeches were made by Junius Davis, Nathaniel Jacobi, Thomas W. Strange, Roger Moore, and others.

At this juncture, the committee of five returned and Rountree reported that it had unanimously adopted the Fishblate amendment. The resolution charged Mayor Silas P. Wright and Chief of Police John R. Melton with "having demonstrated their incapacity to give the city a decent government and maintain law and order." And since their continuance in office was a "constant menace to the peace and welfare" of the city of Wilmington, the two officials were urged to resign.[10] Rountree immediately moved to amend the McRae resolution to include the figure 95 percent for representation of the proportion of whites owning land and paying taxes.[11] The amendment was carried. The figure would later be raised still higher to read: "Of the taxes paid in the city of Wilmington and the county of New Hanover the whites pay 96⅔% while the Negroes pay the remainder 3⅓%."[12] Not mentioned, naturally, were the large numbers of unemployed and improvident whites who paid no taxes.

Then a move was made to appoint a committee of twenty-five to carry out the resolutions. Waddell was made chairman, and prominent members of the group included Hugh McRae, the Reverend J. W. Kramer, Frank H. Stedman, Iredell Meares, E. S. Lathrop, Joseph D. Smith, Frank Maunder, F. A. Montgomery, Junius Davis, J. Alan Taylor, W. C. Galloway, the Reverend J. W. Hervey, Charles W. Worth, Joseph R. Davis, and Preston L. Bridgers.[13] Rountree later complained of being purposely left off the committee by Waddell, "and that was the kind of gratitude he generally displayed." The presence of three members of the Secret Nine made certain that the original group of revolutionaries would be able to continue its direction of the revolt along the lines that it had charted; they continued in contact with the Secret Nine throughout the Rebellion.

The objectives of the conspirators were still cloaked; yet, the euphoria that had been building pervaded the assembly at its adjournment. Some people began to shout, others to shake hands and to slap backs, all exalted at the prospect of achieving their goals. No doubt the conspirators felt this jubilation as the crowd poured into the streets, for the Wilmington Declaration of Independence had been endoresed by many in attendance. The next day, the morning papers would publish in capital letters the names of the citizens, numbering 457, who had signed the resolutions the previous day; there was no concealment, no lack of identification.[14]

That afternoon at three-thirty, the committee of twenty-five met in rooms of the Merchants' Association. Here resolutions were discussed and framed to carry out the objectives of the committee. With Waddell to enforce the resolutions, thirty-two of the more prominent blacks of Wilmington were summoned to meet the committee that evening at six o'clock. The more prominent blacks were Armond W. Scott (attorney), Thomas C. Miller (real estate and pawnbroker), L. A. Henderson (attorney), David Jacobs (barber and coroner of New Hanover County), Carter Peamon (barber and political activist), Frederick C. Sadgwar (carpenter and architect), Thomas Rivers (mortician), Elijah Green (alderman), J. H. Alston (physician), the Reverend W. H. Leak, Dr. T. R. Mash, John Goins (associated with the *Wilmington Record*), John Holloway (postal clerk), the Reverend J. W. Telfair, William A. Moore (attorney), John H. Howe (contractor), John T. Howe (member of the 1897 General Assembly), and Richard Ashe (financier).[15]

Darkness had settled over the aristocratic old Cape Fear Club, which then occupied a large white building on the northwest corner of Front and Chestnut streets. Most of the blacks summoned met the committee at the hour appointed. The whites present were truly representative of the city's economic power and were backed by superior weapons, in both numbers and firepower. The blacks knew this from the beginning; they came with their hats in their hands, their heads bowed to the will of the higher order.

The scene was dramatic. At one end of the room sat the blacks, cowed and terror stricken; at the other end sat the twenty-five white men, with stolid looks on their faces. They were anxious and determined. In the center of the room sat Waddell at the head of the table. All eyes were focused upon him as he read the mass meeting's ultimatum. He then firmly explained the proclamation. In response to a query from one of the blacks as to the meaning of a phrase, Waddell read it a second time. Then he began handing them copies. He told them that no argument would be listened to—no discussion was expected and none would be allowed. They had been invited because they were assumed to be leaders among their people. They were there solely to listen to the ultimatum. The time had passed for words. The demands made by the resolutions must be adhered to without argument, for they would be enforced. Waddell gave them until seven-thirty the next morning to bring a reply to his house. One black said, "Colonel, we are not responsible for this, and we have no authority." Waddell rose. "The meeting stands adjourned" was his only reply.[16] Then going their separate ways, the whites and the blacks disappeared silently into the night.

The blacks went immediately to the barber shop of David Jacobs, located on Dock Street between Water and Front streets. After some deliberation, they drafted the following reply to Waddell's ultimatum:

We, the colored citizens to whom was referred the matter of expulsion from the community of the person and press of A. L. Manly, beg most respectfully to say that we are in no way responsible for, nor in any way condone the obnoxious article that called forth your actions. Neither are we authorized to act for him in this matter; but in the interest of peace we will most willingly use our influence to have your wishes carried out.[17]

Armond Scott was instructed to deliver the reply in person to Waddell's home at Fifth and Princess streets, but he placed it in a mailbox. He knew that his name was on the Secret Nine's enemies list as one of the black politicians earmarked to be banished from the city. What Negro would have had the courage to enter a white community at night under these circumstances? More important, would Waddell receive the message before the deadline?

On the morning of 10 November, the sun rose at six-thirty, brilliant and warm. According to the *Wilmington Messenger,* the temperature at eight o'clock was seventy-one degrees, and no rainfall was predicted. The comfort of the day was intermittently interrupted by currents of cool, salt-laden air from the ocean a few miles away. And except for a few light clouds, the morning seemed serene.

By forenoon, however, the streets presented an unusual sight. Many white men, representing all types of vocations (including the professions and the ministry), were seen proceeding to the armory with rifles on their shoulders. Before eight o'clock, they had filled the armory and were waiting in suspense to learn of the black committee's answer. "Every man," noted the *Messenger,* "brought his rifle and many had pistols also."[18]

The armory of the Wilmington Light Infantry was located on Market between Fourth and Fifth streets. Waddell's residence was near it, on Fifth Street between Market and Princess. That morning he was seen walking unhurriedly in the direction of the armory. He entered the building a few minutes after eight, and found the assemblage already displaying growing impatience, which finally turned into outright dissatisfaction. First, they were angry over the blacks' failure to submit their reply within the specified twelve-hour time limit. Second, they were angry over the absence of Roger Moore, the chief marshal, who, they understood, was to lead them in the event that the blacks refused to comply with the mass meeting's proclamation.

At approximately eight-fifteen, the whites began to grumble and demand immediate action; but a group gathering for a particular objective needs a leader. Walker Taylor received a telephone message that a crowd was at the armory and wanted the military to lead them up to the *Record* office. But Taylor refused. As post commander, it was his duty to disband them. Next, some influential members of the crowd turned to Thomas C. James, commander of the Light Infantry home guard. "What, me lead a mob? Never!" replied James. After some urging and insistence, Waddell agreed to head the expedition.

There was a call for seventy-five men, and about five hundred answered. Waddell lined them up in front of the stately white marble armory with the committee of twenty-five in front. He then shouldered his Winchester and assumed his position at the head of the column.[19] Four abreast (some sources reported they were twelve abreast), the procession began to move at approximately eight-thirty. An eyewitness wrote: "Under thorough discipline and under command of officers, capitalists and laborers marched together. The lawyer and his clients were side by side. Men of large business interests kept step with clerks."[20] The procession moving up Market Street threw the city into a state of excitement; the white schools were let out, saloons were closed, and all business was suspended.[21] While some people watched from the sidewalks or through windows, many men and boys began pouring into the streets. On the line of march, the procession was joined at every corner, swelling it to two thousand persons,[22] and there was a great noise of whistles, yells, and cheers.

The invasion by whites of a black community sometimes was the traditional action that ignited racial confrontations. This was not true of the larger cities of the South and North. Racial violence was most likely to occur in the downtown areas and/or on the edges of the black community and in a "boundary zone separating the black community from the lower-class whites." Not anxious to face a mob of angry blacks, the whites did not go into the heart of the black community.[23] On the contrary, Wilmington presented a special case, because the whites actually invaded the black community heavily armed. When the mob crossed the bridge spanning the railroad tracks and leading into the black community of Brooklyn, its appearance created consternation among some blacks.[24] As the long column of armed men approached the vicinity of the Manly press, a sizable crowd of blacks— men, women and children—could be seen fleeing in all directions.[25]

Manly's press was located in Free Love Hall, a two-story frame structure situated on Seventh Street between Nun and Church. When the marchers reached the hall, Waddell gave a signal and hollered "Halt!" With several men, he advanced to the door and found it locked. Waddell knocked—no answer. He knocked again—still no answer. A few blows forced the door open, and approximately twenty of them entered. Within a few minutes the windows of the building were broken, office fixtures were demolished, and the broken pieces pitched into the streets. As the fragments were tossed out, exultant shouts filled the air. A beaver hat was thrown out and quickly torn to pieces, as was a crayon likeness of Manly. And when a long sign—"The Record Pub. Co."—was cast into the street, a cheer went up.

The next step was to burn the building. Some lamps hanging from the ceiling of the plant were torn down and smashed on the wooden floor, which was saturated with kerosene. A member of the band struck a match. Smoke was soon seen rising out of the upper windows. There were shouts of indignation and commands: "Stop that fire!" "Put it out!" "This won't do it all!"[26] But other buildings were quickly set ablaze, and the fire spread. Men with guns . . . climbed on the roofs and extinguished the igniting shingles.

About twenty feet to the south of Free Love Hall was Saint Luke's Baptist Church, the largest and most handsome black church in the city.[27] It was not the desire of the mob to cause damage to religious property; so one of the men there to destroy the printing press turned in the fire alarm from Box 51 at the corner of Seventh and Nun streets.[28] With the fire burning out of control, the onlookers became apprehensive because of the tardiness of the fire fighters. The public was not aware that the fire department was being intentionally detained on the orders of Fire Chief Charles Schnibben, who had instructed a powerfully built white man named W. T. (Tuck) Savage to hold up the Negro fire unit in its station at Sixth and Castle streets until he sent word that the firemen were actually needed to prevent the blaze from spreading and causing a major conflagration.

Savage did exactly as he had been instructed, restraining the Negro fire

Ruins of the Daily Record after it was gutted by fire. The steps at the right of the Record building are to St. Luke AME Zion Church. (Courtesy North Carolina Collec-tion, University of North Carolina at Chapel Hill)

unit in its station until Chief Schnibben gave him the signal to let the unit leave.[29] When the engine and horses finally came dashing upon the scene, several rounds of ammunition were fired into the air by men who were lined up for more than two blocks in either direction.[30] Negro children in a nearby school were thrown into a state of panic by this; their principal was told that they were free to stay or go home and "no harm should or would come to them."[31] White onlookers and a few blacks stood inactive around the burning building, not knowing what responses their actions might bring. The black firemen, in their red shirts and fire-fighting togs, fought the flames as nonchalantly as if there were no rebellion brewing. "To the everlasting credit of these Negro firemen," one witness reported. "They were the best disciplined firemen I have ever seen."[32] This Negro fire unit had won first prizes and medals in contests throughout the state. Even Chief Schnibben, the white press, and the city had cited it.[33] As the flames succumbed to the floods of water, only the charred frame of the structure was left standing, and this was afterward pulled down by the firemen. An elderly Negro woman watching the scene in awe "stood upon the sidewalk and with all the religious fervor of her race, invoked the wrath of Heaven."[34] The crowd of whites watched her in silent amusement. This was the first act of the tragedy; others were to follow.

3

After the destruction of the Manly press, Waddell claimed, order was immediately restored. In *Collier's Weekly*, he wrote, "I then marched the column back through the streets down to the armory, lined them up, and stood on the stoop and made a speech." He told the crowd: "Now you have performed the duty which you called on me to lead you to perform. Now let us go quietly to our homes and about our business, and obey the law, unless we are forced in self defense to do otherwise."[35] Whether this account is true, rumors were becoming widespread across the city. One rumor had it that three hundred to four hundred blacks at the Sprunt Cotton Compress had discontinued work and were armed, assembled, and preparing to march on the city.

The workers were often contemptuously referred to as "Sprunt Niggers." If on Saturday they got a little drunk and landed in jail, Sprunt always stood their bail. The firm of Alexander Sprunt and Son, cotton compressors and importers, was the largest employer in Wilmington, providing jobs for hundreds of blacks. It exercised careful supervision over the crews of stevedores and ordinary laborers. A few of the blacks held positions of accountability—foremen, checkers, and weighers. Jim Reeves, a cotton weigher, has left one of the more vivid accounts of the origin of the trouble at Sprunt cotton compress. He was very intelligent, and the Sprunts were fond of him. Physically, he was a fine individual, "being large robust and black," of the "pure-breed Afro-American," wrote Red Buck in the *Charlotte Observer*. "Had he been born and reared in Africa, he would be a ruler of many people, and one that his subjects would be proud to look upon." The whites

"A. L. Manly, proprietor of the *Wilmington* (N. C.) *Record*, whose office was wrecked by white men." From *New York Herald*, November 13, 1898 (Library of Congress).

Building that housed the Manly Press with its top floor burned away. Standing in front of it were white men and boys armed with rifles, shot guns and sticks. From *Collier's Weekly*, November 26, 1898 (Library of Congress).

also recognized that Reeves used good clear English, which he had learned from Kate Steward, one of the well-known white boardinghouse keepers in Southport, who had charge of him when he was a boy. He later migrated to Wilmington and began work for the Sprunts. He was at the scales when the riot broke out.

"It sure was a pretty day," Reeves said, recalling the morning of the riot. "The sun was shining and a gentle sea breeze swept about the city. I remember it well; the Negroes were singing 'Carry Me Back to Ole Virginia.'" He suddenly sensed that something was wrong. The first thing that looked suspicious was when Henry Peschau, the ticket collector, came out to the warehouse and whispered something in the ear of his boss, James D. Smith. Then the fire bell rang and kept ringing. The blacks stopped singing. A Negro came running and yelling, Oh my lawd, the Redshirts have killed one man and they are going to get us all. The frightened black man ran toward the Cape Fear River and was never seen again. It has been said that he jumped in the river and drowned.[36]

Meanwhile, the whites rushed in the direction of the cotton compress, located by the river on Front Street. The fire from the press building and the gunfire had excited the blacks. Rumors were circulating that the whites were now going to butcher the blacks at the compress. Rountree stated that he saw blacks rushing in its direction and in a short time there were hundreds of them there.[37] The workers heard that their houses were being burned; this information had been so exaggerated that they thought the whole area of Brooklyn was being burned.

Black women became hysterical and, upon seeing the flames, thought their homes—many of them situated very near—were to be burned. Some of them managed to evade the sentinels set up on every block to stop blacks who might wish to attack the mob that had destroyed the press. The excited women appeared at the compress and told their husbands and relatives that the white people had burned Manly's printing press, were burning their homes, and were shooting guns all over the neighborhood. They begged their husbands to come home.[38] According to a Northern correspondent, there was no violent talk or threats by the blacks. Some of them formed an unarmed body of men rushing from their work to defend their wives and children, they knew not what manner of violence.

Having gotten wind of the gathering of blacks at the compress, the whites also became excited. Those who did not have their guns with them went home and got them. Thomas R. Orrell, for example, was going to work and encountered a great crowd in front of the YMCA building. Someone yelled, "They're fighting at Sprunts, you better go get your gun." So he went home and got it. Don McRae related that he saw a crowd of blacks congregated at Front and Water, and someone said, "Go get your gun." McRae went to his room and got his "riot gun and about seventy-five rounds of riot cartridges, two pistols and a Bowie knife or two."[39] He then started out in the direction of the Sprunt compress. Some of the mob in Brooklyn, reinforced by other armed men, rushed in the same direction and vowed that they were "going gunning for niggers."[40]

When Rountree saw the whites coming toward the Sprung establishment with guns, he became excited and telephoned the armory for the rapid-fire gun, later explaining, "I did so to have it convenient for use if necessary."[41] Rountree's call set off a series of chain reactions. Shortly after the telephone message, rumor had it that a mob of three hundred armed blacks was coming to the city from the compress, and it was suggested by the person who sent the message that the Hilton drawbridge be raised in order to prevent their entrance into the city. This was done, but as was the case with other rumors, the black mob never appeared.[42]

At the compress, the appearance of the whites with guns threw the unarmed black workers into near panic. Observing the whites with guns, one of them asked Rountree, "What have we done?" Perplexed, Rountree later said, "I had no answer; they have done nothing." Meanwhile, some of the angry blacks began to congregate in groups and were heard to say that they were going home to arm themselves so they could protect their families. About that time the sheriff came up and quickly deputized Rountree and several of the whites to go among the blacks and read them the riot act. Rountree recited the act, and soon the blacks began to disperse quietly and slowly.[43] The whites were permitted to remain and, having telephoned for aid, were reinforced by more whites, including elements of the military.

With ships waiting to be loaded, Sprunt, Davis and others, even at the risk of being shot, went among the frightened laborers trying to soothe them and persuade them to go back to work, reassuring them that their families were in no danger. Sprunt had already sent one of his trusted blacks into the Negro community, and the messenger reported to him and the men that no houses, except the one containing the *Record*'s office, had been burned. The men returned to work, some so visibly nervous that they could barely walk.

Nevertheless, some hotheaded whites—among them some recently discharged Spanish-American War veterans under violent leadership—assuming that all blacks were alike and that no group of them should be allowed to assemble in any place, trained their guns on the crowds of blacks and ordered them to run. Threatening "to kill the whole gang of negroes," someone hollered to the whites, "You have just been through the war and so you know about what should be *done*, so let's get started and be through with it."[44]

Stories have come down about the bravery the Sprunts demonstrated in protecting their laborers from the mob. Believing that the whites' guns were meant for use and not for mere intimidation, James Sprunt reportedly had himself hoisted up on one of his big uncompressed cotton bales and said, "Shoot if you will, but make me the victim." Professor Helen G. Edmonds has written that Sprunt "ordered the foreman to barricade the doors; that he ordered the four guns of his pleasure-cruising yacht to be turned on the armed Democrats who then moved on."[45] One eyewitness reported a different version, that the "rioters also shot at Mr. Sprunt's driver and buggy, saying they cared no more for Mr. S's tale [*sic*] than for a bird's."[46]

Sprunt had ordered the laborers either to go back to work or to go home. Some blacks, alarmed for their families, decided to go home. Knowing that the whites were guarding every block, Sprunt asked McRae to accompany his men through the sentinels. He had just started to divide them up, sending one group down Water Street and another group down Red Cross Street, when someone came by and reported that there was fighting between whites and blacks across the railroad. The armed group of whites, including McRae, immediately whirled and veered for action into Brooklyn.

By now Wilmington was becoming hysterical. Aroused crowds of whites could be observed on every corner. Voices and tempers were raised; the leaderless crowd turned and pushed into the streets, shouting loudly.

McRae was moving with a group and saw a seething crowd on Dickinson Hill. Going over to investigate, he was asked to take command. This he did and started to fix a battlefront to drive the blacks back to the river if they came. "I had just gotten the line formed," he recalled, "when some one came up and said, 'This is not right, Don McRae [is] an U.S. Army officer and if found in this business, he will be gotten after by the President,' so they said, 'We will put someone else in command and you can get in ranks.' " Hayden explained the complication: "McRae [was] commander of the active Wilmington Light Infantry that had just returned from duty in the Spanish-American War . . . [and] as Captain McRae's Company 'K' had not been mustered out of the service of the United States Army, the white leaders did not want to get the Federal government involved as it might lead to serious complications or make the whole Revolutionary plan miscarry."[47] Accord-

Scenes from
1898

The remains of Alexander Manly's printing press after the fire at Love & Charity Hall.

An artist's depiction of the destruction of Love & Charity Hall that appeared in a Baltimore newspaper.

W.A. Walker's store, on the southwest corner of North 4th and Harnett streets, where the first killings occured (marked by the X's).

The southwest corner of North 4th and Harnett Streets in 2006.

George Morton's home at 720 North 4th Street. This picture shows Morton, who was Wilmington's Postmaster as well as a Navy Reserve officer, with men he commanded.

The home of William Mayo at 307 Harnett Street. Wounded by a stray bullet while on his porch, Mayo (who was white) became the rallying figure for whites, who then fired into a group of black men at North 4th and Harnett Streets. The shots killed five or six of them.

Peeden's Barbershop was located on the southwest corner of North 4th and Brunswick Streets. It was here that Wilmington blacks were alledged to have plotted to burn the town and massacre its inhabitants. Ten banished blacks were arrested there on November 10.

Authority in Wilmington was enforced by police and the military in the wake of the November riots. In this picture some of them poe outside the John A. Taylor House, used at the time as the armory of the Wilmington Light Infantry.

Black employees of Alexander Sprunt & Sons, where The Cotton Exchange is in 2006. When the mob came to take the blacks working there, James Sprunt interceded to protect them.

ingly McRae took his position within the group as the line was reformed. Surveillance was established, but the blacks never appeared.[48]

Social and demographic factors helped bring on the first bloody confrontation. As noted in the first chapter, Wilmington was perhaps the most integrated city in the South; both whites and blacks lived in each of the five wards. After the Manly press had been wiped out of existence, its destroyers returned to the armory and soon afterward disbanded. Some white men took their guns and went home.[49] Those from the northern part of the city walked down Fourth Street and through Brooklyn. In the meantime, the blacks in various parts of the city had learned of the destruction of the press, and crowds of them assembled. There was much incendiary talk and threatenings. Some talked of revenge while others spoke of returning fire for fire.

Some of the blacks were armed and in a bad temper. Rumors abounded that they had organized a massive retaliation and were to take revenge against the whites who had burned the press. About twenty-five blacks were standing on the southwest corner of Fourth Street at John Brunjes's store as the Brooklyn whites came by with their guns. Suspecting an attack, the whites ordered the blacks away; the blacks refused to move. According to the *Wilmington Messenger*, Norman Lindsay (black) addressed the blacks and appealed to them to disperse. "In the name of God," he said, "for the sake of your lives, your family, your children and your country, go home." They hissed at him. He continued, "I am as brave as any of you, but we are powerless."[50]

The blacks moved doggedly over to the northeast corner of Fourth and Harnett streets and stood diagonally across from their first position. The Brooklyn whites, now joined by others, occupied a position on the west side of Fourth Street, between Brunjes's store and Saint Matthew's English Lutheran Church, a few feet from the blacks' first position. Seeing that trouble was brewing, Police Officer Aaron Lockamy (white) went among the blacks and urged them to leave. He admonished them not to bring on any trouble, that it would be better for them to go home.

"Hell broke loose." Suddenly a shot rang out. A young white man named William Mayo reeled and fell, blood crimson on his right arm. The bullet, according to the *Wilmington Messenger,* had "struck him in the left breast near the arm and came out through the right breast, piercing both lungs." A white woman screamed and called her husband to the window. Again quoting the *Messenger,* "Billy!!" she cried. "There is a white man killed!"[51] The question of who fired the first shot will be considered later.

For a moment silence prevailed; then the crash of gunfire came with a terrible suddenness. The whites had released a fusillade from revolvers, shotguns, and Winchesters. Six blacks fell under the heavy fire, two killed instantly. Two of the wounded jumped up and ran into a small house, but one of them fell dead upon the floor. The other was shot in the left thigh and behind the left shoulder, the bullet lodging in his chest beneath the skin just above the heart. Afterward a running fight ensued. The blacks broke and ran in all directions, with the whites in hot pursuit firing at them, and the blacks firing back as some ran west on Harnett Street.[52] While blacks were unable to purchase guns legally, it is conjectured that some did manage somehow to secure weapons, and some possessed guns already.

Upon hearing of the shooting at the corner, other whites ran from their residences, some seeming to appear out of nowhere with guns. From the corner of Third and Harnett streets, groups of blacks ran down Third Street. Four or five volleys of shots echoed in the rear of houses on Fourth Street. Another volley was heard on Third Street. A black named Sam Gregory ran into a hail of bullets on Third and fell dead between Harnett and Swann streets. A number of blacks allegedly ran toward the scene of the shooting. Several white men at Second and Harnett warned them to go back. The blacks fired several shots, which the whites returned, scattering the blacks back toward the railroad. An unknown black was wounded, but ran as far as the Carolina Central Railroad before he dropped dead.

News of the violence at Fourth and Harnett spread like wildfire throughout the state. The first account of the riot came to the capital, Raleigh, in a telegram to the *Raleigh News and Observer* at eleven o'clock in the morning. It was promptly posted, with bulletins being issued every few minutes. Throughout the day people came to read them and to discuss the situation.

Tensely reading the dispatches of the *News and Observer,* Governor Russell sat shocked and vacillating until official notification was received. On the day before the riot, Colonel Walker Taylor of the Second Regiment, North Carolina State Guard at Wilmington, had wired Governor Russell that "the situation here was serious and that he was holding the military ready awaiting the Governor's prompt orders"; but the governor never acknowledged Taylor's message. The first official notification that Governor Russell received of the trouble came in a telegram from Taylor on the day of the riot. It read: "Situation here is serious. I hold the military here waiting your prompt order."[53]

Governor Russell consulted with Major Charles L. Davis, acting adjutant general of the North Carolina State Guard. The authority for calling out troops rested with Davis, who wired Taylor the following reply:

The Governor directs you take command of Capt. James' company at Wilmington and preserve the peace. Attention invited to Article 2, 28 Regulations N.C. State Guard. Report your action to the Governor direct. By order of the Governor and Commander-in-Chief.[54]

A second wire was received by the governor from George L. Morton, commander of the Wilmington Division, Naval Reserves:

I have ordered the naval reserves not to pressure the peace on order of the sheriff.

The governor approved of Morton's action in another telegram:

> Your action ordering out naval reserves to preserve the peace is approved by the Gov., who directs that you place yourself under orders of Lt. Col. Walker Taylor.

The governor decided to place more troops on readiness to move to the scene. Accordingly, he wired Captain H. J. Hines of the Clinton (North Carolina) Company and Captain G. B. Patterson of the Maxton Company as follows: "Hold your company in readiness to move to Wilmington. Notify railroad company and answer." The acting adjutant general soon instructed the two men to take their commands and report to Taylor at Wilmington.

It is important to note at this point that no official communication was sent to Governor Russell from Mayor Wright. It is safe to assume that the organizers of the Wilmington rebellion—Hugh McRae and other members of the Secret Nine—had already unofficially taken over the city, and that Taylor was taking orders from them.

The telegraph wires clicked and buzzed throughout the state and elsewhere with news of the Wilmington riot. Some flashed, "Negroes Shooting and Killing Whites." Major cities such as Atlanta and as far away as New Orleans offered to send help. A telegram from T. C. DeRosset of Atlanta said: "Please wire situation and who is killed. Give them hell. Had I better come?" Various city officials within the state immediately manifested a zealous willingness to assist the Wilmington whites.[55]

From Oxford, W. A. Graham wired: "Granville will send you 500 men if you need them. Answer quick!" A telegram from J. D. McCall said: "Do you need 500 men? Wire at once." From Rockingham, W. H. McLaurin wired: "Hold your ground. Will carry hundred Winchesters if needed. Answer." Other cities—Dunn, Lumberbridge, Monroe, Wilson, Mount Olive, Fayetteville, Macon, Winston-Salem, Clinton, and Goldsboro—alerted their military forces. Chares B. Aycock, who was to be the next governor, recalled, "There clicked over the wire from Wilmington—'For God sake send 200 men; we have a race riot." In less than half an hour, there were five hundred men at the depot with guns on their shoulders, waiting for the train. Aycock was one of them.[56]

When the violence began at Fourth and Harnett streets, Dr. B. C. Moore, proprietor of a drugstore on the northwest corner of this intersection, telephoned to the armies of the Wilmington Light Infantry and the Wilmington Division of the North Carolina Naval Batallion. "They're fighting over the road," reported Moore.[57] Then the news came in from other quarters. Soon there were yells in the distance; the fire bell began to ring and kept ringing; and once again, excited people began to pour into the streets. A streetcar rolled into the business section, and the conductor reported that blacks had fired into the car. A large number of armed men boarded the car, which sped to the scene of the riot. Those [who] could not get aboard ran on foot to

Fourth and Harnett streets. Meanwhile, a group of young whites boarded another streetcar that had gone around Castle Street, via Sixth, and then up Front Street. They fired out of the car and made such a racket that the fire bell sounded an alarm that had been agreed upon as a signal for the men of every block to assemble at their appointed places.[58]

Soon, more sinister forces were brought into play. Somewhere far out in the old Dry Pond section of the city, the Redshirts had assembled to await a signal—their horses stood pawing and waiting for battle. They had good rifles and plenty of ammunition. The ringing of the fire bell was what they had been waiting for, and they immediately mounted and rode into Wilmington. The Rough Riders were also mounted and ready to ride. All these forces—the Redshirts, the Rough Riders, the military, and the citizens committee—would descend upon the poorly armed black community of Brooklyn.

4

The military prepared as if for war. The awesome Gatling gun was mounted on a large truck drawn by two fine horses, and wagons were drawn by teams of horses. Dragged along with these were two one-pound Hotchkiss cannons.

Taylor had assumed control of the city. A former Confederate officer, Captain William Rand Kenan (father-in-law of Henry K. Flagler, millionaire empire builder of Florida), and Lieutenant Charles H. White were in command of the Wilmington Light Infantry. Captain Harry McIlhenny commanded the squad that operated the machine gun of the Secret Nine, and T. C. James was in charge of the foot troops, a swiftly moving body of men on foot with rifles. Another former Confederate officer and Klansman was Colonel Roger B. Moore, who had discarded his white robe and put on his military uniform with a sword buckled at his side.[59] Spectators witness both Kenan and Moore as they rode the swift-moving wagons to the scene of action.

A throng soon brought traffic to a standstill as the Fourth Street bridge, which spanned the railroad tracks and led to Brooklyn, was blocked by a mob of angry citizens. On the north side of the bridge was the wounded Bill Mayo in an ambulance driven by Frank Shephard, just in his teens.

Father Christopher C. Dennen, pastor of Saint Thomas Catholic Church, was endeavoring to get to Mayo in order to administer the last rites. The priest left his horse and buggy on the south side of the bridge and made his way on foot over the span and through the milling crowd to reach the ambulance. He pleaded with the excited men to clear a path for the ambuland to pass through so that Mayo might be conveyed to the hospital. Shephard finally succeeded in getting the vehicle across the bridge and then brought it to a quick halt. Father Dennen immediately climbed into the

Lieutenant-Colonel Walker Taylor (1864–1937). From *New York Herald*, November 20, 1898 (file, New York Public Library).

ambulance and administered extreme unction to Mayo. Then the driver lashed the horse. The animal raised his hindquarters and went dashing toward the hospital.[60]

Afterward, the military came down Fourth Street and across the bridge. When they arrived at Fourth and Harnett streets, passion and excitement were running high over the shooting of Mayo. James and his foot troops came marching up to the scene, and he shouted, "Halt!" He lined up his men and said, "Now boys I want to tell you right now I want you all to load and when I give the command to shoot, I want you to shoot to kill."[61]

Soon after the military appeared in Brooklyn, word was passed that some of the Negro churches were stocked with men, guns, and ammunition. A detachment from the Wilmington Light Infantry and the naval reserves was detailed to search the black churches. Cannons were turned toward the doors, threatening to blow up the churches if the pastors or officers did not open the doors.[62] They searched all Negro churches and found no guns or ammunition in any of the places, for there was none. After making the hunt, Sergeant J. Van B. Metts recounted the following incident: "We got to the one church and the Naval Reserves lined up across the street and aimed their guns right at the church ready to blaze away and then we went in the church and all we found there was a lot of tickets, 'vote for Dockery.' "[63]

Before the military appeared in Brooklyn, if Thomas Clawson can be believed, whites and blacks were fighting, with gunfire rattling all around, and bullets whistling along Bladen Street. The military arrived and immediately went into action, as intermittent volleys were fired by the Wilmington Light Infantry. Clawson maintained that he was just behind the firing line with a visiting newspaperwoman who wore a crimson Eton jacket. She kept pace with Clawson, always remaining "right at his elbow, and was cool as a cucumber," even "when a volley tore off the top of a [Negro] man's head and he fell dead about twenty feet in front of the news-hawks."[64] With military precision, the soldiers had fired to the cool order of their commander, only to cease when no shots came from the other direction. Clawson wrote eloquently of the military operations, including the "fiery big horses" cutting corners and racing at a rapid rate, carrying the rapid-fire guns through every section of Brooklyn.

Captain Orrell later proudly referred to the Wilmington Light Infantry as "Johnny on the Spot." After the initial confrontation at Fourth and Harnett streets, the whites encountered only intermittent sniper fire. As far as can be ascertained, blacks fired from behind barns, fences, trees, houses and other places that offered protection.

More violence was destined to occur. A shot was allegdly fired at two white men from a small shanty in the southeast area of Sixth and Bladen streets. The whites fired into the house, but no one ran out. Diagonally across the street from this action was Manhattan Park, which was surrounded by a high board fence enclosing a dance hall that was frequented by bad characters. The shooting brought a number of armed men to the scene in double-quick time. The military soon appeared, and when they fired, the crowd went crazy. The hall was pitted with shot holes, and planks in the fence were literally cut in half by .44-caliber bullets.[65] One defenseless and frightened black ran out of the rear of the building and through the yard. Members of the Wilmington Light Infantry hollered, "Halt!" and fired when he kept running. A round of fifteen to twenty bullets stopped him while he was scrambling over the high fence. As one of the shooting party exclaimed, "When we tu'nd him ove' Misto Niggah had a look of s'prise on his count' nance, I ashore you!"[66]

A line of soldiers now advanced with axes, hacked down the high fence, burst open the door, and found six frightened and trembling men. The place was wrecked, and the inhabitants were arrested. One of the blacks was encouraged to run; he proceeded to run for half a block, only to be brought down by a hail of bullets.[67] The others were tied, put in a wagon, and hauled off to jail.

Disarming the enemy is a necessity in all military operations. The blacks of Wilmington were the enemy; to what extent were they armed? "The Negro[es] in this town," a black woman wrote privately to President McKinley, "had no arms (except pistols perhaps in some instances) with which to defend themselves from attacks of the lawless whites."[68] Notwithstanding, some of the blacks did own rifles, at least two of them—Josh Halsey and Daniel Wright—and the command was out to capture and destroy these two men. "When we returned from Manhattan Park," Frank Maunder of the Wilmington Light Infantry told his comrades in 1905, "Sgt. Harris of squad #7 was lined up in front of Hill Terry's house and giving orders to find this negro Halsey." Another eyewitness wrote that Halsey had gone home and went to bed sick with fright. Meanwhile, the Wilmington Light Infantry had "searched every house in the neighborhood. When they reached Halsey's, his poor little child ran in and begged her father to get up and run for the soldiers were coming after him. The poor creature jumped up and ran out of the back door in frantic terror only to be shot down like a dog by armed soldiers ostensibly sent to preserve the peace."[69]

Maunder reported a different version of the killing of Halsey. When the Wilmington Light Infantry found him, Halsey was to be given the privilege of running the gauntlet for his life. Bill Robbins objected and said, "I am sick at the stomach." Maunder growled at Robbins not to "show the white feather or he would shoot him." When the order was given to fire upon Halsey, Robbins snapped his gun and said," I did not hit that man." Maunder replied, "I hope I did for I shot straight at him." Maunder looked down on the ground and noticed that "there were all of Robbins' cartridges and his plunger was out and his gun would not fire."[70]

Daniel Wright was the subject of a most extensive manhunt. He was an active and intrepid politician. When the whites armed themselves, Wright did likewise. Like a man with a contract out on him, Wright was to be hunted down and killed. What was Wright's crime? He was the one accused of shooting William Mayo, and the rumor was magnified as it was passed along. Wright's true role in the Wilmington riot is still shrouded in mystery.[71]

Edmonds introduces him into her study only after the mob surrounded his home; however, she fails to name Wright's crime or to say why the mob was after him. She opens her account with a howling group of Redshirts hurling invectives and demanding that Wright come out of his house. Thinking that he was hiding in the attic, the whites fired several shots toward it. Suddenly a Redshirt reeled and fell from his horse, and another one followed. Wright was using a smokeless and noiseless rifle, firing into the group, killing two members of the Redshirts, Hill Terry and George Bland. A torch was applied to the house; Wright was riddled with bullets as he ran out.[72] Still another version of his death was that the Secret Nine had perhaps given orders to the Wilmington Light Infantry to find Wright. An Indian guide was engaged in the pursuit.[73] He led a detachment of twelve men from the Wilmington Light Infantry to a small house. The soldiers burst open the door and seized Wright, who was told of his crime. He denied that he had shot Mayo, but a case would be build against him. Wright's house was searched, and in a closet were found a double-barreled shotgun and a .44-caliber Winchester. The Winchester had a shell in it that had recently been fired. The man accused of shooting Mayo was described as having one thumb off, and it was found that one of Wright's thumbs was missing.[74]

By the time Wright was captured, an angry crowd had gathered. As he walked back with his captors, "some one knocked him down with a piece of gas pipe," drawing blood.[75] When the bleeding man got up, someone yelled, "String him up to a lamp post." About that time, a member of the crowd suggested that Wright be given the privilege of running the gauntlet. They turned him loose, and someone yelled, "Run, Nigger, run!" The sand was so deep and yielding it was almost impossible to walk, and when he had gotten about fifty feet, at least forty guns of all descriptions were turned on him. "He was riddled by a pint of bullets, like a pigeon thrown from a plunge trap."[76] Wright lay bleeding profusely in the street for half an hour before he was taken to the city hospital, where he lingered on until death released him the next day. Some say he lived for two days. Doctors said that "they never saw one man with as many shots in him as he had."[77]

A strange twist in the Wilmington plot was the tragedy of the black barber, Carter Peamon, who sought no public office and owned no weapons. Before the initial confrontation at Fourth and Harnett streets, Peamon might have prevented the bloodshed at Ninth and Nixon streets. Rumors were afloat that angry blacks were grouping at the Sprunt cotton compress. The white leaders sent M. F. Heiskel Gouvenier, Captain James I. Metts, and another man to investigate the situation, and Peamon accompanied them as peacemaker.[78] Some infuriated blacks were assembled, all right, and the sight of the white men may have added to their anger. In any event, the blacks decided to hold Gouvernier and his associates hostage in retaliation. Peamon argued strongly against this move, and after several hours of wrangling the whites were released. When the three whites returned with Peamon and reported the incident, the whites became angry. They now demanded Peamon's scalp. Despite the fact that he had perhaps saved the lives of the three white men, the whites demanded that he be killed in reprisal. Gouvenier's entreaties saved Peamon.[79] The enraged whites then insisted that Peamon be banished from Wilmington. First he was jailed and then taken out and put aboard a switch engine and sent out of the city on the Wilmington line via the Columbia and Augusta Railroad. Some Redshirts or Rough Riders may have gone ahead of the train. Word reached the city later that Carter Peamon was dead. Someone brought back the news that he had jumped off the moving locomotive and was shot to death by some white men.[80] Of the thirty-two black representatives who had met with Waddell, Carter Peamon was the only one to die violently, and this despite his role as mediator between whites and blacks.

White assaults on individuals or small, isolated groups of blacks were always a common characteristic of race riots. There is an abundance of documentation to support this generalization. Certainly these riot patterns were manifested in the riots of Atlanta (1906), East St. Louis (1917), and Chicago (1919). It must be noted here that such violence was always initiated by small gangs, far fewer than fifty persons and composed of teenagers and yound men (this was not the case at Wilmington). During such confusion, "the crowds were large, most persons were spectators or bystanders furnishing encouragement and a sense of anonymity for the attacking gangs."[81] Immediately after the violence at Fourth and Harnett streets, bands of

A graphic scene of the race riot as visualized and drawn by H. Ditzler of *Collier's Weekly*, November 26, 1898 (Library of Congress).

whites, Rough Riders, and Redshirts moved into the Negro sections to "hunt niggers," some with the intent to "kill every damned nigger in sight." One witness said that he had seen six Negroes shot down near the Cape Fear Lumber Company's plant and their bodies were buried hurriedly in a nearby ditch. Another described the killing of nine Negroes by a lone white marksman, allegedly after they had fired on him through the shanty window. Fire was set to the building, and the rifleman killed them one by one as they filed out of a shanty door in Brooklyn. Still another told how an unoffending, deaf Negro was shot and killed because he had failed to obey a command to halt that he never heard. Another described the slaying of a Negro after he had approached two white men on the wharf; his carcass was tossed into the Cape Fear River.

Some whites claimed that blacks were killed accidently by sniper fire.

"Late in the afternoon," reported the *Messenger*, "while a crowd was on Fourth Street bridge, over the tracks of the Atlantic Coastline, a black allegedly fired a shot from the railroad yard at a position near Third Street, a little east of the railroad car shop. He was instantly riddled with bullets, and was lying dead last night where he fell."[82] A soldier said that a Negro "snapped an army musket at him while he was doing guard duty, and he shot him dead."[83]

Jane Murphy Cronly witnessed two soldiers harassing a black man on his knees. One soldier was threatening to shoot him; the other warned against it. The would-be victim was a uniformed mail carrier; after a little while the man "was allowed to go."[84] Cronly, referring perhaps to the initial bloodshed at Fourth and Harnett streets, recorded in her diary: "Some blood was drawn by a colored man it is claimed, for I suppose a few armed colored men hearing the uproar, had appeared on the scene, and then the carnage began. It is pitiful to hear the accounts of reliable eye-witnesses to the harrowing scenes. We are just shooting to see the niggers run! they cried as the black men began to fall in every direction."

Jane Murphy Cronly condemned the actions of the military. She also wrote that "some Naval Reserves and a small squad of the Home Guard Light Infantry," in addition to some Spanish-American War veterans, "being still in the services, had finally appeared on the scene, but if they did any good . . . I haven't heard it, except for one instance. Mr. Buck Buckheimer rode up and down among the rioters, calling out, 'Shame, men; stop this. Stop this. Don't you see these dead men!' " She charged the Wilmington Light Infantry with most of the massacre, contending that "it has much to answer for." She punctuated her account by charging them with shooting blacks "down right and left in a most unlawful way, killing one man who was simply standing at a corner waiting to get back to his work."[85] Another black woman wrote President McKinley that a man "was told to get out of the way and before he could do so he was shot in the neck—this was not put in the papers."[86]

Driven by pathological hatred, some whites used the race riot as an excuse for ruthlessness against even the most docile blacks. The police force had disappeared; every white man with a Winchester on his shoulder was a law unto himself. A Philadelphia editor wrote that "there was not one white man under arms who did not have some score to settle with a Negro rankling in his breast, which would have been a fair excuse for a shot for luck, any-way."[87] This is one reason, reported the *Atlanta Constitution*, "why so many farmers went into Wilmington . . . They had long waited for an opportunity of this kind."[88] According to correspondent Charles Francis Bourke of *Collier's Weekly*, the Redshirts and Rough Riders were responsible for most of the blacks' misery. According to Harry Hayden: "There were ignorant whites, 'poor-bockers' or 'poor white trash' (as they were called in Wilmington and in the South) who did some dastardly deeds under the cloak of the rebellion. Perhaps thinking that violence was a method of demonstrating white supremacy, the poor whites, in their own ignorant and primal way, vent their unrestrained spleen against innocent . . . and harmless Negroes."[89]

Could bloodshed have been avoided in the initial confrontation at Fourth and Harnett streets? Who fired the first shot—whites or blacks? Newspapers screamed out their headlines: Negroes Fire First Shot. The wounding of William Mayo was part of the mystery, and there are several versions of the story. According to George Rountree, "a half grown Negro boy fired the first shot!"[90]

There were other ambiguities. According to Hayden, Mayo was wounded as he was "standing on the sidewalk in front of his home, [and] Dan Wright . . . fired this shot from his Winchester rifle as he stood behind a tree two blocks away."[91] But Bourke reported "a bad nigger running amuck shot a white man named Mayo."[92] There are several versions of the incident in the *Messenger*. One is an account given by Frank McAllister, a white night yardmaster for the Atlantic Coastline Railroad who had been on duty the previous night. His residence was situated next door to Saint Matthew's Church on Fourth Street near Harnett, almost in the line of the shots fired by the blacks and whites. He had only been home a short while when the violence erupted. McAllister made the following statement to the reporter and later signed an affidavit:

> At 11 'clock I started to go to bed [he sleeps during the day] when my wife called me to the window. "Billy," she said, "there's going to be trouble out there." I jumped up and hurried to the window and saw a white man [evidently policeman Lockamy] on the northeast corner of Fourth and Harnett streets, demonstrating with both hands, laying them off rapidly, to a negro. I heard the white man say, "Go on now, it will be better for you." The negro went about ten paces and pointed a pistol at the white man. I saw the negro shoot."[93]

This account contradicts an earlier version. The assumption is that McAllister was sleeping, and his wife, perhaps having first rushed to the window, recalled the scream and said, "Billy!! There is a white man killed!" (see p. 119).

Other versions of the shooting in the *Messenger* maintained that the whites had fired first. The following account sheds additional light on what may have occurred. When a *Messenger* reporter reached the scene, "two blacks were lying dead, one on the broad pavement under the awning at Walker's store, and one in the gutter just in front of the store." The reporter was told that a wounded man was seen running into the house at 411 Harnett Street. The newspaperman went to the house and knocked on the door, but there was no answer. He then went to the rear door of the house, went in, and "found there women moaning. One man was lying dead on the floor. Another wounded man was in bed." This man gave his name as George

Henry Davis; he had a bullet near his heart, which was felt by the reporter. In agony, Davis managed to mumble that the "white man fired the first shot."[94]

Professor John Spencer Bassett, a historian at Trinity College (now Duke University), wrote to Herbert Baxter Adams: "The Press was destroyed . . . the initial [cause] of the riot . . . and Negroes made no resistance. In a Negro quarter in the suburbs some armed white men met some Negroes standing on the street. There was no claim that the Negroes were doing wrong. They were ordered to disperse [and] they refused. They were fired into. It is claimed that [the blacks] fired first. I don't think many white people who understand things in the state believed the charge. After this the riot was on."[95]

Professor Bassett had first-hand information about both white supremacy campaigns and the riot. Writing to a friend of the white supremacy campaign, he said, "I might write you a whole book . . . [and] I took pains to ask about it from many sources." Continuing the letter, he said: "The campaign has been one of passion. It has ended up in a riot at Wilmington—. . . a riot directly due to the 'white man's' campaign."[96]

4

By three that afternoon, a gradual and uneasy quiet had settled over the city. Blacks already at home remained there, but those returning home from work could not pass without a challenge unless accompanied by their white employer. White soldiers and citizens, including boys as young as twelve years old, held up all blacks who passed on any street and all who went toward Brooklyn.[97] Blacks, especially men, approaching any corner would hear a sharp voice call out, "Halt!" Sometimes the guards would emphasize the order with the muzzle of a murderous-looking rifle or a self-cocking revolver. The leader might ask, "Where are you going, Sam?" or "John" or even "nigger." The black would timorously state that he was going home. He was then searched, more or less roughly. No names were called, and no attempts were made at disguise; sometimes the parties had known one another for years. At the completion of the search, the black man was passed on to the next corner, where he encountered another group, and the entire process might be repeated.

The experiences of Frank Maunder are interesting and instructive. Assessing his labors, he said that he had held up and searched at least twenty-five Negroes and found nothing except an old case knife. He later recalled one incident when a Negro came along with a bag on his back. He was asked what was in it and answered "Nothing but onions and potatoes." Maunder searched it and found "onions and potatoes," and an old case knife, which he kept while passing him on to the next block.[98]

During this era, many whites gave valuable assistance, enabling some blacks to escape from harm and even death. Some blacks found sanctuary in white homes.

The Wilmington race riot was a lesson in black survival. Earlier in this chapter, Jim Reeves and Kate Stewart were introduced. Along with the cultural training Reeves received from Stewart as a boy, as an adult he had learned to carry the whole of his 225 pounds with dignity. On 10 November 1898, he dropped the dignity Stewart had molded in him as a boy; the riot gave him such a fright that he never quite recovered.

With the riot in full blast, Reeves became more frightened by the hour. He asked his foreman, James D. Smith, to accompany him home, which the latter agreed to do. The two men went to Red Cross and Second streets—two blocks away—but when Reeves saw the guards with guns on every corner, he became frightened, stopped, and whispered to Smith, "For God's sake, let me go back to the office." "All right," Smith said. Reeves went back, and Smith promised to bring him his dinner, but when Reeves entered the office door, he "saw a drove of men with guns coming down the street." He then "made a rush and jumped clear over the rail into the paymaster's room" and ran into the private secretary's office, thinking that he would be safer there. When he turned around, however, he could see everybody in the streets. "Lots of men looked at him through the glass." He and the men exchanged curious glances. With all the bosses gone, he reasoned that he would be safer upstairs in the cotton sample room. As he got to the steps, he heard a volley of shots, and he thought that the men with guns were "hot after him." He rushed up the steps and made a dive into a big pile of samples and "went clean to the bottom and the cotton closed over him." He maintained that he "never heard a thing, for I was fifteen feet deep and did not get any air, just thought I was getting some. My bosses hunted for me a long time, but could not find me. They didn't look in that cotton for they didn't think I could live in there. It was pretty poor living . . . but was lots better than being shot at."[99]

Reeves finally emerged from his place of concealment, and the first person he saw was one of his bosses, who offered to accompany him home. He lived on Eight Street, between Red Cross and Warren, eight blocks from the compress. His boss promised to signal him past the first guards, and they would then signal him on. He made out all right until he arrived at Five-Point Alley, where two fifteen-year-old boys were stationed. The boys stood back in the alley a little, and he did not see them until they hollored, "Halt! Throw up your hands!" Reeves heart thumped with fear, his knees shook and he felt weak and faint throughout his whole body. "I came pretty near falling," he said, "but fell on my knees and threw my hands up. I began to pray to the Lord to save me, for I knew that these boys didn't have no better sense than to shoot me dead. My heart was in my mouth. I thought that my time had come."[100] Some people might have classified Reeves as an "Uncle Tom," but he knew the behavior pattern to display for survival. The boys asked, "Do you have a pistol?" Confused, he answered "Yes, sir; no, sir; yes, sir; no, sir." The boys just laughed and told him to go on. Continuing homeward, Reeves traveled on to Fifth Street until he came upon a well and stopped for a drink. Just as he let down the bucket, he heard somebody say, "Jim, is that you?" Startled, he almost fell into the well. It was Walker Taylor, who then sent him on a short errand. Completing the task, he went into his house and shut the door.

According to Reeves, he stayed there "three days and nights without anything to eat or drink." While the riot was going on, he did not hear much, but he saw enough through the cracks to let him know that the house was the best place for him. The white bosses at the Sprunt cotton compress looked for him for two days. When he finally left his home, his landlord, a black policemen, had run away. As soon as Reeves could leave town without arousing suspicions, he did.

Reeves was among the respectable blacks who migrated from Wilmington. He became the popular headwaiter at the Hotel Lafayette in Fayetteville. Red Buck wrote: "He was a favorite with the traveling public, entrusted and appreciated by his employer, and respected and feared by those who worked under him. None but the chronic kickers disliked Jim Reeves."[101]

5

After the shooting was over and events had quieted down, the streets were dotted with men—some still lying where they fell. An abmulance from the city hospital with a large Red Cross banner on it was observed driving around the black community. As the driver commanded the horses to halt, the animals shied at the dead body of a black, lying huddled up in a collapse that marked sudden death. Quickly dismounting for an examination, and satisfied that there was no sign of life in the person, the driver remounted, struck the horse with a whip, and dashed on toward the next body. At the next corner lay the body of another man, presenting a gruesome spectacle of red blood oozing from a ghastly wound in the forehead. There were also the wounded men, who lay moaning in the streets until they were picked up and crowded into the jim crow wards of the city hospital. There were also wounded whites, the most seriously injured being William Mayo. Two others were Bert Chadwick, who was shot in the arm, and George Pizer, who was only slightly wounded.[102]

Included among the wounded blacks were Daniel Wright, and young Frank Shephard, who had driven the ambulance that had earlier carried Mayo to the hospital and that had returned and carried Wright to the hospital. Wright was riddled with thirteen bullets; some sources say he was shot in seventeen places. Among the other wounded blacks were Henry Davis, shot in six places; George Miller, shot in two places; and John Dow, also shot in two places.[103] Dr. John Sconwald, who dressed the wounds of Mayo, Pizer, and Chadwick (all white) and who gave his professional service to several black men, stated that all were wounded by .44-caliber balls. Some of the injured blacks eschewed professional aid at the hospital perhaps out of fear. For example, Dr. C. D. Bell was sent for and found a black badly wounded at his home on Davis Street, between Second and Third. He had been shot in the right side and right arm, but the doctor did not learn his name. One unidentified black was found dead under the residence of Mrs. W. H. Straus (white) on Fourth Street, between Harnett and Swan. During the height of the riot he had crawled under the house and had died during the night.[104]

Considering how the city was garrisoned and the whites armed, the results could have been predicted. What about postmortems of the tragic event? Newspaper and historical sources differ in their estimation of the number of deaths. The *Wilmington Morning Star* reported seven deaths. The conservative *New York Times* reported nine Negroes were killed, compared to the fifteen reported in the *New York Herald,* and the *Richmond Daily Times* reported sixteen killed.[105] Writing in his memoirs, Alfred Waddell wrote that "about twenty [blacks] were killed."[106]

Historians have unintentionally perpetuated the cover-up by concentrating on newspapers explaining the Democrats' story, of which no single one was trustworthy. Consequently, the few accounts by historians of the era are badly flawed. For example, historian J. G. de Roulhac Hamilton recorded twelve deaths. Josephus Daniels of the *News and Observer,* writing in later years, recorded eleven deaths. Indeed, these figures are too low, and incorrect, since both took their data from Democratic sources of which none agree. The coroner, a black barber named David Jacobs, had the dead removed to the D. C. Evans funeral establishment on Second Street. Fourteen bodies were viewed by large crowds; Jacobs impaneled fourteen coroner's juries. They rendered the identical verdict in all fourteen deaths: that the deceased came to their deaths by gunshot wounds inflicted by persons unknown.[107]

At the same time, another drama was being enacted elsewhere. It took place on the morning after the riot in a little rickety shanty establishment for the very poor. The scene was gruesome. On the bare floor stretched six dead black men, and their bodies told the story of the previous day. They were dressed in their street clothes, just as they were shot down; these were their burial clothes, too. Three men were busy making crude pine coffins. Around the corpses "stood Negro women with sad faces."[108] There were no other men present. The dead were either husbands, lovers, or relatives. It is possible that these six were not counted in the published death tolls. Wilmington had many blacks who lived in abject poverty, and some of them may have secretly buried their own dead. "How many blacks were killed," the editor of the *Wilmington Messenger* correctly concluded, "will never be known." Their friends and families concealed their deaths for fear of implication in some way in the offenses committed.[109]

When one goes beyond standard historical accounts, manuscripts, and documents, to utilize the oral tradition, it becomes apparent that the Wilmington massacre could take on bizarre dimensions. There were some witnesses who contend that "over one hundred were killed in the internecine street fighting," while some "creditable persons" say that "two hundred and fifty Negro dead were scattered on the streets of Wilmington" on that fateful day.[110] One white eyewitness reported, "Wagon loads of Negro bodies were hauled through the streets of Wilmington."[111] A similar scene was supposedly witnessed by a black schoolteacher. To a relative in Boston she wrote that from her porch she "saw carts pass with men thrown up there like dead animals they were taking . . . out to bury. . . . Now you won't find that in history because they don't want that—No! there's not liable to be, but that's true. They didn't allow it to be published."[112]

These reports tend to exaggerate the extent of the casualties; moreover, persisting even today in the oral tradition is the bizarre legend of the Cape Fear River—stories of the river being saturated at the mouth with bodies of black men. The Reverend Mr. Kirk wrote that hundreds of blacks were killed and their bodies dumped into Cape Fear River.[113] Professor June Nash of New York University interviewed the town librarian, who said, "We'd soon forget it . . . I heard the river was full of bodies."[114]

Several years ago a white history major at the University of North Carolina at Chapel Hill, who asked to remain anonymous, said during an interview: "My grandparents told me the Cape Fear River was saturated at the mouth with dead Negroes. And you know what? The Cape Fear is a very large river."

What makes oral history fascinating is that it generally contains some germ of truth. Some blacks in Wilmington definitely will not be quoted, but they will say in private that the mob threw many of their victims into the Cape Fear River. On the other hand, some said that the amount of violence at the Cape Fear River was exaggerated. Mabel Sadgwar and Felice Sadgwar concluded that "there was enough violence without stocking the river with dead bodies."[115]

6

When the floodwaters of the riot gushed over Wilmington, an exodus of both whites and blacks ensued. Some whites with economic means had already sent their families out of the city. When the riot began, the whites who lived in Brooklyn quickly found shelter at designated churches and schools, which were well guarded by citizen committees, but no precautions had been made for the blacks of Brooklyn, many of whom fled to the woods for survival. The *Messenger* reported that "a crowd of at least 500 men, women and children were on the road and in the woods beyond Smith's creek bridge."[116] "The roads," in the words of the *Caucasian,* " were lined with [blacks], some carrying their bedding on their heads and whatever effects could be carried." November nights were sufficiently cold to have caused suffering for the hundreds of blacks who fled into the woods. The *Caucasian* reported, "It was pitiable to see the children hurrying in fright after their parents." Many of the blacks had fled in panic without taking a quilt or blanket; they huddled without any protection overhead and with nothing but the ground to sleep upon.[117] And the forest would be their refuge for two days.

An eyewitness, correspondent Charles Francis Bourke of *Collier's Weekly,* has left a vivid description of the drama: "Bone-chilling drizzling rain falls sadly from a leaden sky, dripping from the moss-laden housetops and pattering among the sodden leaves and pine mask. Yet in the woods and swamps, innocent hundreds of terrified men, women and children wander about, fearful of the vengence of whites, fearful of death, without money or food, insufficient clothes."[118] Noting the plight of the children, he said: "Wrapped in the mother's tattered shawl, the little ones whimpered in the darkness and rain. Whispering and crawling things of the night keep them company. Fearing to light fires, listening for chance footsteps crushing fallen twigs, shuddering and peering gray-faced into the darkness, wailing, wait-ing—they knew not for what . . . In the woods, in the night, in the blackness of the pines, I heard a child crying and a hoarse voice crooning softly a mournful song, the words of which fell into my memory with the air: 'When de battle's over we kin wear a crown, In the new Je-ru-sulum.' "[119]

Long before the dust had settled on Wilmington, Colonel Taylor, "armed with a telegram from [the] Acting Adjutant General of North Carolina, had proclaimed marital law."[120] The city, which was practically being run by the committee of twenty-five, became a formidable fortress; at the main bridge into Brooklyn was stationed that night a rapid-fire gun under the command of Captain Kenan, two rapid-fire machine guns were also transported to the Negro quarters and advantageously placed.

The whites had the support of the Wilmington Light Infantry and the naval reserves, as well as of citizens performing sentinel duty in their respective communities. These forces were augmented by out-of-town military units: help was summoned from Fayetteville and 150 men responded, and three companies of state guards from Kinston, Clinton, and Maxton were ordered to the city and reported to Taylor. Finally, 200 special policemen were sworn in and placed on duty.[121] All over the town, men with Winchesters stood picket over their quiet homes and sleeping families. If the whites were expecting the blacks, they were disappointed.

5

Act 2—An American-style Coup d'État

1

THE Secret Nine and the Reformers—opportunists to the end—made the riot a smoke screen for their violent and revolutionary seizure of the city government from the legally elected Fusionist regime. They also had other special events planned—this was to be the second act of the drama.

It was pointed out in the Preface that any reexamination of a significant historical theme presupposes an analysis of new kinds of data, and this definitive study not only investigates a number of unanswered questions about the Wilmington race riot, but the extensive research is based on a number of previous unexplored sources. Completely ignored by historians and others are the New Hanover County Town Council Minutes (Wilmington, N.C., 1898–1911, F and G). The importance of these minutes can hardly be overestimated. They take one behind the scenes before, during, and after the coup; they also raise important questions. One entry shows that the mayor and his board had met three days earlier. The next entry, on page 15, shows that a special meeting was held on 10 November at 12:50 P.M. and that Mayor Wright presided. Only five aldermen were present: Andrew J. Hewlett, John G. Norwood (black), H. C. Twining, D. J. Benson and W. E. Yopp. Absent were Benjamin Keith, Andrew J. Walker (black), and Elijah M. Green (black). The other two memebers of the board, one of whom was black, cannot be accounted for. By this time, Waddell had already led a mob that destroyed the *Record*'s press, and the killings had occurred at Fourth and Harnett streets. The police department was helpless and had, in effect, completely melted away, while the revolutionary leaders were carrying out their carefully laid plans. Instead of the mayor declaring a state of emergency and telegraphing Governor Russell for help, however, at one o'clock that afternoon he and his Board of Aldermen concerned themselves with the enactment of a prohibition ordinance. This law made it "unlawful for any person or persons to sell or give away in the city of Wilmington any whiskey, wine, beer, ale, brandy, or other intoxicating drinks between one o'clock p.m. Thursday, November 10, 1898 and November 14, at 12 o'clock noon."[1]

On the next two pages (16 and 17), the minutes show that thirteen new men were sworn in as aldermen; no date or time is recorded, nor is there any indication of who was in charge.[2] This was a violation of the city charter, which mandated a ten-member Board of Aldermen. Then they proceeded to elect one of their members as mayor and to select some citizen to fill the vacancy created by the election of the mayor. Immediately following the recording of the thirteen aldermen's names, the entry shows that Waddell took the oath as mayor of the city of Wilmington.[3]

The record also shows that Waddell repeated his pledge, as did other members of the revolutionary Board of Aldermen. All this means that the town council minutes show double entries.

Meanwhile, clandestine groups were holding caucuses. One group of conspirators—a committee including James H. Chadbourn, Jr., George Rountree, and Iredell Meares—met at the Cape Fear Club. It is not clear what this group had in mind, but Rountree had sent Chadbourn on a mission and told him to see his people and get them ready. As to the time, it is surmised that this cabal met soon after the first shooting at Fourth and Harnett streets, or at least before noon that day.

Meanwhile, another committee meeting had been scheduled at the Seaboard Air Line Building. Charles Worth alerted Rountree and told him to go over to Waddell's meeting. Rountree immediately went on this mission and soon located the group. There he found John Bellamy, who like himself was not a member of that committee. There were a number of strangers in attendance, assumed to be visiting correspondents.

It should be recalled at this point that Waddell had earlier led the mob that destroyed the Manly press. He was now the mainspring of this intrigue and proceeded to call the meeting to order, explaining that the purpose was to select a mayor and a Board of Aldermen. Rountree arose, stating that he was invited by a member of the committee and he "had something to say to the committee if they cared to hear." He wanted to know if the committee represented the businessmen of the city. This inquiry ignited a heated debate, during which Bellamy arose and said that Rountree "was there by invitation and did not like that sort of talk."[4]

When this impasse was finally surmounted, the committee issued a mandate to Mayor Wright and his Board of Aldermen to meet in City Hall. Frank H. Stedman and Charles W. Worth were commissioned to call upon the mayor and his men.[5] As delegated by Waddell and his cabal, Stedman and Worth called on Mayor Wright and his associates, who included the Populist chief of police. They were asked to surrender their offices because of their weakness and inability to preserve law and order in the city. Mayor Wright stated that he would not prefer to do so in the face of this crisis.

Meanwhile, Waddell and his group had assembled at the Merchants' Association Building with other members of the committee of twenty-five to hear Stedman and Worth's report. According to the *Messenger,* this took place about three o'clock in the afternoon. At this juncture, the entire committee decided to bring pressure to bear on Mayor Wright and his board.

With Waddell again in front, onlookers saw the group of men striding in the direction of City Hall. Magnetlike, their appearance drew men and boys into the street behind them; others watched from the sidewalks or out of nearby windows—all were looking for action. On reaching their destination, they went into City Hall, while the crowd was milling about making great noises, yelling and whistling. Waddell ordered the mayor to call a special meeting, which was done at four o'clock with Mayor Wright presiding. Some conspirators insisted on getting all ten aldermen there. Failing to do so, they went ahead with their scheme, despite the absence of aldermen Keith, Merrill, Green, and two others. The group demanded that the mayor and his board resign immediately, but Wright refused to quit under fire. Some told him to take a look at the crowd in the street. He eased over, looked out the window, and saw the streets filled with men walking with rifles in their hands—men whose pockets "bulged out ominously."[6] By this time, the crowd around the building was in a dangerous state.

Mayor Wright quickly changed his mind and decided to resign. Then Stedman, Worth, and J. Alan Taylor took over (the last was a member of the Secret Nine). By wards, each of the aldermen and then the mayor resigned as dictated by the above three men. The resignation of the aldermen from the First Ward was read and accepted, and a person was then nominated and elected by the committee of twenty-five. So continued the process as the committee selected its nominees, continuing until the mayor, the Board of Aldermen, and all the city officers had been replaced by Democrats.[7] Alderman Keith was out of the city and Alderman Merrill was ill, so these two men still remained on the board. They were, however, forced to resign within two days. As would be anticipated, the three black aldermen never showed up. Hugh McRae and Taylor declined to qualify as aldermen until two days later; they wanted to be free to act independently in the unfinished business of the Secret Nine.

Beginning with the Populist chief of police, the entire police department was forced to resign. Edgar G. Parmele was named chief of police by the new board, and M. F. Heiskel Gouvenier was appointed assistant chief of police, with John J. Furlong being designated as captain of the Police Department. Parmele was duly sworn in as chief of police of the city of Wilmington, and he immediately came forward and took charge of the police force.[8]

With the resignation of Silas P. Wright, the office of mayor fell vacant. As one might have anticipated, Waddell was unanimously elected mayor of the city of Wilmington and came forward and had the oath of office administered to him by Martin Newman, Jr. Then the new mayor took the chair and made a few remarks. He said that all the members of the board no doubt felt like he did "in this crisis," and while he thanked the board for the honor conferred upon him, he did not "desire the position, and hoped soon to be relieved," as he accepted it only as a "duty in this grave crisis." He implored the members to cooperate with him "in the most extraordinary conditions which confront us." He called God to witness that he would employ his efforts to sternly enforce order and suppress violence.[9]

With perhaps a feeling of remorse, Alderman Worth moved that a vote of thanks be given to the retiring board. The motion was tabled. Alderman King moved that the mayor be authorized to have two hundred special policemen sworn in immediately. The minutes were carried, and with no further business, the meeting adjourned.[10]

At this time the elitists and the poor whites parted along traditional class lines. Those who had acted as leaders, having accomplished their objectives, withdrew from active participation in the riot. Several of the ringleaders now began to exert themselves to prevent further disorder. Mayor Waddell's first official act was to issue a proclamation making it clear to everyone that he intended to use all powers to "preserve peace and order." He also asked all people to "co-operate with the municipal authorities in every way possible to secure the permanent establishment of good government." In conclusion, he said, "The law will be rigidly enforced and impartially administered to white and black alike."[11]

2

The Greeks had a word for temporary exilement *(ostrakismos)*, but the Democrats of Wilmington wanted permanent exilement. As pointed out by the *Raleigh News and Observer*, "certain men had long been marked." Immediately after Waddell became mayor, a member of the Secret Nine gave Taylor a list of prominent Republicans, both white and black, to be permanently banished from Wilmington.[12]

Now that the pendulum of the race riot had swung from shooting to banishment, the initial step was to round up the intended victims and imprison them overnight for safekeeping. This task was entrusted to Police Captain Furlong, who along with Thomas W. Wright climbed aboard the wagon and began the manhunt. To assist in this objective, a small detachment of mounted Wilmington Light Infantrymen galloped close behind the wagon.

First, they looked for former mayor Wright but could not find him. It was later learned that the former mayor had left town under cover of darkness. Learning that French was still in town, Furlong stepped up his search, hoping to find him before the Redshirts, who would surely lynch him; but French could not be found.

The search now shifted to the Populist former chief of police, Melton, and the soldiers, dogged in their pursuit, soon found him. Not knowing what was to be his fate—some soldiers were talking of hanging him, while one said, "God help Melton"—he looked like a condemned man being led to the gallows. "I shall never forget," Metts later recalled, "how Melton looked as he sat under a tree in front of the Armory; he could not eat and when some of the boys went upstairs and took a rope with a noose in it and threw it at his feet, he turned just as white as a sheet."[13]

Furlong had orders to bring in the black, Thomas Miller, who was charged with declaring that he would wash his hands in the white man's blood before night, but the real reason was that his continued presence made a travesty of white supremacy. He was a wealthy and astute real estate broker, businessman, and the only pawnbroker in the city. According to the black oral tradition, Miller was to be banished because many whites owed him money, and some desired to take over his extensive real estate holdings.

When the soldiers arrived at Miller's house, his daughter was on the veranda and, realizing that her father was in danger, told the men that he was not at home. Furlong pushed past the girl, gave several sharp knocks on the door, entered the house, and confronted Miller without being properly introduced. Miller was ordered to accompany Furlong to jail for safekeeping for the night. Miller obstinately refused, but when the police captain motioned for bystanders to assist him, he consented to go along. Miller's daughter rushed to his side and was again pushed away. Like a criminal, Miller was led to the wagon, and he climbed aboard. His daughter, weeping and wailing, trotted and walked behind all the way to the jail. At one time during this ordeal, Miller said he would "rather be dead than to have to suffer such humiliation." One of the men tersely told him to jump from the wagon and his last wish would be granted instantly.[14] Miller kept complaining, and the soldiers could not keep him quiet. "He talked and talked until Ed McKoy's gun went 'click, click' and he kept a little quieter."[15]

United States Commissioner Robert H. Bunting was also scheduled for banishment. He was looked upon with abhorrence ostensibly because he had tilted the scales of justice in his court to favor blacks, while severely punishing whites. The real charge went deeper: for some time he had violated Southern law by cohabiting with an attractive fair Negro woman—perhaps a mulatto. Already a crowd was milling about the house, yelling for the commissioner. Some of its members were drunk, and they were in a dangerous state by the time the soldiers arrived. Neither the commissioner nor his wife were at home, and this was fortunate. While some of the hoodlums milled about yelling obscenities, there was talk about pulling the commissioner's house down. Then the hoodlums crashed through the front door. These poor whites had never seen such things. First they ransacked the house, smashed the furniture, and stole some objects. Then they tore from the walls two large gold-framed portraits of Bunting and his Negro wife and nailed them to a tree on the corner of Seventh and Market Streets. They were tagged for identification: "R. H. Bunting—white" and "Mrs. R. H. Bunting—colored."[16] The Southern order tacitly approved of white men's illicit relations with Negro women, but not marriage. Meanwhile, the commissioner had gone to the armory and asked for protection, and from there he was placed in jail for safekeeping.[17]

Some of the leading blacks who had met the evening before with Waddell and the committee of twenty-five had already vacated their holdings. One of them was Armond W. Scott; likewise, L. A. Henderson asked for a military escort to the railroad for himself and his family.[18] In a local paper, special reference was directed at the Reverend J. Allen Kirk, pastor of the Central Baptist Church: "The Negro who came from Boston here to lead the Negroes in their depredation had better take his departure and shake the dust from his feet."[19] The Reverend Mr. Kirk headed the Ministerial Union, which had helped Manly relocate his press and which had asked the blacks to endorse the *Record* by supporting the newspaper. During the riot, he sequestered himself in the black cemetery, later scrambling through the woods and swamps to safety.

By dusk, all of the men earmarked for banishment who could be found were lodged in jail for safekeeping. But the searchers had not found French, who, according to rumors, was still hiding in town. Meanwhile, the Redshirts and the Rough Riders became more restless and bold as darkness fell upon the city. During the night there was a chilling rain; notwithstanding, there arose among the Redshirts and Rough Riders wild talk of a lynching bee. In fact, there was a prearranged lynching party set for the night of 9 November, which did not take place, because Manly had been the intended victim. Now wanting any justifiable victim, they intensified their search for French. The Redshirts and the incensed mob sought in vain to locate him, but "the maddened mobsters could find no trace of French."[20] They then turned their horses sharply up the road that led to the city jail.

Reports quickly spread throughout the city that some horsemen were going to storm the jail and seize the blacks imprisoned for safekeeping and scheduled for banishment the next morning. Phones buzzed among Mayor Waddell and other town officials. Walter G. McRae, the new sheriff of New Hanover County, and Roger Moore were instructed to go to the jail and protect the prisoners. Father Dennen, the Catholic priest, was also told to go there and talk to the mob. The Reverend Mr. Strange remembers receiving an urgent phone call to "go there and talk to the mob."[21] Soon thereafter the lynch mob arrived at the jail, bent on taking the prisoners.

Various suggestions and arguments were advanced by the men in the crowd in an effort to persuade Moore and McRae to leave the jail for just a short time. Both were keenly aware of the motive behind the proposal and remained on guard. Father Dennen, so it was said, stood firmly in the doorway, telling the angry men that they would have to walk over his dead body

Members of the Wilmington Light Infantry and Naval Reserves escorting captured blacks to jail. From *Collier's Weekly*, November 26, 1898 (Library of Congress).

in order to get at the prisoners. About ten-thirty, a picket comprising some sixty troops was placed on duty to protect the jail.[22] Perhaps the rain played some role in dampening the spirits of the Redshirts.

The next morning dawned clear but a bit chilly, and the streets showed dampness from the rain of the previous night. People were streaming into town, first congregating around the city jail and then lining the street leading to the railroad station, as if waiting for a parade; all seemed amused and excited at what was about to happen. The blacks were the first to go. Under the command of Lieutenant Commander George L. Morton, the soldiers with fixed bayonets walked on each side as Williamson (a South Carolinian), R. B. Pickens, the Reverend I. J. Bell, Isaac Luflin, Ira R. Bryant, and Thomas C. Miller passed by. The crowd cheered and hurled racist slurs.

Deeply shaken by this event, Miller made the ignoble journey with grief and humiliation. He was Wilmington's most successful black, and his wealth had set him apart from most whites and far more blacks.

The six men were escorted to a "north bound train and placed in a special car with a guard under orders to carry them beyond the limits of the state."[23] As the train moved off slowly, the crowd filled the air with cheers and yells. The engine gathered speed, each revolution of the wheels putting greater distance between the banished and Wilmington. Stretching into the distance, the whistle pierced the air repeatedly.

At two o'clock that afternoon a northbound train arrived for its special mission, the banishment of leading white Republicans. A still larger crowd had assembled to watch this event, again lining the streets from the city jail to the railroad station. Excitement was generated when the crowd around the jail began to murmur and to point. Someone shouted, "There's French!" A greater sensation was created when the crowd recognized him, along with

Melton, Bunting, H. Gilbert (a policeman), James Larglin (a clerk on Front Street), and Charles McAllister (a merchant). To prevent French's lynching, James V. Allen had secretly hidden him in a room in the Orton Hotel on Front Street. The very sight of Fench infuriated the spectators. Various charges had been trumped up against him. Formerly a carpetbagger, he had settled in Wilmington and had become a member of the General Assembly. He was also a former postmaster. The whites never forgot a speech he had made in which he had said, "I would like to spin a rope to hang every Democrat in North Carolina."[24] But now he was hated most because he was the political organizer of the blacks and was accused of coddling them for their votes.

For some reason, the soldiers had discarded their fixed bayonets. As if drawn by a magnet, an angry throng, including many young ruffians, poured into the street and followed the prisoners. While the soldiers marched on each side of them hoping to prevent violence, there arose from the sidewalks an "angry murmur far ahead like the ocean tide,"[25] as the men moved along. When they reached the station with French, there was silence for a moment—then like a trumpet, a voice blasted out, "Hang him!" Pandemonium broke out. Accompanying vulgar phrases were shouts of "Hang him! Hang him!" The soldiers faced down the mob, but found themselves unable to protect their prisoners.[26] Members of the mob dragged French out into the open to a telephone pole on Front Street. A noose was thrown over his head and placed about his neck, and the rope was tossed over the arm of the pole and pulled. French was now half choked and gasping for air. Then there was another sudden commotion at the appearance of Stedman and two other influential Democrats.

As spokesman, Stedman made it clear to the mob leaders that the town was not going to be disgraced by a lynching. He followed this with the stern warning that if French were to be hanged, the guilty parties would surely stand trial for murder. There was a deathlike silence, and the rope was released. Fench fell upon his knees, hastily got up, ran toward the train, jumped aboard, and cringed on the floor beneath the seats in one of the coaches.[27] The climax of this drama brought whistles and cheers from many spectators.

As the train began to pull off, Bunting and Gilbert fought to maintain their composure as long as they could, but at times it was beyond their strength, and as the train pulled off, both men burst into tears.[28] Bunting was being snatched from his comfortable home. Gilbert and Melton were forced to leave behind a wife and five children each. In contrast to this sad scene was a crowd of hundreds of cheering people. The exiled men arrived at New Bern via the Atlantic Coastline Railroad. There they were met by a committee of citizens who notified them that they were not welcome. At six o'clock that evening, they were escorted to the steamer *Neuse,* which sailed for Elizabeth City, while notice was sent to that city "to keep them moving."[29]

It was now time for the Democratic coterie to pay their debts, but it was inevitable that there would be many disappointments in the distribution of the spoils. There just were not enough jobs to go around to all of the whites Manly had dubbed as "poor bocras" living throughout Wilmington and New Hanover County. Promises had been made to them for their assistance in the killings and the banishment of the blacks from the city.[30] Then there were the politicians hankering for public offices. None of these people, however, possessed the educational qualifications to fill the few clerical positions. Even if this had not been the case, these jobs would have been reserved for members of middle-class white families.

Another great disappointment for the poor whites involved the luxurious homes of the blacks, which had always been the envy of the destitute. Because of their acute racism and poverty, if given the opportunity, they would have destroyed the property of affluent blacks, but these homes were not destroyed because the demogogues had promised to turn over to the poor whites the confiscated property of the wealthy blacks in return for their assistance. In the end, however, they reneged on that promise, and this disappointment helped to intensify further the hatred between blacks and whites. The conspirators never had any intention of letting these low-class whites into their community; in fact, they were considered even more abominable than blacks.

At three o'clock on the same afternoon as the banishment, Mayor Waddell called a special meeting for the purpose of reorganizing the Police Department. Chief of Police Parmele reported that he had on duty only four regular policemen that morning. Walker Taylor spoke about the seriousness of the situation and offered the assistance of the military. It was agreed to keep the town under martial law until the reorganization of the police force was completed. The following day, the Board of Aldermen appointed a special committee to select competent men for the Police Department. Meanwhile, a provisional police force of thirty-seven men was appointed; it was staffed with former members of the mob—Redshirts and Rough Riders included— and in time all would become regulars. The pay was one dollar per day, and there were more than enough takers.[31]

Victims of the coup's ax also included the all-black health board, the superintendent of streets (black), the cattle weigher (black), the clerk (black), the day janitor and messenger at city hall (black), and the lot inspector (black). White Republicans included the city attorney, the treasurer, and the superintendent of garbage. Some new jobs were created. One of them went to M. D. Croom at $30 per month to keep the downtown section clear of cattle and hogs, which were running at ease in the streets, creating a filthy condition.

Next, an all-white fire department was reorganized and reduced from five to three companies. Charles Schnibben, one of the local saloon owners, who had held the position of fire chief under the Fusionist administration, made sure that he was on the winning side; he was retained in his old position. The Redshirt leader, Mike Dowling, was appointed foreman of Hose Reel Company No. 3 at forty-five dollars per month.[32]

Similar to the time when the Fusionist forces toppled the Democrats from power, leaders of the coup made a clean sweep of public offices, and resignations were demanded from all non-Democrats. The town council minutes were full of resignations read and accepted. On 12 November, the resignation of Alderman Keith from the Third Ward was read and accepted. Two days later, upon motion of Alderman Worth, J. Alan Taylor and Hugh McRae were unanimously elected aldermen from Keith's ward. Taylor and McRae came forward, took the oath of office, and took their seats as aldermen.[33] Positions were declared vacant for those refusing to tender their resignations, as Waddell and his cohorts proceeded to fill them with men selected by the new administration.

Recalling at this point the resolution adopted at the mass meeting of 9 November, which promised "in the future to give to white men a large part of the employment heretofore given to Negroes," the influential *Messenger* reminded the new city officials of the promises and resolutions adopted. It was hoped that the promises would "not end in empty declarations, or idle words, but in deeds." In support of the white labor movement, the paper alleged that the "white laboring men in this city have not been treated fairly in the past. They have been discriminated against, and the Negro favored." In the words of the *Messenger,* it was the "natural and invincible duty of every white man to remember first his white brother . . . stand firmly, consistently, continuously by the men of your own race. . . . Blood should be thicker than water in Wilmington. Forget not, neglect not your true friends in time of uneasiness, distress and anarchy."[34]

Unique in the history of labor movements was the Wilmington crusade to substitute white for black labor.[35] Such a movement had been initiated before the riot. On 27 October, 1898, a white labor union had been organized, with the express purpose of cooperating with the businessmen of the city in matters of securing white men to take the place of blacks who might be discharged from their jobs.[36] A constitution and bylaws governing the deliberations of the organization were adopted and signed by the members. They showed that the object in forming such a union was "the sole protection of white labor in every channel."[37]

One of the mainsprings of the organization was Mike Dowling, who also served as its president. The union naturally, had the active support of the Secret Nine, especially Walter L. Parsley, at whose home they had mapped out the riot scheme. Furthermore, the union could count on strong support from Hugh McRae, owner of a large cotton mill, at whose home the riot organizers occasionally met.

Next the union set up the White Labor Bureau. W. E. Worth served on its executive board, and he urged all employers who wished to change from black to white labor to examine the applications on file with the secretary of the bureau. Soon many businessmen were answering Worth's call.

Mayor Waddell and the town officials had already set the stage for white preference in municipal jobs, but to the chagrin of the white labor union, municipal wages were reduced and remained drastically low. If the white man wanted preference in employment, he had to work for the same wages as the black, which reduced him to the black man's living standard, making a travesty of the doctrine of white supremacy. Notwithstanding, the white labor union quickly gave up the struggle for higher wages and made it clear that whites would work for the same pay that blacks received and "would sweep floors, carry bundles and [the] like."[38]

As the white labor movement exerted pressure, jobs formerly thought to be beneath white men became lily-white. White men were hired to truck the bales of cotton and even work in the holds of the ships which take on the cargoes of cotton. They were also employed in the cotton compresses and in guard work. By early December 1898, only a few firms were not in hearty accord with the white labor movement, which also secured employment for white women. Generally, the positions of domestic maids, cooks, and such were the only jobs available during this era. Black women had performed this labor for two or three dollars per week.[39]

The movement to substitute white for black labor was meeting with success throughout the city. An especially encouraging feature of the movement was its strong endorsement by the business leaders. The union held its meeting in the office of the Merchants' Association. Some of the principal speakers were businessmen, including Hugh McRae, Walter Parsley, and Thomas W. Clawson. In their speeches they always told the members of the union what they wanted to hear: that they would substitute whites for black labor as soon as possible. At the same time, a special committee of the union was canvassing the merchants, manufacturers, contractors, railroads, and others to encourage such employers to make the substitutions. In arguing for white preferences in labor matters, Dowling, the union's president, stressed the superiority of whites over blacks in both "morals and industrial sense."[40]

To what extent did efficiency suffer in the citywide movement for substitution of white for black labor? To what extent was Dowling typical of the numerous poor whites? While a mainspring in the movement for substitution, he had preached fervently that whites were superior to blacks in both efficiency and morals. Notwithstanding, in March 1899, as foreman of Fire Engine Company 2, he was ordered before the Board of Audit and Finance and dismissed from his post for "incompetency, drunkenness, and continued insubordination."[41]

Employers were soon complaining that the whites were poor workers. This was especially true in the heavy industries, such as the lumber mills.

One said that he tried a few whites at his mill and quickly discovered that they could not count and pile the lumber and run the mills. Another said that it often takes two white men to perform one Negro's task. It was, indeed, ironic that dependable and efficient black laborers were leaving the city in alarming numbers.

4

Focusing attention again on the hundreds of blacks who had fled into the woods to escape the turbulence, one finds that shooting by the boisterous Redshirts was heard periodically in Brooklyn far into the night.

The morning of 11 November dawned damp, clear, and cold, and the plight of those who were forced to sleep in the open air exacted pity. The sunrise exposed a crowd of women and children huddled about a large fire they had built, but others were afraid to do this for fear of signaling the whites of their whereabouts.

Humanitarianism, ironically, is a trait of Southern white Christians. It was pointed out in the previous chapter that country whites were first to provide some comfort for these blacks, but there was a paradox: at the mere sight of white men, black children screamed and ran to their mothers for protection, and this apprehension would be engraved in their memories for many months. The refugees were so thoroughly frightened that the whites could not induce them to believe that it was safe to return to their homes. The persuasion continued, however, and gradually the blacks drifted back into the city, only to find that their jobs had been taken over by whites. Consequently, a Negro migration was set in motion. There have been race riots in the nation before and since, but never had one set in motion a black exodus.

It was stated in the preface that a black diaspora was at the center, the very heart of the racial massacres. There are several ways of forcing people to disperse, and racial violence is one way. Still another way is to eliminate jobs. The whites favored the Negro exodus; their purpose was quite clear—to provide more jobs for the surplus of poor whites.

As an immediate consequence of the terror, hundreds of blacks packed their bags and left Wilmington. Some went west and south, but the majority went to Philadelphia, New York, and other Northern cities. A large number left the city on railroad tickets sent to them by relatives. One railroad official, who was in a position to know, told a reporter of the *Wilmington Star* that the exodus of Negroes from the city seemed to continue without abatement. Blacks could be seen crowding ships, railroad stations, and coaches. The *New Bern Journal* reported: "Between forty and fifty colored people—male and female with a number of children—arrived here last night over the Atlantic Coast Line from Wilmington for the North. Yesterday over 300 left that city coming this way."

On the whole, the blacks who were forced to leave, with few exceptions, had no political following or aspirations. Whether politically active or not, however, they were the special targets of the Secret Nine. The more affluent ones lived in residential sections near prominent white families. These were protected from the viciousness of the mob by the white elite during the riot. Ironically, it was this class of whites that took the lead in organizing the mob. After the riot, however, they gave the middle-class blacks throughout the city twelve hours to get out of town.

How did the massacres affect those sections of the city long integrated by black and white "achievers"? Made destitute by the riot, the black achievers who were fortunate enough to find buyers sold their property at prices far below market value. Other less fortunate ones, whose psyches were now pervaded with a genuine fear and distrust of their white neighbors, readily abandoned their property, which was subsequently sold for taxes. Prominent whites acquired the property, along with other choice pieces of real estate they had long coveted. Today, reputable blacks will point out to interested persons vast real estate holdings formerly owned by blacks. As one black told Professor Nash: "I could spot properties and things like that, the white people got rich off the money and properties that they stole from Negroes. My grandfather had a plantation, just acres and acres of it; not a trace of it can be seen today. He owned almost a whole city block, and others too, but none of that now. He was a carpenter, my father was a carpenter and a cabinet maker."[42]

The massacres also pushed into migration the entrepreneurs who had formerly owned more than 90 percent of the downtown eating establishments. Other victims included more than 80 percent of the city's barbers (see pp. 23–25). Also forced to flee the reign of terror were prominent merchants, lawyers, physicians, clergymen, and various craftsmen, including carpenters who were both architects and housebuilders.

There is more to this gloomy story. When the fire department was reduced from five to three companies, the city was stripped of its crack all-black Cape Fear Engine Company, which had protected Brooklyn since 1873. This outfit had the reputation of being the best in the state. Decorating the walls of the firehouse were trophies won in many tournaments for skilled fire fighting.[43]

The blacks quickly lost their majority: in 1890, Wilmington's black population was 2,593 more than its white population; by 1900 the whites held a small majority, which was destined to grow much larger.[44] Two whites and one black had comprised the school committees, until the hand of the coup reached out to the committees, weeding out old members, including the one black committee man. In the future, there would be no spokesman for the black schools. The ax fell on all the black policemen. This meant, in effect, that Redneck officers, with their frustrations and aggression personalities would now patrol the black community.

The uprooted—the black artisans, along with the unskilled laborers—

found themselves in distant places. Whether migrating North or South, the skilled craftsmen encountered the lily-white labor unions. The common laborers who migrated North came into competition with whites performing what down South was called nigger work. And in Wilmington, the poor whites were willing to accept 'nigger wages' as quid pro quo for black exclusion from most menial occupations as well as trades.

The middle-class blacks who stayed in the city—ministers, teachers, businessmen, and doctors now confined to the black community—soon discovered that their social and political values as citizens had attenuated to the status of the town's lowest blacks.

And finally, in the wake of the riot, the true feelings of the Wilmington blacks can only be conjectured. And for those blacks who elected to remain in the community of Brooklyn, where many of them knew personally one or more of the riot victims, the pain did not easily go away, and there was a lingering sense of sadness. Their reaction to the world about them was passive and subdued, and they were slow to smile. Such scenes were reflected most strikingly in their eyes that haunted the mind, as if asking questions about the riot that were not easily answered.

On Sunday morning following the riot, the Reverend Peyton H. Hoge said to his congregation of the First Presbyterian Church: "Since we met in these walls we have taken a city. That is much. But it is more because it is our city that we have taken . . . not by investment and siege, not by shot and shell, but as thoroughly, as completely as if captured in battle."[45]

In contrast, the black churches of Brooklyn were empty and their pulpits silent. Nearby, a grief-stricken black woman wrote to President McKinley, "And to day [Sunday] we dare not go to our places of worship."[46]

The next day, the bright and sunny morning of 14 November, the strains of "Dixie" and the sound of marching feet again brought many of the people of Wilmington into the streets. The crisis of the city was over, and the military was leaving. The naval reserve in their jaunty white uniforms and grimy troops in blue, carrying blanket rolls and packs, marched toward the railroad station. High-spirited spectators greeted the troops along the route, and small handkerchiefs fluttered from the windows of residences and hotels, and gay morning dresses appeared on the balconies. At the depot, the officers in command lined up their men and called for three cheers for the hospitable and courteous people of Wilmington. Then in a steady and orderly fashion, the railroad coaches were soon jammed with the troops and their equipment of war. "Bevies of pretty girls stood on the platform outside and tearfully begged cartridges for remembrance."[47]

The whites of Wilmington had been most hospitable to the military, which had come into town to protect them from what now turned out to be a phantom—the Negro menace. "The white women of the town fed the soldiers as they stood guard upon the street corners. Coffee was prepared in 50-pound lard cans, buckwheat cakes were stacked high on large platters, eggs were fried by the dozens, and other items of food were served to the troops and guardsmen by the housewives all over the city."[48] When correspondents arrived in town, they were met by a cordial committee, who saw that they, too, were wined and dined. The purpose was clear: they would report the Democratic story as the town officials wanted it reported. There was one last gesture of cordiality. Boxes of cigars appeared mysteriously and from unknown sources, and their contents disappeared in the twinkling of an eye.

As the train pulled out, the shrill rebel yell pierced the morning air. When Wilmington had faded in the distance, the troops broke into song and indulged in revolver practice from the platforms and car windows. Thus, the city of Wilmington—the setting of a violent coup—had been evacuated, and "Johnny has gone marching home again to the accompaniment of the inevitable Hooray!"[49]

The Negro as the enemy—a phantom, if ever one existed—was visible, but a threat more imagined than real. However, white Wilmingtonians paranoically imagined or saw what was not there.

6

Beyond the Borders of the Maelstrom

1

THE Wilmington racial crisis attracted national attention. Northern newspapers, led by the influential *New York Times* and the *New York Herald,* ran
eye-catching headlines.[1] The *Washington Post* and the *Atlanta Constitution*
did the same for their regions, while prestigious magazines such as *Collier's
Weekly, Harper's Weekly,* and *Forum* joined in notifying the public.
"M'Kinley Consults Alger," announced the *New York Herald.* President
William McKinley considered the event to be serious and worthy of the
immediate attention of his cabinet. Secretary of War Russell A. Alger expressed the majority sentiment when he concluded that the conditions in
Wilmington were "a disgrace to the State and to the Country."[2] Attorney
General John W. Griggs was not in the nation's capital during the fury of the
riot, but the urgency of the conflict caused him to rush back to his office. On
the night of 11 November, he "was for some time in conference with the
President." In fact, the story of the events in North Carolina became the
subject of widespread discussion and comment throughout the Justice Department.[3]

Meanwhile, sources outside McKinley's cabinet speculated on the question of federal intervention in Wilmington. And there loomed the paramount
question: Would the president dispatch troops into North Carolina to restore
law and order and depose the revolutionary government in Wilmington?

The *New York Herald* bureau in northwest Washington, and its reporters
and correspondents kept in close contact with the Wilmington events. In
fact, during this crisis the *Herald* was the most active newspaper outside the
South. It was aware that no official communication had come from North
Carolina touching on the race riot; beyond newspaper reports, President
McKinley received no communication from state officials. The *Herald* was
quick to point out the "Rights of the President"; referring to the Wilmington
situation, the president's attention was called to section 5,299 of the Revised

Statutes, which informed him that it was both lawful and his duty to employ "the army and naval forces of the United States, or use other means necessary for the suppression of insurrection, domestic violence, unlawful combinations or conspiracies of any state that obstructs or hinders the execution of the laws of the United States." Moreover, in such cases the president can use these measures whenever constituted authorities of any state are unable to protect or for any cause fail in or refuse to protect for the people of a state "any of the rights, privileges or immunities or protection named in the constitution."[4]

Having received no instructions or advice from the officials in Wilmington, President McKinley refrained from commenting on the situation. It soon became evident to the president that Governor Russell had no intention of seeking federal assistance. In fact, the governor declined to comment at all on the troubles in Wilmington.[5] According to the *New York Times*, President McKinley decided against federal intervention to unseat the revolutionary government (since he believed this would further aggravate the race conflict) unless the violence was resumed.

But there would be no more violence. The Secret Nine and conspirators of the coup, along with other Wilmington officials, had planned for the riot to be swift, with objectives and goals achieved within a short time. On that day, 10 November, they overturned the old order in a few hours, and between eight in the morning and three in the afternoon, the entire drama had been acted out. The actors—Redshirts, Rough Riders, and all—had performed their roles to perfection and without a visible prompter. In less than two days, as far as President McKinley was concerned, the question of the Wilmington race riot had become a nolle prosequi; that is, the federal government would pursue no further action in the affair.

Notwithstanding President McKinley's benign neglect of the Wilmington event, the issue was kept alive by people of conscience who had firsthand information, and by those who were personally touched by the riot. And to these forces must be added black newspapers, leaders, and civil rights groups—all censuring both the president and the Department of Justice, while seeking federal intervention in North Carolina.

A week after the riot, Benjamin F. Keith wrote his friend Senator Marion Butler and asked him "to try to get a newspaper man to come to Wilmington, investigate and get the facts." He emphasized that the "local papers had not told the truth and there were things down here that honest people ought to know." He called the riot "the saddest thing that ever happened, and it was awful to know the true conditions of affairs." He mentioned also the blacks who had been in the woods "like stray cattle" in the "bad weather," and the "innocent Negroes killed." With a bit of cynicism, he said: "I fear our city is doomed . . . If one should disapprove publically, he would have to leave at once . . . What I have written," he cautioned Senator Butler, "keep it to yourself [or] I would have to leave and probably not alive."[6] Perhaps Keith had hoped that Senator Butler would have enough clout to instigate a congressional investigation.

On 9 November, two days after Keith wrote his letter, B. F. McLean, an attorney and United States commissioner of justice for the eastern district of North Carolina, wrote to Attorney General Griggs: "I deem it my duty as officer to inform you of what was done down here. . . . You have no idea of the trouble we are having with the Red Shirts unless you were here." Among other things, he related how some whites had organized themselves into the "White Union," had armed themselves with Winchesters, and for three nights prior to the election had made hideous raids over the county "yelling and shooting into the houses of innocent Negroes." In conclusion, he asked, "Are not these people liable for indictment under U.S. laws 5506-7-8-9 R.D.?"[7] He followed up this correspondence with another letter dated 3 December 1898.

Two days later attorney C. M. Bernard, also of the Department of Justice for the eastern district of North Carolina, inquired of Attorney General Griggs about the "possibility of initiating a Congressional investigation of the violation of the election statutes of the United States respecting United States officers and citizens in the exercise of their constitutional rights and privileges at an election held in North Carolina in November, in 1898; and if justified, to send bills of indictment and vigorously prosecute the guilty parties." Bernard complained that he was "powerless without a complaint from somebody, or a witness or witnesses," and he had no reliable information from "any witnesses except from newspaper reports . . . No one has made complaints to me," he wrote. "I do not know where the court process can reach Mr. Bunting, Mr. Gill . . . [and those] whose names I cannot now recollect. From the last information I have these parties were in Washington, D.C. If your Department can locate these parties I will have them come at once, or if your Department could notify them to come here at once, it would save time and greatly facilitate these matters."[8]

Bernard persisted in his efforts to bring to justice and to punish the guilty parties.[9] Several months later, he contacted the attorney general again about the matter. Thinking that his letter of 1 April 1899 "had been overlooked," he asked the attorney general for a reply, while offering several suggestions as to how he might assist his office. "First the assistance of one or two first class men, particularly selected and especially adapted to this work, from the Secret Service, or detective service, to go into each community, and to secure the necessary information and names of necessary witnesses for the trial and conviction of the guilty parties." Anticipating some difficulty, he explained that in "some instances they would have to ferret out the members of an organized, masked band of men, who broke up the election, assaulted members of the election Board, taking the ballot boxes, and shooting one of the election inspectors." In other instances, they would have to "locate members of bands of red shirts, their names, residences and time and places of meetings, and follow some into the state of South Carolina." As for Wilmington, he noted that it would "be necessary for the two Federal agents to go into and associate with the roughs and toughs" in certain wards of the city "who were incited and led and directed by other men of higher official and social standing, and who have profited by this work, and who should be made examples of. This was the storm center from which emanated most of the election crimes and intimidation." "If true bills of indictment could be found by the Grand Jury," he further noted, then at least "two able, courageous attorneys of integrity would be needed to assist the Government in the prosecution of the cases." Aware that what he was asking was exceedingly difficult, he cautioned the attorney general that a failure to convict would, in his opinion, be more harmful than beneficial.[10] But already, what Bernard was hoping for had quickly faded like a distant mirage.

2

One day after their banishment from Wilmington, the exiles—United States Commissioner R. H. Bunting, C. H. Gilbert, and the Populist chief of police, John R. Melton—arrived in Washington, D.C. They called on the United States Department of Justice and concomitantly sought an interview with President McKinley. Their problem was further complicated by the prior arrival of prominent victims of the Phoenix, South Carolina race riot.[11]

At a crossroads country store, a mere spot on the map designated as Phoenix in Greenwood County, and in neighboring communities, election day riots had resulted in the death of one white man and at least twelve blacks. Included among the wounded were three members of one of the most influential white families—the Tolberts (leading Republican and federal officeholders)—who were forced to flee the intensity of the violence.

Leading Republicans, the Tolberts were well-educated, wealthy planters, and their combined landholdings exceeded ten thousand acres with numerous black tenants. Formerly large slave owners, they had opposed secession, yet four members of the family fought for the Confederacy. The head of the family was Major John R. Tolbert, Sr., a former scalawag and currently collector of customs at the Port of Charleston. His son, Robert Rhett Tolbert, accompanied by some Republican politicians, hastily departed for Washington, D.C., after the shootings. On 10 November, he and Solicitor General Richards called at the White House and had an extended interview with President McKinley. He related to the president the story of his experiences in South Carolina, entering into minute details of the trouble on election day. The president listened attentively to the recital, but gave no indication of what action, if any, might be taken. However, he requested Tolbert see the attorney general and give him a full statement of the situation.[12]

Soon afterward, the ranks of the Wilmington exiles were increased by the sudden appearance of Armond W. Scott. Scott was granted an interview with Attorney General Griggs, as were Bunting and Melton. However, a conference with the president did not occur.

Bunting and Melton persisted in their efforts to see the president. On Christmas Eve of 1898, listing their address as "318 Pennsylvania Avenue N.W., Washington, D.C.," they forwarded a jointly signed letter to President McKinley. "We the undersigned," they began, "were driven from Wilmington, N.C. our home for the reason, we were republicans and stood up for the Republican Party." On reminding the President of their destitute status, they said: "We have been here for six weeks with very little means to subsist on. We have made every effort to get employment and have failed. We can't return to our families, and have been notified through the public press at Wilmington, N.C. that if we return we would be killed." The two men asked the president to use his office to secure them "employment in the government services." In an apologetic tone, they continued: "We would have called on you and laid our trouble before you, but we know your time is too valuable, hence we take this method of reaching you." They wished the president a "Merry Christmas and a Happy New Year." Bunting and Melton added a postscript to their letter: "We would like very much to have an interview with you for then we can explain our case more satisfactory."[13]

Quite understandably, black citizens wrote President McKinley the most distressed letters, some of them full of pathos. On 14 November 1898, Della V. Johnson of Wilmington wrote, "I beg you [for help] in the face of justice, in the face of the constitutional wrongs, and for the sake of humanity."[14] The next day the president received an anonymous letter from a distraught woman who said: "I am afraid to own my name but for God sake help . . . the colored people know that the old Confederate flag is floating in Wilmington, North Carolina. The city of Wilmington is under confederate laws."[15] Still another unsigned letter said, "For the sake of humanity send us protection." It asked the president "not to believe those [white] papers."[16] In calling the president's attention to the plight of the blacks, Wilhelmena Anderson wrote, "I have a feeling I am nothing but a poor washer woman [but] excuse my writing as I never went to school in my life."[17]

The most comprehensive letter was dated 13 November 1898, the Sunday following the riot. The writer headlined her letter "Please send relief as soon as possible or we perish."[18] The writer was probably a schoolteacher, and she wrote authoritatively about the riot. The evidence suggests that she made no errors or faulty analyses. Because it is so informative, her letter is quoted almost in its entirety.

"I a Negro woman of this city appeal to you from the depths of my heart, to do something in the Negro's behalf. The outside world only knows one side of the trouble here, there is no paper to tell the truth about the Negro here in this or any other Southern state. The Negro in this town had no arms (except pistols perhaps in some instances) with which to defend themselves from the attack of lawless whites." In citing the time the turbulence began she said, "The riot broke out on the 10th Thursday morning between eight and nine o'clock when all Negro men had gone to their places of work." And as to the leaders of the mob, she put the blame on "Col. A. M. Waddell, John D. Bellamy and S. H. Fishblate." She also accused the whites of "firing Winchester guns . . . as they marched from the Light Infantry Armory on Market Street up to seventh down seventh to Free Love Hall [which was owned by a society of Negroes, and where the Negro daily press was] and set it afire and burnt it."

Among the weapons, she noted that the whites had a "Hotchkiss gun . . . [and] Colt rapid fire guns." Concerning the role in the riot played by John D. Bellamy, she identified him as a rabble-rouser and accused him of deliberately inciting the whites by telling them that "in addition to the guns they already had they could keep back federal interference, and he could have the soldiers at Ft. Caswell to take up arms against the United States."

The mob proceeded to the *Record*'s office and the building was burned. "After destroying the building," she wrote, "they went over in Brooklyn, another Negro settlement mostly, and began searching every one and if you did not submit, [you] would be shot down on the spot. They searched all the Negro churches . . . They found no guns or ammunition in any of the places, for there was none. And to satisfy their blood thirsty appetites would kill unoffending Negro men to on their way from dinner." Of the iniquitous role played by the Spanish-American War veterans and the out-of-town military, she said: "The men of the 1st North Carolina were home on a furlough and they took high hand in the nefarious work also. The companies from every little town came in to kill the negro. There was not any Rioting simply the strong slaying the weak."

She also spoke about white boys, not yet in their teens, carrying guns, along with the special police. Condemning this action, she said: "Every white man and boy from 12 years up had a gun or pistol, and the negro had nothing, his soul he could not say was his own. Oh, to see how we are slaughtered, when our husbands go to work we do not look for their return. The Man who promises the Negro protection now as Mayor is the one who in his speech at the Opera house said the Cape Fear should be strewn with carcasses."

She did not refrain from expressing her sentiments about Manly and his press. "Some papers I see," she wrote, "say it was right to eject the Negro editor. That is all right but why should a whole city full of negroes suffer for Manly when he was hundreds of miles away? And the paper had ceased publication. We were glad it was so for our own safety. But they tried to slay us all."

She was distraught over the fact that Wilmington had lost its most prominent black citizens, while the shiftless blacks were allowed to remain. "Some of our most worthy Negro men," she pointed out, "have been made to leave the city. When our parents belonged to [the whites] why, the Negro was all right [but] now, then they work and accumulate property they are all wrong. The Negroes that have been banished are all property owners to considerable extent, had they been worthless negroes, we would not care."

She also expressed compassionate concern about the exiled whites, inquiring of the whereabouts of G. Z. French, deputy sheriff; John R. Melton, chief of police; Silas P. Wright, mayor; and R. H. Bunting, United States commissioner. "We don't know where Mr. Chadbourn the Post Master is, and two or three other whites. I call on you the head of the American Nation to help these humble subjects. Will you for God sake in your next message to Congress give us some relief? If you sent us all to Africa we will be willing or a number of us will gladly go. . . . We are loyal [and] we go when duty calls us."

Near the end of the letter, she asked President McKinley some searching questions. "Are we to die like rats in a trap? With no place to seek redress or to go with our Grievances? Can we call on any other Nation for help? Why do you forsake the Negro who is not to blame for [our] being here? Is this land of the free and the home of the brave? How can the Negro sing My Country tis of thee?"

In reminding the president of America's compassion for foreign people while ignoring that same attribute for blacks. She said: "This Grand and Noble Nation who flies to the help of suffering humanity of another Nation and leave the Secessionists and born Rioters to slay us. Oh, that we had never seen the light of the world. For Humanity sake help us, for Christ sake do. We the Negro can do nothing but pray. There seems to be no help for us. No paper will tell the truth about the Negro."

She ended her letter with these words: "Today we are mourners in a strange land with no protection near. God help us. Do something to alleviate our sorrows if you please. I cannot sign my name and live. But every word of this is true. The laws of our state is no good for the Negro anyhow. Yours in much distress."[19]

The reactions of the black press to the Wilmington race riot were predictable. Harry Smith, the angry black editor of the *Cleveland Gazette*, railed at whites and blacks alike: Dancy for leaving the scene and the Department of the Army for disarming the veteran Tenth Cavalry at Huntsville instead of dispatching them to Wilmington.[20] The *Richmond Planet* called the Wilmington Massacre "a relic of the Middle Ages." "We challenge a comparison of this slaughter," the paper said, "with the atrocities of the Turks in Armenia [1894], and the murder of colored men without parallel since the St. Bartholomew Day Massacre." From a safe distance in Richmond, the paper advised blacks to defend their homes and "kill a few of their murderers and then send up a prayer to God before they leave for the unknown country."[21]

Cited by historian Benjamin Quarles as the ablest Negro editor of his day, the uncompromising T. Thomas Fortune, of the *New York Age*, organized a mass meeting at Cooper Union to protest the Wilmington race riot and invited many prominent blacks, but not Booker T. Washington. He concluded that "the subject was altogether foreign to Professor Washington's work."[22]

As chief spokesman for black Americans, Booker T. Washington kept silent on the Wilmington controversy. For those who are familiar with his social, economic, and political philosophy, his attitude comes as no surprise. Washington's position was in keeping with his conservative and submissive doctrine of accommodation and doing nothing to agitate racial antagonism. On the other hand, one could also anticipate that his aggressive counterpart, W. E. B. Du Bois would certainly not be complacent. Being the mainspring behind two protest conventions in the North,[23] he responded to the Wilmington crisis in hopes of pricking white American democratic consciousness. Blacks in urban centers throughout the North and West staged mass meetings and rallies to protest the Wilmington atrocities. All sent strong resolutions to President McKinley, the Justice Department, or members of Congress. Too redundant to cite all, only the following are included: the colored residents of Washington, D.C.; the colored people of Asbury Park and Elizabeth, New Jersey; the colored citizens of Mount Vernon, New York; Pittsburgh, Pennsylvania; Chicago and East Saint Louis, Illinois; Cincinnati, Ohio; and Denver, Colorado.[24] Black activists of Massachusetts censured President McKinley's plea of constitutional inability to cope with the Wilmington crisis. They reminded him that where there is a will with constitutional lawyers and rulers there is always a way.

The National Anti-Mob and Lynch Law Association wrote to Marcus Alonzo Hanna, an Ohio industrialist, United States senator, and McKinley's campaign manager during the 1896 presidential contest. Aware that he possessed enormous power within the Republican party, the organization asked him to use his influence to investigate the recent outrages in the Carolinas. The association said: "The treatment of the Armenians by the Turks and the cruelties of the Spaniards is nothing [compared] to the willful murders at Wilmington, N.C.; this happened in a Christian land; our civilization is said to be the best in the world, yet the world cannot furnish an example of butchery." The association debunked the idea of the futility of federal interference, and reminded Hanna to "remember how Grover Cleveland had come to the rescue of Chicago when that great city was threatened with destruction by the strikers, and that too without the consent of the Governor of the state." The association also pointed out that the "Federal Government was paramount to any state Government, when the Constitution was violated and the lives and property of citizens were in danger of destruction."[25] Mark Hanna, like his fellow senators, was not interested in the rights of black citizens. Their major concern was Republican Prosperity.

Nevertheless, black leaders continued to call public attention to the urban racial violence that inflicted a wound on the nation's reputation. As Kelly

Miller, a black educator at Howard University, wrote, "The crime, murder, violence, and lawlessness that were daily disgracing the . . .[nation] are unsurpassed in frequency of occurrence, length of duration, and atrocity of perpetuation of like occurrence in any part of the civilized world."[26]

3

What has become of Alexander L. Manly? In his memoirs, Josephus Daniels said that Manly had "gone to New Bern but could not be found there. He seemed to have disappeared off the face of the earth."[27] He had fled to Asbury Park, New Jersey; then he went to Washington, D.C., and worked for the black Congressman, George H. White (see pp. 98–99). Perhaps while in the employ of the latter, he was able to get an interview with President McKinley. Manly reported that the president greeted him very cordially, then the meeting suddenly terminated almost as quickly as it had begun. The president had assumed that he was talking to a white man, But when he realized that Manly was a Negro—and worse, the alleged instigator of the riot—the President ordered him out of the White House.[28]

Manly was often asked about the controversial editorial, and he would tell his listeners that "there were some features about the case which he could not make public at present, as the safety of others might be affected." When asked if he intended to return to North Carolina, he replied that "that was a question he could not answer at present."[29] He did, however, give one interview to the press and said: "The whole trouble at Wilmington was caused by the minconstruction of an article in my paper. Extracts from this editorial have appeared in Northern newspapers. The part, however, that shows my innocence of any intended disrespect to or slander of the white people has been studiously ignored."[30]

Manly had already assessed his own future before the eclipse of Congressman White's political career in January of 1901. From Washington, D.C., he migrated to Philadelphia. He lived in an apartment building at Eleventh and Walnut streets, becoming the building's superintendent (actually he was the janitor). Since that position did not occupy all of his time, he secured a job as a painter.[31]

Since trade unions in the North practically proscribed black membership, Manly's son Milo was asked, "When your father came to Philadelphia, did he pass for black or white?"

He passed for white. . . . He came in and found [that] in order to get a job in the painting field—No Negro painters were getting any kind of work that amounted to anything; when he went to work for a company he didn't realize it at first, he simply went and applied for a job as a painter and they hired him thinking he was white. So he let them keep right on thinking it."[32]

Like other blacks who had to flee Wilmington, Manly had owned property. The Negro lawyer L. A. Henderson had lost his home and all his property during the riot.[33] Milo Manly was asked; "What happened to your father's property?"

"Ha!!" he answered with derisive laughter, then proceeded to relate what had happened. After the riot (the date cannot be verified) while the elder Manly was working in Washington, D.C., he was notified from Wilmington that he had not paid his taxes and that they were going to auction off his property, a practice that had been done numerous times in the past "with a whole lot of Negroes and whites."

The young lawyer and friend, Armond W. Scott, was also in the District of Columbia and "was engaged to go to Wilmington to try to present his tax receipts that his father kept to show that he had paid them and so forth." Scott had been riding in the buggy with Manly when the latter fled from Wilmington. How was it possible for the two to fool the Redshirts successfully? Milo Manly provided the following information:

"The whole Scott family was half Jewish. The original Scott was a Jew, and all of them inherited the business ability to make money. Scott went to Wilmington with receipts to show that his father had paid his property taxes. There are two versions as to what happened. When he got to the court house, there were some people in the waiting crowd who knew him. Either Scott became afraid and burned them up to keep the mob from getting him, or the mob took them away from him. At any rate, the receipts were burned, and the "property knocked down and sold." Alex Manly "tried years later to revive something about it, but town officials contended that without any written proof, there was not anything that he could do about it . . . Those at the courthouse who tried to look into the matter discovered the records had been so altered or stolen or lost that there was nothing to show that the Manlys actually owned that property. The whole thing was cleaned out from under them."

Records of property were kept in the county courthouse, and Manly was asked, "If someone should make an investigation, would a record of the Manly property be located?"

"I doubt it," he answered, "because it has been checked and checked quite a few times to see if anything could be uncovered."

After Scott returned to Washington, D.C., from Wilmington empty-handed, he and Alex Manly remained friends, but their future relations were somewhat chilled. President Franklin Roosevelt later appointed Scott as a judge in Washington, D.C. John Campbell Dancy, Jr., would on occasion chide him, saying, "Wilmington did you a favor by running you out of town; they ran you right into a judgeship."[34]

The next inquiry concerned Tom Miller; Manly was asked if he knew him.

He answered, "I didn't know him personally; I knew of him, because my uncle married his widow."

"Do you recall whether he owned real estate?"

"He sure did; he was quite a wealthy man. He left a good bit of property to his wife—his widow—and some of it came down to his daughter, who is now dead."

"Do you think the whites may have taken over some of Miller's property?"

"The story is they took most of it . . . It was simply a carrying through of the carpetbagger era because the Northerners went down and stole property from the Southerners right and left. . . . So the Southerners got back to the group below them in the same way. It's something that is going on in America today. Look at the Indians trying to fight back; fortunately they've got a piece of paper to show, but if they didn't have that piece of paper, where would they be?"

Thomas C. Miller's Caucasian appearance, wealth, and social standing seemed to place him in a class by himself. Considered in an economic sense, he was Wilmington's most successful black citizen. He had enough money to buy out half a dozen of the Democrats, including Waddell (who banished him from Wilmington), not to mention the numerous poor whites, who lined the streets and jeered him with racial slurs at the time of his banishment. Wealth was nullified by racism. Miller was characteristic of one of W. E. B. Du Bois's models—the "Talented Tenth"; but what happened to him during the riot reflected the plight of the black middle class of his era. The achievement of a high cultural level in Western society was unacceptable to the white supremist who subscribed to the Proto-Dorian doctrine—that is, the lowest white is better than the best black man. As Wilbur J. Cash explained in his classic *Mind of the South,* the plantation and wealth had degraded the poor whites in many ways. Blacks in the "big house" might sneer at them. Nevertheless, "how much their master might agree with them," he could never do this in public. "Come what might," poor whites would always be classed socially above blacks and could find solace in the Proto-Dorian doctrine of white supremacy.[35]

Where Tom Miller migrated after being banished from Wilmington remained a secret, well guarded by relatives and not known by even his close friends.[36] He was shaken with grief by the course of events and by a social system that had robbed him of both his dignity and his wealth. Shortly after the riot, he became more and more withdrawn. According to the little available information, he died soon afterward.

Manly mirrored the true dilemma of the American color line—straddling two incompatible worlds—neither black nor white. For black Americans as white as the Manlys and possessing talent, nothing should have stood in the way of advancement. It is ironic that blacks who could have passed over into the white race but who decided to cast their lot with the black race became the most determined foes of the American caste system. The late Walter White, former executive secretary of the National Association for the Advancement of Colored People, is perhaps an example of the Manly tradition.

After the race riot, according to the oral tradition, some of Wilmington's most fair-skinned Negroes just walked out of their houses and closed the doors behind them. Some relatives were to spend a lifetime searching for loved ones they would never find. Their relatives had crossed the color line into the larger society. Some of the Manlys crossed the color line, but they never lost contact with their families. Manly himself was very light complexioned and could have passed as a "voluntary Negro." As his son Milo said, "My father's family looked so much like whites, sometimes I wondered myself." When questioned about the Manlys' crossing the color line, he replied: "All of them at one time or another have done that—it was so easy to do . . . They all looked like whites, except my uncle Laurin, and he looked more Indian. . . . He took somewhat after his mother. Nothing that I've ever noticed was negroid about any of my father's family . . . Several of my uncles passed as white after the riot down there in Wilmington. It was the only way they could make a living. . . . I've personally had to pass time and again in my own work."

One of Manly's brothers made up his mind that he was not going to be a Negro. Not that he was ashamed of his race; rather he decided that he would avail himself of "every possible opportunity to attain a white man's success, and that, if it can be summed up in any one word, it means money." In the larger white world, he ultimately became captain of one of the country's largest trans-Atlantic steamships.[37]

One of the Manlys neither crossed the color line nor migrated to the North, but he did leave North Carolina for other parts of the South. His son, Lewin R. Manly, a graduate of Howard University, is presently a successful dentist in Atlanta, Georgia.[38]

All in all, "they consider themselves Negroes, but they could have easily gone over on the other side and stayed." As Milo Manly explained: "My father and his brothers used to get together, but those of us who didn't look quite white enough would stay away . . . That much is true of Negro families across the country that came up in this way."

Alex Manly eventually set up his own painting business, and soon afterward purchased a house in a "solid Irish neighborhood."

"That was easy," said his son. "My father went there to get the house—he looked Irish, and dropping into an Irish brogue [was] so easy it wasn't even funny."

Thus, his Irish neighbors thought Manly was a "part of the clan" until his wife appeared on the scene.

Carrie Manly was half Indian, a woman of striking beauty with a radiant personality. She was also gifted with a magnificent voice and was a former member of the Fisk University Jubilee Singers. There is currently a large portrait of her hanging in Jubilee Hall at the university in Nashville.

Although not as common today as it was a generation ago, the practice of blacks drawing the color line themselves indeed reflects rigid class consciousness. Light-complexioned blacks often required and sometimes demanded that members of their families marry only mulattoes. Milo Manly was asked if his mother's bronze complexion was a handicap in her courtship and marriage into his father's family. He answered, "No . . . it was just the opposite. My mother's family sort of objected to her marrying a man who looked white."

Then he proceeded to relate what happened after his father's Irish neighbors saw his mother for the first time.

"My mother came along with me . . . small, very fair even as a little tot . . . My mother was brown; they thought she was his housekeeper or something of that sort, and then they found out that my father and mother were married. They closed down on us so fast that it wasn't funny. What is known as a 'spiked fence' went up between us from the front door down to the street." The fence remained well-grounded for some time. For a while afterward, his father had to walk him to school. In time the tension eased after an unusual incident occurred.

"Well, one afternoon there at the house my mother heard from next door groans, coughing, screams, and so forth. The daughter named Ann rushed to the door screaming, 'My mama's dying! Mama's dying!' or something like that. I remember that incident too well, even though I was small at the time . . . and was going to school in the first grade. My mother just rushed right on out, right on into the house, and found Mrs. White, who was a big florid woman, gasping away for air. I was scared, just like all the other kids. My mother grabbed her and whatever she did to her, I never did know. But got her to breathing, got her straightened all out."

When the doctor finally arrived and learned what had happened, he told all of them that Mrs. Manly had "saved Mrs. Whites's life, because she had an attack of indigestion, and was choking and she had probably swallowed her tongue—or something like that . . . Well, the next morning when my father went out to work, the spiked fence was gone. From that point on we could do no wrong in that neighborhood. And when we moved to the community of Lamont, the White family . . . was one of the first to come out here and visit."

One final remark on Milo Manly's father: In the building where he established his painting business, one room was equipped as a gym for boys. One day at the gym, he ran into a bouncer who was a handyman in a whorehouse. Manly observed that he was a natural boxer and induced him to come to the gym. Soon the fellow was instructing other men in the art of self-defense. That young, powerfully built young man was Jack Johnson—the future heavyweight boxing champion of the world. It is claimed in Philadelphia that Manly gave the world one of the greatest heavyweight champions of all time.[39]

Milo Manly was asked if he had any letters or other documents that would shed additional light on his family. He produced a letter from his mother.

On 14 January 1956, Carrie Manly wrote one of her final letters to her two sons, and with deep insight and compassion, she said: "My dear boys . . . Did I finish the love story in that last letter? The thought of the newspaper made me cut it short, but I am going to try to finish it. Really, there can be no finish."

Then reflecting on the tragic event of 10 November, she continued: "I have to tell you about the Wilmington, North Carolina riot. This happened before we were married. Mr. Manly answered in an editorial a statement a lecturer made uncomplimentary to the women of his race. It got under his skin, so to speak. The *Daily Record* sent it out to the World, it turned the Southern cities from North Carolina to Alabama upside down. They said Alex Manly had defamed white womanhood and the big black burly coon must not live. Five hundred white men went hunting on horseback to lynch him, then came the riot. They burned the *Record* Office to the ground."

Wilmington's interpretation of the Manly editorial and the destruction of his press flashed across the Atlantic to England. Continuing, she said: "I have a picture of the *Record* Office in flames. I was in London at the time and I read in the London *Chronicle* that trouble was brewing, and it would only be a matter of time before they would catch the editor, as he had escaped to the swamps and the bloodhounds were on his trail. I stood on the stage that night to sing my solo and my voice quivered and stopped." A doctor was hastily summoned, and he came backstage and said that she must have had a shock. "You know boys . . . my voice has never been the same since. You see . . . all I knew about bloodhounds is what I have read in *Uncle Tom's Cabin*. This was something terrible." The manager would not let her sing for a week, but paid her the full salary. In retrospect, she wrote, "When I think of the hardships we had to go through . . . I don't see how Alex stood it."

Then she recalled the happy days she had "spent with the boys" on the paper. Milo Manly interrupted at this point. "My mother," he explained, "before she went to Europe would go down to the office and help them set type."

As she neared the end of her letter, her thoughts became more engrossed in her family's past—her husband; the children she had brought into the world, nursed and reared; and the home she had kept. The deeper her soul penetrated, the more the subject absorbed and grew larger. Carrie Manly ended her letter in a pensive mood and with no angry words. "I have a copy of that paper," she said in conclusion. "It is yellow, falling to pieces, as it is fifty-six years old. I should let the dead bury the dead. Every man connected with the paper has gone to his grave, there will be no more sorrow to arise."[40]

7
The Wilmington Race Riot in Historical Perspective

1

AMERICAN race riots can be logically divided into the following periods: Reconstruction and Post-Reconstruction, Progressive era, Red Summer, riots of Harlem (1935; 1943) and Detroit (1943), the housing riots in Cicero, Illinois (1951) and the anti-desegregation violence in Clinton, Tennessee (1950s), and the widespread ghetto insurrections of the 1960s. Even a survey comparison of the Wilmington incident with selected riots of each of these above periods, however, is too complex to be accomplished here. A brief historical survey is offered as an alternative.

Focusing first on the political riots, the Wilmington riot was an extension of that type of racial violence, so typical of the Reconstruction, post-reconstruction, and Progressive eras. One must exercise caution, however, in labeling each riot of the Reconstruction era as politically motivated, for interwoven always was the ideology of whites to maintain Caucasian supremacy. This was particularly true of the one that occurred at Memphis on 1–2 May 1866, when whites went on a rampage and tried to destroy the entire new black community. When peace was restored, two whites and forty-six blacks had been slain.[1] Since blacks had not yet received the right to vote, socioeconomic undercurrents were the major causes of the riot.

Two months later, a riot erupted at New Orleans and was clearly politically motivated. Here a mob—supported by the police—assaulted a black suffrage convention. When the smoke cleared, thirty-seven blacks and three of their white supporters had lost their lives.[2] This riot foreshadowed a reign of terror in Louisiana, beginning early in the 1870s, after the whites organized the Whites League. Their objective was apparently to overthrow the radical government by violence.[3] On 13 April 1873, a massacre occurred in upstate Louisiana at Colfax. Here a clash between black militia and armed

165

whites left two white men and an estimated seventy black men dead, half of the latter killed in cold blood after they surrendered. In late August 1874, the Whites League murdered six Republican officeholders at Coushatta, near Shreveport. Two weeks later, on 12 September, New Orleans was again the scene of a riot involving the Whites League on one side and the police and state militia on the other. Thirty persons were killed and one hundred wounded.[4]

In 1876, racial violence flared up in South Carolina, a state with a population ratio that exceeded four blacks to each white. The Black Belt was in constant turmoil, particularly in Edgefield County, where the star of "Pitchfork" Benjamin Tillman was rapidly rising. The crux of the problem who would rule: A white minority (Democrats) was trying to maintain dominance over another white minority (Republicans), who controlled a formidable Negro bloc. At the town of Hamburg, a minor Fourth of July incident between a Negro militia and two white men set the stage for a bloody racial clash. Four days later, the episode escalated into a pitched battle among two hundred whites, who imported heavier arms and munitions. Several blacks were killed in an attempt to escape, and five were slain after being captured. President U. S. Grant "personally branded the Hamburg massacre 'cruel, bloody-thirsty, wanton, and unprovoked.'"[5] Hostilities persisted intermittently through the election of 1876. The famous compromise of 2 March 1877 and President Hayes's inauguration two days later marked the end of the Reconstruction era. The next month, the new president withdrew the last of the federal troops from South Carolina, Louisiana, and Florida, and home rule in the South was completed. Blacks not only continued to vote in large numbers in most parts of the South, however, they also held public offices.[6] Thus the political riots were destined to continue until total black disfranchisement became a fait accompli in the South.

The first political riot of significance in the post-Reconstruction era occurred at Danville, Virginia in 1883. Again, the Democrats exploited the passions of the poor whites with a cry for white supremacy and white solidarity, and instigated an election-eve race on "the color-line issue" to insure the triumph of their party in the legislature.[7] And three days before the Wilmington massacre, a vicious election day riot erupted at Phoenix, South Carolina (see p. 154). Twelve blacks were captured and shot execution style. Then mobs of 'white cap' riders roamed the countryside of Greenwood County shooting and hanging an indeterminate number of Negroes.

The Wilmington race riot was representative of a watershed. As stated by Thomas R. Cripps of Morgan State University, "The Wilmington massacre effectively announced that white violence against blacks for the next quarter of a century would be organized, collective in strength and in daylight, and against concentrations of blacks in their own ghettos."[8]

Focusing now briefly on the riots of the Progressive era, that period in American history which historians mark roughly by the end of the Spanish-

American War and the nation's entrance into World War I. During the first decade of the Progressive era, riots broke out in the South at New Orleans in 1900 and in Atlanta in 1906. In the North riots occurred in New York in 1900; Springfield, Ohio, in 1904; Greenburg, Indiana, in 1906; and Springfield, Illinois, in 1908. The worst of these was at Atlanta, on the hot Saturday afternoon of 12 September, with the town full of country people for the day. Unlike the Wilmington massacres, the riot in Atlanta exploded without warning after the *Atlanta Journal* had for months carried on a "nigger-baiting" gubernatorial campaign with Hoke Smith and Tom Watson (a political boss) on one side and Clark Howell and the regular Democrats on the other. Papers began hitting the streets shortly after noon. The second and third editions were extras. Then the *Atlanta Evening News* got in on the action. It published four extras in six hours. Their theme in headlines "eight inches high" reported Negro attacks upon white women. With the white heat worked to a frenzy, a racial volcano erupted and anarchy reigned for four days.[9]

At least two riots of the Progressive period erupted at East Saint Louis, Illinois, and Houston, Texas, in 1917. The former occurred in May after blacks shot into a car and killed two white detectives whom they mistook for a gang of whites who had shot up Negro homes earlier in the evening. The riot began the next morning and involved the burning of boxcars, homes, and slayings of "unspeakable horror." When it finally ended, in addition to the deaths, there were thousands of blacks injured and an estimated six thousand homeless.[10]

In September, almost the same chemistry that produced the East Saint Louis riot generated the Houston riot. After much goading, insults, and assaults by whites, the all-black Twenty-Fourth Infantry broke into the army ammunition storage room and marched on the police station. Seventeen whites were killed in the riot that followed. The military kangaroo court was swift and exacting. Thirteen black troups were hanged for murder and mutiny; forty-one imprisoned for life, and forty held pending further investigation.[11]

The Houston and East Saint Louis riots were only the prelude to those in the period dubbed the Red Summer, during which spontaneous racial violence raced through many American cities like an angry river.

James Weldon Johnson, noted black writer, diplomat, and former secretary of the NAACP, originated the title Red Summer to describe the race riots that bloodied the streets of more than twenty towns and cities—North and South—in the six-month period from April to early October 1919.[12] The riots of the Red Summer first struck at Charleson, South Carolina, followed by those at Long View, Texas; Washington, D.C.: Omaha, Nebraska; Knoxville, Tennessee; and Chester, Pennsylvania, with the most violent ones occurring at Elaine, Arkansas, and Chicago.

Chicago seemed the top of the world for the thousands of Southern blacks who had migrated North during World War I in search of employment and freedom. It was, in fact, one of the most de facto segregated cities in the North. On the Michigan lakefront, an imaginary line divided not only the beach but the water itself into white areas and black areas. On 27 July of the Red Summer, several black youths on a homemade raft drifted past the invisible line. A lone white man began stoning them and struck one of the boys, who drowned. Blacks later attacked a white policeman who had refused to arrest the guilty party. The riot that ensued raged on through the night and the next day. Despite the efforts of the National Guard, it lasted for eleven more days. Order was restored only after fifteen whites and twenty-five blacks had been killed.[13]

The racial violence that occurred in the rural area around Elaine, Arkansas, could be classified as a pogrom. The riot was nonpolitical, but economically motivated. Sixty-eight black tenant farmers had organized the semisecret Progressive Farmers and Household Union of America to challenge their landlords accounts, and had commissioned a white law firm for legal action. If this failed, a strike was imminent. Expecting danger, the black farmers had armed themselves. Rumors had it that they were plotting a riot. A shooting incident outside a black church resulted in the death of one white man and the wounding of a deputy sheriff. News of the Hoop Spur Church clash spread quickly, and white men poured in from other parts of Arkansas and neighboring towns of Mississippi and Tennessee, all totaling an emergency posse of five hundred men. In the face of all this, the frightened black men fled into the woods and canebrakes as a reign of terror began. It was reported that they were hunted down by a white mob and slaughtered like animals, and at least five white men were killed as well. The estimated number killed ranged from thirty men to several hundred men.[14] A still more bizarre account is a statement by George Washington Davis, a black man from Pine City, Arkansas, who claimed that 103 black Masons had died and that he, as acting secretary, had paid their death benefits; in addition, he said, seventy-three blacks who were not Masons died along with "fully 250 white men."[15]

During the year that followed the Elaine massacre, scattered minor racial conflicts were reported in several parts of the country. The largest one was a political riot in Ocoee, Florida. It was precipitated when a few blacks attempted to vote. That fall, the Klan was very active in several Florida cities, intimidating black voters, and had taken part in the election riots at Ocoee.[16] Three years later, another serious race riot occurred at Rosewood, Florida. here a white mob invaded the black community in search of an alleged rapist. Six houses and churches were burned, and five blacks and two whites were slain.[17]

The Tulsa race riot of 1921 was the most serious of the post–World War I era. This event certainly had the ingredients of a race war, which propelled this conflict into a new dimension. It was the first riot "in which aircraft were employed . . . and the press and general populace used the term 'war' and other war terminology such as 'prisoners,' 'skirmish line,' 'concentration camps,' 'casualties,' 'refugees,' 'rehabilitation,' 'reconnoiter,' 'aid station,' and 'reconnaissance' in describing the riot."[18]

An inflammatory editorial in the *Tulsa Tribune* of a trivial incident provided the white heat for that riot. On 30 May, it accused Dick Rowland, a nineteen-year-old bootblack, of attacking a white woman in an elevator in the Drexel Building on South Main Street in downtown Tulsa. Rumors reached the black community of a possible lynching, and about seventy-five blacks (most armed) gathered at the jail to prevent it. A white man attempted to wrest a gun from one of the blacks; the weapon discharged and a riot ensued.[19] The first exchange of gunfire was at point-blank range. Both races quickly dispersed and sought shelter, but by midnight, fierce and bloody fighting had begun and would continue until dawn. Meanwhile, the ranks of the whites continued to swell. Their fury was evident by numerous and heinous outrages. One of the macabre acts was "tying a rope around the neck of a black corpse, securing it to the rear bumper of an automobile, and dragging the body through the business district."[20] After the reign of terror, at least ten whites and twenty-six blacks suffered violent deaths, but reliable statistics on the number of people killed or wounded do not exist. A squad of black grave diggers declared that 150 blacks died. Thirty-six bodies were found and buried without church funerals and without coffins. And according to the oral tradition, "many truckloads of black bodies were dumped into the Arkansas River, buried in mythical trenches, burned or otherwise disposed."[21]

Tulsa's black community had experienced a holocaust, and its economic losses were enormous. Between thirty and forty blocks were reduced to rubble by the torch. Fire, looting, and vandalism had demolished the black business section, while 314 homes had been looted, but not burned. Now fewer than 1,115 homes had been destroyed; consequently, 4,291 blacks were homeless.

There is a footnote of irony here. Sarah Page, who accused Dick Rowland of attacking her, had been in Tulsa for only a short while and a sheriff described her as a "notorious character." Rowland was set free soon after the riot, and in September of that year, all charges against him were dropped.[22]

The interim between the Tulsa event and World War II marked a transitional era from the old-style to the new-style riot. The latter embodied a new spirit of resistance and even retaliation among blacks. The new-style riot, concluded August Meier and Elliot M. Rudwick, "first appeared in Harlem in 1835 and Detroit in 1943, where Negro attacks were mainly directed against white property rather than white people. The Detroit race riot of 1943, one of the more serious racial conflicts in American history, brought death to nine whites and twenty-five Negroes and had affinities with both the older and the more recent variety of race warfare."[23] Finally, it should be mentioned that both the Harlem and the Detroit riots presaged the turbulence of the 1960s—the protest riots.

These urban disorders of the sixties "would appear to be the result of release of frustrations and rebellion against the past—a protest against centuries of being the outsider in America."[24] They had no American precedent, and they profoundly shocked both white and black citizens. Beginning in 1964, urban riots swept the Chicago suburb of Dixmoor, Harlem, Bedford-Stuyvesant section of Brooklyn, Rochester, Philadelphia, and the New Jersey cities of Jersey City, Elizabeth and Paterson. The next year a formidable riot occurred in Watts, the black ghetto of Los Angeles. The following summer witnessed similar chaos in New York, Cleveland's Hough section, and in Chicago.[25] In 1967, there was still more violence in Tampa, Cincinnati, and Atlanta, with the most serious riots in Detroit and Newark. Property damage in Newark was estimated at $10,251,000. The death toll came to twenty-three, including a white detective, a white fireman, and twenty-one blacks. Of the blacks, six were either women or children. Detroit's bloody statistics—40 deaths, 2,250 injuries, and $250 million in property losses. Then in April 1968, Dr. Martin Luther King, Jr., was assassinated. This tragedy triggered a new wave of black anger. In more than a hundred cities, they "swiftly unleashed their anger in a paroxysm of burnings and looting."[26]

Urban violence subsided after the riots triggered by the King assassination, yet many of the underlying causes remained at the end of the 1970s. The Miami riot of May 1980 shocked countless Americans, black and white. What the riot demonstrated, among other things, was that the decade of the 1970s had simply smothered racial flames while the ashes still smoldered, and there was much speculation on a renewal of the ghetto insurrections of the 1960s. But what triggered this three-day Miami explosion was a verdict of not guilty from an all-white, six-man jury in the trial of several Dade County policemen.[27] No review is necessary here. Their acquittal in this case reflected a failure of our American criminal justice system.

" 'History never repeats itself,' said Voltaire, 'man always does.' Thucydides, of course, made that principle the justification for his work."[28] The tendency of the American phenomena called race riots to strike more than once in the same cities certainly gives validity to Thucydides' premise.

2

The social and demographic questions involving race riots have been given special attention by scholars in the past two or three decades. To show both differences and similarities, and to further establish the uniqueness of the Wilmington riot, an analogy of this city's social patterns will be briefly compared with Chicago and East Saint Louis during their riots.

Unlike those of Chicago and East Saint Louis, the black community of

Wilmington was not threatened by the hostility of surrounding white ethnic groups. There was nothing in its history that would ever suggest the ideal type or type case of "riot involving direct 'ecological warfare' between the residents of white and black neighborhoods."[29] In East Saint Louis and Chicago, the violence erupted in the downtown business sections, where the whites inevitably outnumbered the blacks—this was in contrast to Wilmington, where the total black population outnumbered the white population. It is important to emphasize here that during the weeks immediately preceding the coup, at which time racist rhetoric increased, armed Redshirts stalked the streets, and the state Democratic party made it clear that they were whipping up a White Supremacy campaign which did not preclude violence.

In those days, bold invasion of whites into the black community was a common riot pattern in the South. The violence did not occur in Wilmington's downtown business section, but in the heart of the black community, where the whites ignited the violence by burning a Negro press. This raises a fundamental question, Why did not the blacks, like those in Tulsa and Chicago, take measures to fight off their attackers?

The day began with blacks not expecting trouble, since the greater majority had not voted in the election, in which the Democrats were overwhelmingly victorious. Early that morning, most blacks had gone quietly to their jobs—unarmed. They were not aware that some dreadful event awaited them. In contrast, that very morning the heavily armed whites had assembled at the local armory. Merchants had absolutely refused to sell blacks weapons of any description or any gunpowder. Their only arms were a few old rifles, pistols, and, according to the oral tradition, axes. Crowds of spectators and bystanders provided the backdrop and the plaudits for the mobs—splinter groups of white men (some inebriated), half-grown boys, and Redshirts. To this was added the military, heavily armed with rifles, cannons, and a Gatling gun—acting out a psychological war game and riot prone.

As in slavery times, the odds were heavily against the blacks, and when the fury of the mobs bore down on them, it was a one-sided affair. No effective resistance had been made by any blacks. The mobs flocked spontaneously into the black community, with their appetites whetted by the initial encounter, where one white was wounded and a few blacks killed. Far down the streets and along the intersecting thoroughfares, fleeing blacks heard distant voices and the ominous refrains, "Kill the niggers! Kill the damned niggers!"

The whites were crying for vengeance. The initial confrontation and the wounding of William Mayo roused the whites to a frenzy. Soon afterward, they were running through the streets yelling, "A nigger killed a white man!" Notwithstanding the extenuating circumstances underlying the provocation and the fact that a number of black men lay dead in the streets, the slaying of a white by a black man was an unforgivable sin. The concept had been bred in the white consciousness long before there was an entity called the South. Spontaneously, a white mob, presenting a formidable appearance, congregated in the black community of Brooklyn. The black defense, if there was any, quickly melted away.

The Wilmington race riot—unlike other racial disturbances—did not explode during a period of war or international unrest. "Indeed, war throughout American history has provided a setting conducive to racial violence," as Professor William M. Tuttle, Jr., explained in *Race Riot: Chicago in the Red Summer of 1919.* "Draft and labor riots between the races broke out frequently during the Civil War." The Red Summer was in 1919, the first year of peace after one of the most disruptive wars in history. "Race riots engulfed Detroit and Harlem in 1943, during World War II. And most of the riots," he concluded, "were contemporaneous with the military violence in Vietnam."[30]

Considering all the above, it is interesting to note that the Wilmington event did follow close in the heels of the "Splendid Little War—the Spanish-American War. There is no evidence that the war had any great impact in North Carolina; however, there were Spanish-American War veterans in Wilmington, and they, as Redshirts, contributed to the violence.

Another salient fact must be included here. The large majority of riots, Tuttle noted, "erupted in the summer when the weather was hot and uncomfortable, and when many people were restless and susceptible to the commission of acts of violence."[31] This does not apply to Wilmington during the month of November 1898.

In considering the seriousness of the Wilmington race riot—other than its death toll—one must take into account such other factors as size of population, ratio of the black population to the total population, and duration of the event. Wilmington's total population in 1890 was 11,324 blacks and 8,731 whites—in contrast to Atlanta with its population of about 80,000 whites and 50,000 blacks; East Saint Louis with a total population of about 70,000; and Chicago with a black population of about 110,000 in 1920.[32] Atlanta's riot erupted on 22 September 1906, and the first and bloodiest night of rioting was brought to an end when the rain began to fall mercifully at three o'clock in the morning, clearing the streets of the last violent men. The riot continued for two more days; the results were one white man and twenty-five black men perished.[33] Between 28 May and 30 May, and again on 17 June 1907, East Saint Louis experienced embryonic racial confrontations. The full fury of the riot exploded on 2 July and left in its wake nine whites and about thirty-five blacks dead.[34] On 27 July 1919, the Chicago riot exploded, and thirteen days of violence ensued in the oppressiveness of the ninety-five degree heat. Thirty-eight people were killed, including fifteen whites and twenty-five blacks.[35]

In contrast to the riots of Atlanta, East Saint Louis, and Chicago, the tragic events at Wilmington were crowded into the brief space of approximately six hours. During this time the mob had invaded the black community of Brooklyn, demolished the *Record*'s newspaper office and set it on fire, shot up the black community, and killed and wounded a large number of blacks. Concomitantly, a political coup unfolded, and its leader was elected mayor. All in all, it is concluded that the Wilmington massacre was the most intense in the nation's history.

The Wilmington episode of 1898 was a pogrom which repeated a pattern of racial violence "that harked back to the Memphis and New Orleans riots of 1866."[36] For the latter two events, as well as for those that transpired in Atlanta (1906), East Saint Louis (1917), Chicago (1919) and other urban localities, there were official estimates of the death count. But in Wilmington there was no official list, suggesting a minimum of fatalities. Newspaper accounts and both primary and secondary sources, indeed, are not in agreement on the magnitude of Wilmington's death toll. The wide discrepancies in reporting the fatalities lead to the conclusion that evidence was suppressed. The total casualties will never be known, and the truth lies somewhere between the figures published in the newspapers and the unpublished figures in the manuscripts. More significant, in light of the magnitude of the total crime, the actual death toll is most important; for in a democratic society to weigh the event in purely quantitative terms diminishes the humanity of each individual. The fact that a situation came to exist in which even a single life, white or black, could be lost under such conditions was a tragedy.

With the ending of the Civil War, as this chapter demonstrates, race riots relentlessly persisted; they spanned the Reconstruction, Post-Reconstruction and Progressive eras, as well as that period designated as the Red Summer, when blood was spilled in more than twenty Northern and Southern cities. In the classic, *An American Dilemma* (1944), Gunnar Myrdal discussed race riots. And observing their significant decline, he wrote: "Their devastation and relative fewness make them landmarks in history."[37] Nevertheless, history has not sustained Myrdal's thesis, as reflected by ghetto insurrections of the 1960s, the violence identified with the Wilmington 10 during the 1970s, and renewal of such turbulence in Miami in 1980 and 1982. Accordingly, the persistence and implications of phenomena known as race riots remain profound problems for American democracy.

Epilogue

1

IN time, of course, the city of Wilmington returned to 'normalcy,' a normalcy paid for by a series of rationalizations and falsifications whose intent was to deny the town's guilt. But still there remained that infamous Thursday, 10 November 1898; the nagging ethical question still demands an answer, Before the bar of historical justice, who might Clio, the muse of history, hold accountable for the Wilmington catastrophe?

Immediately after the violence, whites unburdened their guilt by blaming blacks for creating an explosive climate in Wilmington; from them came one-sided accounts. Ministers and journalists were first to speak out and to find grounds to relieve their consciences and advance moral explanations for the riot. With the purpose of reaching a national audience, the Reverend Alexander J. McKelway, a leading churchman, humanitarian, and the editor of the *North Carolina Presbyterian,* published an editorial in *Outlook* under the title, "North Carolina Revolution Justified." Defending the actions of whites in the events leading to the coup, he rationalized that law and order had broken down under the Fusionists. In consequence, the very foundation of Wilmington's government was terrorized by a criminal element of blacks, lawlessness reigned supreme, and the white citizens were forced to arm themselves for protection of their lives and property.[1]

Another outstanding clergyman, Josiah W. Bailey, editor of the *Biblical Recorder,* the official organ of the North Carolina Baptists, concluded that revolutions were never lawful, "but often right." He believed that the "people of Wilmington were moved in their actions by the same spirit that led their forefathers to battle for their freedom on these shores." As for the calamity that befell the blacks, he said that they could "lay the bodies of their dead to the charge of their representative Manly and to his vicious publication."[2] Reaching a still wider audience, *Harper's Weekly* defended the Democrats of Wilmington and charged that the Republican party had turned Wilmington over to the control of alien races—blacks and carpetbaggers. Echoing, in effect, the themes of both the Reverend Mr. McKelway and the Reverend Mr. Bailey, *Harper's Weekly* told its readers that there

174

was chaos and inefficient government in a "city once so peaceful." The new government, however, soon found itself incapable of maintaining law and order and providing an efficient government.[3]

Josephus Daniels, owner and editor of the *Raleigh News and Observer* (and later Woodrow Wilson's secretary of the Navy), years later, with no apology, and expressing the majority sentiment, still saw no need to condemn the conduct of the Wilmington citizens. Both for posterity and for his own generation, he recorded in his memoirs in 1941 that the riot "was an armed revolution of white men of Wilmington to teach what they believed was a needed lesson."[4] "Who could help the inevitable?" asked the *Raleigh News and Observer*. It made no atonement for the bloodshed, when it concluded: "Surely a few things in the history . . . were more painful, yet it had to come. Death only could settle the score and bring peace, which had become a necessity."[5] No doubt many Southerners of the era would have agreed with Fred L. Merritt, who wrote in the *News and Observer*: "Here is the cause of bloodshed in Wilmington. It was the editorial slandering of white women, published by the Negro Alex Manly in his paper—the *Daily Record*."[6] Northern publications joined hands with the *News and Observer*.

Correspondent Henry L. West wrote in the *Forum*: "A Negro editor published an editorial, defaming the virture of poor white women in the South. This fanned the flame of Anglo-Saxon resentment to white heat."[7] Reporting the Wilmington race riot in New York, the *Literary Digest* said, "The chief cause alleged was an editorial printed in a paper edited by a mulatto named Alex L. Manly."[8] Nevertheless, succinctly stated—the Manly editorial was not the cause for the Wilmington massacre.

Charles W. Chesnutt, in his novel, *The Marrow of Tradition*, was right on target when he said: "Its [the Manly editorial] great offensiveness lay in its boldness: that a Negro should publish in a newspaper that white people would scarcely acknowledge to themselves in secret . . . The article was a social *lèse majesté* in the most aggravated form." But the truth of the issue was that "a peg was needed to hang a *coup d'etat*, and this editorial offered the requisite opportunity. It was unanimously decided to republish the obnoxious article, with comments adopted to fire the inflammable Southern heart and arouse it against any further self assertions of the Negro in politics or elsewhere."[9]

Considering in retrospect the volatile racial climate in Wilmington and the rest of North Carolina in 1898, the Manly editorial was untimely, but the argument that he should never have written it can be ruled out for a variety of reasons. He was certainly acting in his own right and exercising a fundamental tenet of the United States Constitution—freedom of the press. Manly was a humanist, endowed with a strong sense of black awareness; nevertheless, this article touched white Southerners in their most sensitive consciousness. Perhaps a similar article in a Northern newspaper would have created no controversy other than angry comments among some white readers, but coming from a black man in the South, it could not fail to create a sensation. Had Manly been white, the same rules of political, social, and moral conduct, would not, in the very nature of things, have been applied.

Some Southerners maintained that the blacks were given ample time to avoid the calamity that befell them. They pointed out that Waddell gave the blacks twelve hours in which to answer the ultimatum of the committee of twenty-five. They charged Armond W. Scott with a dereliction of duty, and the reason for his actions will forever remain an enigma.

In the aftermath of the chaos that engulfed Wilmington, blacks were portrayed as the culprits responsible for the volatile conditions that led to the riot. Not one white man was willing to stand up and publicly defend the blacks. Nor did any of them write in defense of blacks in their private letters except Benjamin Keith's correspondence to Senator Marion Butler.

From the white ranks came one other lonely voice, that of Jane Murphy Cronly (see pp. 128, 203). Defending the blacks, she wrote: "For the first time in my life, I have been ashamed of my state and of the Democratic party in North Carolina, and I hope I utter the sentiments of many other women when I lift up my voice in solemn protest against the proceedings in Wilmington, North Carolina on last Thursday, November 10th. It will ever be a day to be remembered in my heart with indignation and sorrow." She strongly condemned the riot as being unnecessary, for the election had been carried in favor of the Democratic party, and the blacks "had quietly accepted the fact." In defense of the blacks, she maintained that the charges against them were "utterly and entirely false." Continuing this defense, she noted that property had "never been in danger from blacks here, who have been as good a set of people as could be found anywhere." It was ironic that the very people who had "been villifying and abusing them had entrusted to them the care of their little children. . . . In spite of all the goading and persecuting that has been vented upon them for months, they have gone quietly on and have been almost obsequiously polite as if to ward off the persecution they seemed involuntarily to have felt to be in the air." Cronly hoped in vain that a stronger voice than hers would be lifted up in defense of a much-injured race, but such was not the case.[10]

John Spencer Bassett, teacher, historian, and author, privately condemned the riot as "justifiable at no point" and without historical or constitutional justification. "The whole thing," he told his friend Herbert Baxter Adams, "was not necessary because in two months the Democratic Legislature will meet and can and will change affairs in Wilmington."[11] Bassett had detached himself from the political climate and was opposing the prevailing sentiments in North Carolina. To speak out publicly would have infuriated the white majority and brought its entire wrath upon him.

Political opportunism, inextricably interwoven with economic grievances and racism, was clearly one of the causes of the riot. Certain prominent whites, including former congressman Waddell, stood to gain the power and prestige that went with top-level public offices. In a detailed letter that a black woman had written to President McKinley, John D. Bellamy was singled out as one of the white men active in the riot. Bellamy wanted to be elected to Congress. It is also significant that Waddell—leader of the mob and mayor elected after the coup—and Edgar G. Parmele—chief of police—were both unemployed at the time of the riot.[12] Other unemployed whites were William Rand Kenan, who before being replaced by John Campbell Dancy, was collector of customs at the Port of Wilmington. His assistants were Parmele, deputy collector and chief inspector, and V. S. Worth, special collector.

It is conjectured that Waddell was a political opportunist. His memoirs are rather vague on his activities after he lost his congressional seat to Daniel L. Russell in 1889. He appeared suddenly in Wilmington while the Secret Nine was planning the coup. Even with his connection with the riot well known, some correspondents and others have tried to whitewash him. Charles Francis Bourke of *Collier's Weekly* wrote that Waddell was a "mild-mannered gentleman, extremely conservative and the last man one . . . would expect to find mixed up in a bloody revolution."[13]

In writing to his friend, Thomas Nelson Page of *In Ole Virginia* fame and undisputed champion among the glorifiers of the Old South and the plantation legend, Waddell expressed no remorse and rationalized that the riot was the only course for settling the race problem. "The good old Anglo-Saxon way of waiting until government becomes intolerable, and then openly and manfully overthrowing it is for the best."[14]

On 26 November 1898, *Collier's Weekly* ran a front-page editorial on the Wilmington event. It was headed, "The North Carolina Race War, by Alfred M. Waddell." In this article, Waddell defended his involvement in the riot. According to his interpretation, the people came to him when the crisis arose, and there was a universal demand that he should take charge. They made him chairman of the citizen's committee of twenty-five. He admitted that the change of government "was certainly the strangest performance in American history." Yet he mentioned that there was no flaw in the legality of the government. It was the "result of revolution, but the forms of law were strictly complied with in every respect and there was not a single illegal act committed in the change of government."[15] While recognizing that the event was "legally and technically" a radical revolution, he saw it as a "spontaneous and unanimous act of all the white people and was prompted solely by an overwhelming sense of its absolute necessity in behalf of civilization and decency."

In reality, the editorial in *Collier's Weekly* was not written by Waddell. About a week after it appeared, he said: "The article resulted from a conversation which Bourke of that paper took down as I talked to him. I think I would have written better than that." Writing privately to Edward A. Oldham, Waddell admitted receiving a "bushel of abusive and infamous letters, and printed material." (These materials must have been destroyed, for they are not among his papers.) In defense he said: "I certainly shall not answer the newspaper lies about our revolution. I thought that I might sometime give the facts to the *Post* or some magazine."[16]

Meanwhile, the next General Assembly had set in motion the machinery for the vindication of Waddell's illegal administration. The legislature amended the city charter, making provisions for a primary election to be held on 10 March 1899, to nominate candidates for mayor and chief of police. Alderman Edgar G. Parmele was elected chief of police, while Waddell was elected mayor by a large majority over John J. Fowler and Frank H. Stedman.[17] The revolutionary government was now a legal body.

Waddell ran for reelection as mayor in 1903. Questions now arose about his honesty and integrity, and aspersions (perhaps politically motivated) were then cast on his character. Ironically, he had to face in his election individuals who had aided him in the coup—former mayors John Fowler and S. H. Fishblate, as well as Edward Johnson and William Springer.[18] Waddell continued as mayor of Wilmington until his defeat in 1903; then his political career ended.

Some time after the riot, Waddell began to assess his future, of which he seemed rather pessimistic. To his friend Oldham he wrote: "I am, you know, no politician, and know nothing about wirepulling. To be a Senator would be very gratifying, of course, and if the people want [me] in that capacity, I would accept it." He believed that he could "beat any man in the State and certainly so if the incoming Legislature had to choose; that two years is a long time for laying pipe and fixing things." In the back of his mind perhaps Waddell knew that he could not beat Furnifold Simmons, the czar of the state Democratic party who was destined to serve six terms in the United States Senate.

Waddell still hoped to be elected to Congress, and his friends organized on his behalf. George A. Latham, editor of the *Newbernian,* tried to promote him for Congress, but he never regained his seat in the face of cliques and cabals, conspiracies and intrigues. His friends also tried to promote him for the Senate, claiming that the state legislature has utterly ignored this [eastern] section of the State in distributing its highest honors. R. B. Henderson wrote about Waddell's claim upon the Democratic party and gave reasons that he should be rewarded. Later there appeared a campaign announcement: "Hon. Alfred M. Waddell considered for United States Senate to succeed Marion Butler."[19] But the Waddell bandwagon soon came to a halt. The credentials of the leader of the mob, and of the coup making him mayor of Wilmington, were not enough for a seat in the halls of Congress.

Were there other prominent whites, in addition to Waddell, Bellamy, and Parmele, who stood to gain from the riot? One cannot say with certitude who they were or what their actual social and economic status was; but one might speculate that there were people whose families had been aristocrats during slavery times. Some of these people found themselves in competition with the black bourgeoisie, notably the enterprising businessmen and successful attorneys. For there was grumbling among the white professional classes, that black lawyers, especially such skilled ones as Armond Scott and L. A. Henderson, had too much business, while black entrepreneurs, located conspicuously downtown, deprived white businessmen of legitimate sources of income to which they thought they were entitled. With families to support and social status to maintain, they saw many blacks living better than they were.

Foremost in Negro-baiting, election fraud, and violence, the racism of poor whites was far more virulent than the wealthier, more conservative white supremacists. In light of limited economic opportunities in Wilmington, it is surmised that some had been professional politicians with no other means of livelihood other than public offices. Like many of their kind throughout North Carolina's Black Belt, they found themselves unemployed after the municipal elections of 1897. Finally, it has been clearly demonstrated that an environment of racism and poverty abetted the intensity of the violence. All in all, these socioeconomic factors help to explain why the coup took the shape it did and why it succeeded.

Everyone had an ax to grind; accordingly, the little Democratic coterie and the leading businessmen fashioned a well-defined conspiracy. They fixed the date of 10 November 1898, and set the hour and the course their revolution would pursue. The result to be achieved—the city government was to be wrested from the Republicans and their black allies. Their plan was also to arouse white sentiment in order to effect the coup and assure the ascendancy of the Democrats.

Political and economic opportunities were merely the tips of the iceberg; the larger issue was black disfranchisement. At the opening of the next General Assembly, the clarion call came from Wilmington.

The cabal of local Democrats and the leaders of the state Democratic party envisioned the complete elimination of blacks from future participation in North Carolina politics. They were resolved to checkmate both the Negro voters in the Black Belt and the white Republicans who controlled them. The conspirators had adroitly planted George Rountree in the General Assembly expressly for that purpose. "The chief reason for my accepting the nomination in '98 to the legislature," Rountree wrote much later in a personal memorandum, "was to see if I could do something to prevent a recurrence of the 1896 political upheaval by affecting a change in the suffrage law."[20] When the next General Assembly convened, the Speaker of the House appointed, by previous agreement, a special joint committee of prominent lawyers of both houses, under the chairmanship of Rountree. "I as chairman," he later confessed, "did all the work."[21]

Since Negro suffrage was assured by the United States Constitution, ways had to be found to circumvent it. In 1890, Mississippi, with an "understanding clause," contrived the principal technique for voiding the Constitution on a racial basis. Modifications of the scheme were incorporated in the constitution of South Carolina in 1895 and Louisiana in 1898. The infamous grandfather clause, invented in Louisiana, was the device finally agreed upon for disfranchising blacks in North Carolina. It permitted illiterate and propertyless white men to vote if their fathers and grandfathers had voted prior to 1867—the year blacks were enfranchised.

The suffrage amendment was the major issue in the gubernatorial election of 1900. Once again, the Democratic leaders pulled out all the stock themes of "Negro domination" and built a statewide white supremacy campaign around it. They again appealed to the passions of the poor whites to do the dirty work of politics for the sake of party unity, white solidarity, and white supremacy. Wilmington was rather quiet during the campaign, but demonstrated its overwhelming enthusiasm for black disfranchisement by casting only two votes against the suffrage amendment.[22]

After North Carolina adopted its grandfather clause, other states followed suit: Alabama in 1901, Virginia in 1902, Georgia in 1908, and Oklahoma in 1910.

In the search for manifestations of Southern Progressivism, some historians have turned to black disfranchisement, which is an absurdity. Historians who advocated black disfranchisement included Joseph G. de R. Hamilton of North Carolina, the noted Francis Butler Simpkins, and William A. Dunning of Columbia University. Dunning viewed enfranchisement of blacks as blind "species of statecraft."[23] In 1900, the gubernatorial candidate Charles B. Aycock, referring to the Wilmington riot, expounded that disfranchisement would avoid future bloodshed. Leading Democrats argued that it would save Southern politics from chaos and corruption by eliminating the illiterate and unqualified voters. As many scholars know, the underlying purpose was "to consolidate one-party rule by disfranchising the opposition."[24]

There were masses of poor and ignorant blacks in the South; on the other hand, the enactment of a grandfather or an understanding clause was a tacit admission by white Southerners that there were also masses of white men in the South in the same class. The grandfather clauses were flagrant violations of the Fifteenth Amendment and were declared unconstitutional by the Supreme Court—but not until 1915. Historians are belated in recognizing this decision as representative of the so-called Progressive Era.[25]

The Wilmington event of 1898 reflected the waves of violence and racial repression then sweeping the nation. Its massacres and coup characterize the period. Historians are in agreement that the Progressive era was the nadir of American race relations.[26] Mob violence, the stalking-horse of anarchy, attained dramatic proportions, as more than one hundred people were lynched in 1900, and the number escalated to more than eleven hundred before the end of the Progressive era.[27] In 1896, the nation's highest tribunal legalized the separation of races in the sweeping decision, *Plessy* v. *Ferguson*. Three years later, North Carolina adopted its first segregation ordinance. During that decade, jim crow laws expressing race and class became fixtures in the South, and the walls of segregation were raised higher and higher. The city of Wilmington followed the pattern, as a maze of signs reading Whites Only and For Colored appeared in almost every place that the two races might conceivably meet.

2

During the year of the Wilmington race riot, Anglo-Saxon rule, social Darwinism, and imperialism were indicative of the national mentality. Under the leadership of the Republican party, the nation had plunged into imperialistic adventures overseas and rushed with giant strides toward colossal wealth. Abstract ethical theories had to be discarded in the face of such exigencies.

Our nation acquired a varied assortment of people of color and, after the Spanish-American War, problems of color became complex. The process of writing Anglo-Saxon laws for colonial people and Southern blacks went forward simultaneously. Scholars like John W. Burgess and William A. Dunning of Columbia University brought academic authority to the support of Southern racial policy.[28] Thus the rights of the white supremacists to define and assign the Negro his place could not be denied Southerners who sought the suppression of blacks.

Statistics on crime were manipulated to portray blacks' degeneration in both morals and progress. Senator Benjamin R. Tillman made speeches to Chautauqua audiences in all parts of the county, popularizing his racial views. The Negroes were "akin to the monkey," an "ignorant and debased and debauched race." Southern writers were using their pens skillfully to popularize Southern racist ideology. There appeared such works as Charles Carroll's "The Negro a Beast; or, In the Image of God" (1900); William P. Calhoun's *The Caucasian and the Negro in the United States* (1902); William B. Smith's *The Color Line: A Brief in Behalf of the Unborn* (1905); and Robert W. Shufeldt's *The Negro: A Menace to American Civilization* (1907). Thomas Dixon wrote his trilogy of historic novels on the race conflict: *The Leopard's Spots: A Romance of the White Man's Burden, 1865–1900* (1902); *The Clansman: An Historical Romance of the Ku Klux Klan* (1905); and *The Traitor: A Story of the Fall of the Invisible Empire* (1907).[29] To these must be added Dixon's screenplay, *The Birth of a Nation,* which became a controversial D. W. Griffith movie.

The waves of racism crested during the early years of President Woodrow Wilson's first administration. "Accustomed by imperial design and judicial decision to thoughts of racial superiority, white America linked Progressive democracy and equality to greater separation from the Negro."[30] Nearly two

THE "JIM CROW" CAR.

Compliments of the Railroad Commission.

The North Carolinian, January 1899 (file, University of North Carolina).

dozen anti-black bills "were introduced in the House and Senate, running the gamut from Jim Crow transportation, regulation of armed force enlistment to prohibition of miscegenation, civil, and repeal of the Fifteenth Amendment. Their sponsors were all Southerners."[31] The Wilson Administration paid considerable attention to the senatorial clout of James K. Vardaman (Mississippi), Benjamin R. Tillman (South Carolina), and Hope Smith (Georgia). In Wilson's Cabinet were Secretary of the Navy Josephus Daniels (North Carolina) and two Southerners Postmaster General A. G. Burleson and Secretary of the Treasury William Gibbs McAdoo. These men pushed for Departmental segregation in civil services. "While segregation orders were conceived and issued by subordinates, it was clear that Wilson made little or no effort to stop them." By the summer of 1913, for the first time, photographs were required on all civil service applications. After a visit to the nation's capital, a despondent Booker T. Washington, said: 'I have never seen the colored people so discouraged and bitter as they are at the present time.' "[32]

Given the whole web of circumstances—historical, sociological, and psychological—surrounding the pervasive racism of the Progressive era, it is not surprising that the racial massacre and coup of 10 November 1898 could have been committed with impunity.

The Democrats put out the charges of Negro rule and Negro domination, which were utterly false and no one knew it better than they. True, there was a black majority in Wilmington; mere numbers, however, do not always confer political power—one need only refer to the black majority in South Africa. It was also true that the 1897 amended city charter violated home rule in Wilmington, but the constitution and the American way mandate governmental transformation by ballot. It took a constitutional amendment to enfranchise blacks, and nothing short of a constitutional revision could have disfranchised them legally, yet Wilmington took a revolutionary step, which resulted in the race riot and the coup d'état. Hypocrisy prevailed, for the Democratic leaders could not alter their time honored script, and the white citizens of Wilmington discarded their veneer of civilization and collectively acted out the ritual drama. The evidence presented in this study clearly demonstrates that the Wilmington race riot did not erupt spontaneously, accidentally, or in a vacuum. This study has exposed the "conscious distortion of history . . . how a society can wilfully turn its back on the truth, choosing instead to wear the emperor's clothes. The fabric of the social order can become a lie, a self imposed delusion that flies apart at the slightest challenge."[33]

The riot had an irreversible political, economic, and social impact upon the city's blacks. Immediately after the massacres, white businesses moved in and filled the economic gaps left by the flight of the blacks. When the turbulence receded, the integrated neighborhoods had disappeared. Wilmington remained, however, one of the most integrated cities in the South; notwithstanding, the race riot left an ineffable blot on the city's reputation and the bitter memories of blacks of the violence perpetrated upon them by whites. For many years, whites and blacks would regard each other with fear and suspicion, which remain, latent, today.

In the North Carolina Black Belt, the legacy of the white supremacy campaigns of 1898 and 1900, the black disfranchisement movement, and the Wilmington race riot are still very much evident. The city provided the sociopolitical backdrop for the controversy known as the Wilmington 10, which emerged out of the turmoil of the 1970s to become a cause célèbre, an international scandal, and a source of embarrassment to the Carter administration.

Describing the conservative mood of this section of North Carolina, Jack Bass and Walter De Vries have written, "In the rural east, where the black population is most heavily concentrated, black registration remained below that of the rest of the state. Not only was the region bypassed by the civil rights movement, but it was also a hotbed of Ku Klux Klan activity in the 1960s, and the Klan in North Carolina was larger and more virulent than any state outside Alabama and Mississipi during that period."[34] From this section between 1892 and 1898, North Carolina elected four blacks to Congress, but not a single one has been elected in the entire twentieth century. Likewise, since the riot the city has never had another black representative on its Board of Aldermen.

Leadership had truly failed. Governor Daniel M. Russell was bound by every consideration of the sanctity of his gubernatorial oath to protect the ballot from violence. He had the power to appeal to the federal government for aid to suppress the unlawful white army and for such force as might have been necessary to preserve law and order; it would have been the duty of President McKinley to answer his call. This might have resulted in political suicide or even assassination for Governor Russell. Yet as chief executive of North Carolina he should have been willing to risk "the hazard of both his fortune and his life in fulfilling the duties which public office puts upon him."[35] On the other hand, after considering the volatile racial climate in the state, one cannot help but gain insight into Governor Russell's predicament—his pessimism and, in the face of the Wilmington crisis, his feeling that he was helpless to do anything about the crisis.

President McKinley also chose to ignore the Wilmington massacres and coup. He knew well that federal intervention would have exacerbated Southern race relations. Taking a benign view of the entire affair, he dropped it as though it never happened. With a presidential administration whose apparent record of blacks was outstanding, having doubled Southern black patronage, one could hardly conclude that McKinley was unconcerned about racial violence and the worsening of the conditions of blacks at the polls. Like other presidents—Rutherford B. Hayes, Benjamin Harrison, Theodore Roosevelt and to a lesser degree, Grover Cleveland—"McKinley manifested the usual timidity on things racial when political contingencies were involved."[36] Indeed, during this era, each of those previously mentioned "admitted that the Negro question, or the Southern question as they called it interchangeably, was one of their greatest difficulties." Thus none of them "were willing to exploit the full potentialities of the presidential office in the interest of racial statesmanship."[37]

In keeping with the white Southern outlook at the dawn of the twentieth century, there were only a few white men who professed that a class of black citizens, constituting a third of North Carolina's population and a majority of Wilmington's, was entitled to some representation in the lawmaking bodies. Perhaps there might have been found, somewhere in the state, white men ready to concede that all men were entitled to equal rights and justice before the law; on the other hand, there were timorous men who shuddered and shrank from civic strife. But where were the courageous white men during the race riot? Both Northern and Southern sentiments became more favorable to publications circulated by the conspirators and their sympathizers.

Only a few white Americans throughout the nation possessed both the courage and the detachment from their own culture to protest. One such racial liberal was the writer Albion W. Tourgée, who had gone to North Carolina "on what he called 'a fool's errant' some twenty years ago to wrestle with the race problem." He had once nurtured the hope that Christianity, coupled with the inherent American sense of liberty and justice, "would be sufficient to solve the race problem short of blood and violence that had marked the travail of liberty in Western Europe." In his opinion, the blatant display of race antagonism was the most dangerous and horrible feature of American life, which now required "divine intervention, since the race problem was beyond remedy by any human means." Tourgée was saddened over the rising tide of Negrophobia, which reflected how far the Americans had drifted from the ideals of the American creed. He saw a correlation "between the race question and the ultimate destiny of American liberty." From his sickbed in Bordeaux, France, he wrote to President McKinley: "I cannot doubt," he said, "that the American republic may pay the price of its own injustice by finding in the race problem the end of its liberties and the destruction of its original character."[38]

On November 19, 1898, an editorial in *The Outlook* correctly stated a proposition: "Revolution is sometimes justified." Nevertheless, it could not justify the Wilmington revolution, which was characterized as "criminal, because it was needless."[39] With all the naked ruthlessness that accompanied this epochal event, Southern presses and pulpits were silent. A few Northern correspondents did regard the Wilmington affair with condemnation. Yet nowhere was there an Émile Zola to write *J'accuse*.

Notes

Preface

1. Arthur S. Link, et al., *The American People: A History* (Arlington Heights, Ill., 1981), 590.
2. *New York Herald,* 11 November 1898.
3. Published by Fairleigh Dickinson University Press, Rutherford, N. J. 1979.
4. William M. Tuttle, Jr., *Race Riot: Chicago in the Red Summer of 1919* (New York, 1974), vi.
5. Tuttle to H. Leon Prather, December 16, 1982.

Prologue

1. Jack Thorne [David Bryant Fulton], *Hanover; or, The Persecution of the Lowly* (N.d., n.p.; reprint, New York, 1969), 6.
2. Griffin J. McRee, "An Imperfect Sketch of the History of the Town of Wilmington" (typescript), Louis T. Moore Collection, North Carolina Department of Archives and History, Raleigh.
3. James Sprunt, *Chronicles of the Cape Fear River, 1660–1961* (Raleigh, N.C., 1916), 6–4; Walter Gilman Curtis, *Reminiscences of Wilmington and Smithville and Southport, 1848–1900* (Southport, N.C., n.d.); Andrew J. Howell. *The Book of Wilmington* (Wilmington, N.C., 1930?), 23–24.
4. J. G. Randall and David Herbert Donald, *The Civil War and Reconstruction* (Lexington, Mass., 1969), 453.
5. C. Vann Woodward, *Origins of the New South, 1877–1913* (Baton Rouge, La., 1951), 309–10.
6. Ibid., 155–56.
7. Howell, *Book of Wilmington,* 154.
8. Henry Bacon McKoy, *Wilmington. N.C.: Do You Remember When?* (Wilmington, N.C., 1936), 70.
9. Harry Hayden. *The Story of the Wilmington Rebellion* (Wilmington, N.C., 1936), 3.
10. *Wilmington Star-News* 11 January 1976.
11. June Nash, "The Cost of Violence," *Journal of Black Studies* (December, 1973), 160.
12. Dickson J. Preston, *Young Frederick Douglass: The Maryland Years* (Baltimore, Md., 1980), 142.
13. Carl Wittke, *The Irish in America* (Baton Rouge, La., 1956), 126–27; Leon F. Litwack, *North of Slavery: The Negro in the Free States, 1770–1860* (Chicago, 1961), 162–63.
14. *New York Herald,* 11 November 1898.
15. Woodward, *Origins of the New South,* 207–08.
16. C. Vann Woodward, *The Strange Career of Jim Crow* (New York, 1966), 53–54.
17. *Wilmington Business Directory, 1897* (Richmond, Va., 1897), 11, 271.

18. See p. 44.

19. Helen G. Edmonds, *The Negro and Fusion Politics in North Carolina, 1894–1901* (Chapel Hill, N.C., 1951), 89.

20. John Campbell Dancy Collection, Private Papers and Correspondence, in the Andrew Carnegie Library at Livingstone College, Salisbury, North Carolina.

21. *Charlotte Star of Zion*, 10 November 1898.

22. *Wilmington Business Directory, 1897*, 261–77 passim.

23. Ibid., 274.

24. Felice Sadgwar and Mabel Sadgwar, interview with author, Wilmington, North Carolina, 6–8 April 1977.

25. *Wilmington Business Directory, 1897*, 11; Nash, "Cost of Violence," 159.

26. The names of the black attorneys were L. A. Henderson, Armond W. Scott, William A. Moore and L. P. White (Edmonds, *Negro and Fusion Politics*, 163–64).

27. John Campbell Dancy, *Sands against the Wind: Memoirs of John C. Dancy* (Detroit, 1966), 70.,

28. *Wilmington Business Directory, 1897*, 261–77 passim.

29. Woodward, *Origins of the New South*, 361. See also George B. Tindall, *The Emergence of the New South 1913–1945* (Baton Rouge, La., 1967), 161–65.

30. Wilbur J. Cash, *Mind of the South* (New York, 1941), 166.

31. Woodward, *Origins of the New South*, 110.

32. Gunnar Myrdal, *an American Dilemma: The Negro Problem and Modern Democracy* (New York, 1944), 597–98.

33. Dancy, *Sands against the Wind*, 60.

34. Ibid., 68.

35. Ibid., 64.

36. Harry Hayden Papers, Duke University, 38.

37. Dancy, *Sands against the Wind*, 67.

38. Ibid., 65.

39. Ibid., 67–68.

40. Ibid., 69.

41. Ibid., 70

42. Ibid., 63.

43. Ibid., 65–66.

Chapter 1

1. V. O. Key, *Southern Politics in State and Nation* (New York, 1949), 4.

2. Ibid., 5.

3. H. Leon Prather, Sr., *Resurgent Politics and Educational Progressivism in the New South: North Carolina, 1890–1913*, (Rutherford, N.J., 1979), 19–20.

4. Ibid., 23.

5. U.S. Bureau of the Census, *Twelfth Census of the United States, 1900*, 1:466–67; ibid., 2, cxxxii.

6. U.S. Bureau of the Census, *Eleventh Census of the United States, 1890*, 1:473.

7. Van Bokkelen v. Canaday, North Carolina Supreme Court 10 June 1875.

8. *Wilmington Messenger*, 26 March, 1897.

9. *Constitution of the State of North Carolina*, 1875–76, art. 7, sec. 14.

10. *Private Laws of the State of North Carolina*, 1895, chap. 121.

11. *Ordinance of the City of Wilmington, North Carolina* (Wilmington, 1897).

12. *Private Laws of the State of North Carolina*, 1895, chap. 121.

13. *New York Herald*, 20 November 1898.

14. *Private Laws of the State of North Carolina*, 1897, chap. 150.

15. W. N. Harriss et. al. v. S. P. Wright et. al. (Raleigh, N.C., 1897), 2.

16. Benjamin F. Keith, *Memories* (Raleigh, N.C., 1902), 79–80.

17. *Cases Argued and Determined in the Supreme Court of North Carolina* (September term, 1897), North Carolina Reports 131:173.

18. *Wilmington Messenger* 11, 12 March 1897.

19. Ibid., 21 March, 1897.

20. Ibid.

21. Ibid.

22. Ibid.

23. Keith, *Memories*, 82.

24. *Wilmington Messenger*, 23 March, 1897.

25. Daniel L. Russell, *Appointment Book, 1897*, North Carolina Department of Archives and History, Raleigh.

26. *Wilmington Messenger*, 26 March 1897.

27. Ibid.

28. Keith, *Memories*, 84.

29. *Wilmington Messenger*, 26 March 1897.

30. Ibid.

31. Ibid.

32. Ibid.

33. Ibid., 27 March 1898.

34. Ibid.

35. Ibid.

36. Ibid.

37. *Cases Argued and Determined in the Supreme Court of North Carolina* (September term, 1897), 131:173.

38. *Wilmington Messenger*, 21, 22 April 1897.

39. Ibid., 23 April 1897.

40. *Cases Argued and Determined in the Supreme Court of North Carolina* (September term, 1897), 131:178–79.

41. Ibid., 180.

42. Ibid., 181–82.

43. Ibid., 182–83.

Chapter 2

1. Harry Hayden Papers, Duke University, 7.

2. Ibid.

3. Ibid.

4. Ibid.

5. Ibid., 11.

6. Ibid., 7.

7. Iredell Meares, "The Wilmington Revolution," an account in the Edmund Smithwick Papers, North Carolina Department of Archives and History, Raleigh.

8. *New York Herald*, 11 November 1898.

9. Meares, "Wilmington Revolution."

10. Ibid.

11. Ibid.

12. Ibid.

13. *Wilmington Messenger*, 4 September, 18, 19, 27, 28 October, 4, 4, 6, 7 November 1898.

14. *Atlanta Constitution*, 11 November 1898; *Literary Digest*, "Race Troubles in the Carolinas," 625. 26 November 1898, 623.

15. Harry Hayden, *The Story of the Wilmington Rebellion*, (Wilmington, N.C., 1936), 4.

16. *Wilmington Messenger,* 27 October 1898.

17. "Political Campaign of 1898," undated newspaper clipping, University of North Carolina.

18. Ibid.

19. *Literary Digest,* 26 November 1898, "Race Troubles in the Carolinas," 623–27.

20. Alexander J. McKelway, "North Carolina Revolution Justified," *Outlook* 31 December 1898, 1058.

21. *New Bern Journal,* quoted in *Wilmington Messenger,* 18 September 1898.

22. *Wilmington Messenger,* 4 September 1898.

23 *Wilmington Star,* 27 October 1898.

24. *Wilmington Messenger,* 21 September 1898.

25. *Statesville Landmark,* quoted in the *Wilmington Messenger,* 18 September 1898.

26. McKelway, "North Carolina Revolution Justified," 1058.

27. "Governor Jarvis Talks" (editorial), *Raleigh North Carolinian,* 14 July 1898.

28. Josephus Daniels, *Editor in Politics* (Chapel Hill, N.C., 1936), 284.

29. Fred Rippy, ed., *Furnifold Simmons, Statesman of the New South: Memoirs and Addresses* (Durham, N.C., 1936), 17–19.

30. *Wilmington Messenger,* 4 September 1898.

31. *Wilmington Business Directory, 1897,* 10.

32. *Charlotte People's Paper,* 19 August, 9 September 1898.

33. *Fayetteville Observer,* 8 September, 20 October 1898.

34. *Constitution and By-Laws of the North Carolina White Supremacy Clubs* (Raleigh, N.C., 1898), 1–5.

35. Josephus Daniels, *Editor in Politics,* 147–49.

36. *Raleigh News and Observer,* 4 August 1898.

37. George Rountree, "Memorandum of My Personal Recollection of the Election of 1898," 2, Henry G. Connor Papers, Southern Historical Collection, Wilson Library, University of North Carolina, Chapel Hill.

38. Ibid., 3.

39. Ibid., 3–4.

40. Ibid., 4.

41. Benjamin F. Keith, *Memories* (Raleigh, N.C., 1902), 99.

42. Ibid., 104–5.

43. Keith to Butler, 11 October 1898, Marion Butler Papers, Southern Historical Collection, Wilson Library, University of North Carolina, Chapel Hill.

44. *Wilmington Messenger,* 7 September 1898.

45. Ibid., 6 October 1898.

46. Ibid.

47. Ibid., 8 October 1898.

48. *Appleton's Annual Cyclopaedia,* 1898, S.V. "Race Troubles and State Election."

49. Rountree, "Memorandum," 4.

50. *Wilmington Messenger,* 18 October 1898.

51. *Winston Union Republic,* 27 October 1898. Copies of this letter were delivered to the *Raleigh News and Observer, Charlotte Observer,* and *Raleigh Post;* each paper declined to publish it.

52. Rountree, "Memorandum," 9–10.

53. Thomas R. Cripps, introduction to *Hanover; or, The Persecution of the Lowly,* by Jack Thorne [David Bryant Fulton] (n.d., n.p.; reprint, New York, 1969), iii–ix.

54. *Wilmington Messenger,* 21, 23, 25, 27 August 1898.

55. Henry L. West, "The Race War in North Carolina," *Forum* 26 (January 1899): 582.

56. Beth G. Crabtree, *North Carolina Governors, 1585–1974* (Raleigh, N.C., 1974), 82, 87; Samuel Ashe et al. (eds.), *Biographical History of North Carolina* (Greensboro, N.C., 1907), 6:354–55; William S. Powell, *The North Carolina Gazeteer* (Chapel Hill, N.C., 1968), 311.

57. Milo Manly, interview with author, Philadelphia, Pennsylvania, 25 May 1977.

58. Ibid.

59. Felice Sadgwar and Mable Sadgwar, interview with author, Wilmington, North Carolina, 6, April 1977.

60. Clawson, "Wilmington Revolution."

61. *Wilmington Daily Record,* mutilated copies on microfilm, New York Public Library; *Collier's Weekly,* 23 October 1898, 5.

62. Thorne, *Hanover,* 13.

63. Wilbur J. Cash, *Mind of the South* (New York, 1941), 115.

64. Thorne, *Hanover,* 13.

65. H. Leon Prather, Sr., *Resurgent Politics and Educational Progressivism in the New South: North Carolina, 1890–1913* (Rutherford, N.J., 1979), 152–53. See also Thomas W. Clawson, "Exhibit A" copy of a controversial editorial the *Wilmington Record,* August 18. Clawson Papers in the Louis T. Moore Collection, North Carolina Department of Archives and History, Raleigh, N.C.

66. *Progressive Farmer,* 30 August 1898.

67. Dancy to Bruce, 30 July 1899, John Edward Bruce Collection, Schomburg Center for Research in Black Culture, New York.

68. Quoted in Josephus Daniels, *Editor in Politics,* 286–87.

69. *Wilmington Morning Star,* 9 October 1898. This was a reprint allegedly taken from Manly's *Record.*

70. Nash, "The Cost of Violence," 159.

71. J. Allen Kirk, *A Statement of Facts concerning the Bloody Riot in Wilmington, N.C., November 10, 1898* (n.p., n.d.), 2.

72. Gunnar Myrdal, *An American Dilemma: The Negro Problem in Modern Democracy* (New York, 1944), 561–62.

73. *Congressional Record,* 51st Cong., 1st sess. (1891), 707–08.

74. Gunnar Myrdal, *An American Dilemma,* 1977.

75. *Ibid.,* 1975.

76. John Hope Franklin, "The Great Confrontation: The South and the Problem of Change," *Journal of Southern History* (February, 1972), 6.

77. Anne Firor Scott, *The Southern Lady: From Pedestal to Politics, 1830–1930* (Chicago, 1970), 4.

78. Winthrop D. Jordan, *White Over Black: American Attitudes Toward the Negro, 1550–1812* (Chapel Hill, N.C., 1968), 7–8.

79. Myrdal, *An American Dilemma,* 114.

80. Carl N. Degler, *Neither Black Nor White: Slavery and Race Relations in Brazil and the United States* (New York, 1971), 101–02.

81. Mydral, *An American Dilemma,* 114.

82. Franklin, "The Great Confrontation," 6.

83. W. E. B. DuBois, *The Souls of Black Folk* (New York, 1924), 106.

84. *U.S. Bureau of the Census: Negro Population, 1790–1915* (Washington, D.C. 1918), 208.

85. Eugene D. Genovese, *Roll Jordan Roll: The World the Slaveholder Made* (New York, 1972), 421–22.

86. Franklin, "The Great Confrontation," 7.

87. Genovese, *Roll Jordan Roll,* 423.

88. Franklin, "The Great Confrontation," 7.

89. Genovese, *Roll Jordan Roll,* 482.

90. Ibid., 483.

91. Ibid., 490–91.

92. Jordan, *White Over Black,* 150–52.

93. Genovese, *Roll Jordan Roll,* 422.

94. *Montgomery Advertizer,* August 16, 1887.

95. Ibid., August 17, 1887.

96. Ibid., August 16, 1887.

97. Ibid., August 17, 1887.

98. Ibid.

99. Ibid.

100. Ibid., August 18, 1887.

101. Association of the Wilmington Light Infantry, Minutes, 14 December 1905, Personal Accounts of Members' Experiences in the Wilmington Riot, 1, University of North Carolina.

102. *Collier's Weekly,* 26 November 1898, 5.

Chapter 3

1. *Wilmington Morning Star,* 18 October 1898.

2. *Fayetteville Observer,* 27 October 1898.

3. Dancy to Bruce, 30 July 1899, John Edward Bruce Collection, Schomburg Center for Research in Black Culture, New York.

4. Thomas W. Clawson, "Exhibit A" (copy of a controversial Manly editorial in the *Wilmington Record,* 18 August 1898, Clawson Papers, in the Louis T. Moore Collection, North Carolina Department of Archives and History, Raleigh.

5. Ibid. See also Josephus Daniels, *Editor in Politics* (Chapel Hill, N.C., 1936), 296–97.

6. *Wilmington Messenger,* 22 October 1898.

7. *Fayetteville Observer,* 22, 27 October 1898; *Raleigh News and Observer,* 22 October 1898.

8. *Wilmington Messenger,* 22 October 1898.

9. *Raleigh News and Observer,* 22 October 1898.

10. *Wilmington Messenger,* 22 October 1898.

11. Ibid.

12. *Fayetteville Observer,* 22, 27 October 1898; *Raleigh News and Observer,* 22 October 1898.

13. Alexander J. McKelway, "North Carolina Suffrage Amendment," *Independent,* May–August 1900, 1955–57.

14. Jonathan Daniels, *Tar Heels: A Portrait of North Carolina* (New York, 1941), 72.

15. *Washington Post,* special to *Wilmington Messenger,* 25 October 1898; *Raleigh News and Observer,* 25 October 1898.

16. *Wilmington Messenger,* 25 October 1898.

17. *Washington Post,* special to *Wilmington Messenger,* 25 October 1898.

18. *Raleigh News and Observer,* 28 October 1898; *Asheville Daily Gazette,* 28 October 1898.

19. Keith to Butler, 11 October 1898, Marion Butler Papers, Southern Historical Collection, Wilson Library, University of North Carolina, Chapel Hill.

20. George Rountree, "Memorandum of My Personal Recollection of the Election of 1898," 6–7, Henry G. Connor Papers, Southern Historical Collection, Wilson Library, University of North Carolina, Chapel Hill.

21. Alfred M. Waddell, *Some Memories of My Life* (Raleigh, N.C., 1908), 51.

22. *Collier's Weekly,* 26 November 1898, 16.

23. Waddell, *Some Memories of My Life,* 245.

24. Keith to Butler, 17 November 1898, Butler Papers.

25. Rountree, "Memorandum," 7.

26. *Wilmington Messenger,* 25 November 1898.

27. Ibid., 25 October 1898.

28. *Wilmington Morning Post,* 25 October 1898.

29. Sprunt to Russell, 24 October 1898, Alexander Sprunt and Son Papers, office files 6138–6410 (1898), Duke University.

30. Harry Hayden Papers, 32–33, Duke University.

31. Foster to Sprunt, 30 October 1898, Sprunt Papers.

32. Daniel L. Russell, *Letter Book, 1897–1901*, 49, North Carolina Department of Archives and History, Raleigh.

33. Ibid., 50.

34. *Wilmington Messenger*, 27 October 1898.

35. Ibid., 29 October 1898.

36. *Goldsboro Argus*, special to *Raleigh News and Observer*, 21 October 1898; *Fayetteville Observer*, 20 October 1898.

37. *Wilmington Messenger*, 28, 29 October 1898.

38. *Raleigh News and Observer*, 29 October 1898.

39. *Asheville Daily Gazette*, 30 October 1898.

40. Henry L. West, "The Race War in North Carolina," *Forum* 26 (January 1899): 580.

41. *Wilmington Messenger*, 3 November 1898.

42. Benjamin F. Keith, *Memories* (Raleigh, N.C., 1902), 98, 102.

43. Rountree, "Memorandum," 5–6.

44. *Raleigh News and Observer*, 1 November 1898.

45. J. Allen Kirk, *A Statement of Facts Concerning the Bloody Riot in Wilmington, N.C., November 10, 1898* (n.p., n.d.), 3.

46. Hayden Papers, 9–10.

47. Thomas W. Clawson, "The Wilmington Race Riot of 1898," 7, Clawson Papers in the Louis T. Moore Collection, North Carolina Department of Archives and History, Raleigh.

48. Carrie Manly, "Love Letter to My Sons," 4 January 1954 (in possession of Milo Manly, Philadelphia, Pennsylvania).

49. Ibid.

50. *Literary Digest*, "The Race Troubles in North Carolina," 625. 26 November 1898.

51. *Raleigh News and Observer*, 1 November 1898; *New York Herald*, 1 November 1898; West, "The Race War in North Carolina," 580.

52. Rountree, "Memorandum," 4–5.

53. *Atlanta Constitution*, 9 November 1898.

54. West, "Race War in North Carolina," 580.

55. Iredell Meares, "The Wilmington Revolution," an account in the Edmund Smithwick Papers, North Carolina Department of Archives and History, Raleigh.

56. Clawson, "Wilmington Race Riot of 1898," 10.

57. Meares, "Wilmington Revolution."

58. Association of the Wilmington Light Infantry, Minutes, 14 December 1905, Personal Accounts of Members' Experiences in the Wilmington Riot, 2, University of North Carolina.

59. Jack Thorne, [David Bryant Fulton], *Hanover; or, The Persecution of the Lowly* (d., n.p.; reprint, New York, 1969), 51. See also Helen G. Edmonds, *The Negro and Fusion Politics in North Carolina, 1894–1901* (Chapel Hill, N.C., 1951), 165.

60. *Atlanta Constitution*, 10 November 1898.

61. Wilmington (North Carolina) Town Council, Minutes, 5 November 1898, North Carolina Department of Archives and History, Raleigh.

62. [Jane Murphy Cronly?], "An Account of the Race Riot in Wilmington, N.C., in 1898, 5, Cronly Family Papers, Duke University.

63. *Outlook*, "North Carolina Race Conflict," 707–09. 19 November 1898.

64. *New York Herald*, 20 November 1898.

65. Ibid. See also Josephus Daniels, *Editor in Politics*, 302.

66. Cronly, "Account of the Race Riot," 5.

67. Kirk, *Statement of Facts*, 5.

68. Cronly, "Account of the Race Riot," 5–6.

69. Wilmington Light Infantry, Personal Accounts, 3.

70. *Wilmington Messenger*, 9 November 1898.

71. *Progressive Farmer*, 29 November 1898.

72. Cronly, "Account of the Race Riot," 1.

Chapter 4

1. Anonymous letter 9 November 1898, Hinsdale Family Papers, Duke University.

2. George Rountree, "Memorandum of My Personal Recollection of the Election of 1898," 10, Henry G. Connors Papers, Southern Historical Collection, Wilson Library, University of North Carolina, Chapel Hill.

3. *Wilmington Evening Dispatch*, 9 November 1898.

4. *Wilmington Messenger*, 10 November 1898.

5. *Appleton's Annual Cyclopaedia*, 1898, s.v. "Race Troubles and State Election."

6. Harry Hayden, *The Story of the Wilmington Rebellion* (Wilmington, N.C., 1936), 10.

7. Benjamin F. Keith, *Memories* (Raleigh, N.C., 1902), 109.

8. Rountree, "Memorandum," 12.

9. Hayden, *Story of the Wilmington Rebellion*, 12.

10. *Wilmington Messenger*, 10 November 1898.

11. Harry Hayden Papers, 14, Duke University.

12. Henry L. West, "The Race War in North Carolina," *Forum* 26 (January 1899): 581.

13. Hayden Papers, 15.

14. *Wilmington Messenger*, 10 November 1898.

15. Hayden Papers, 15.

16. *Wilmington Messenger*, 19 November 1898; West, "Race War in North Carolina," 584.

17. *New York Herald*, 11 November 1898.

18. *Wilmington Messenger*, 11 November 1898.

19. West, "Race War in North Carolina," 584.

20. *Wilmington Messenger*, 11 November 1898.

21. *Wilmington Evening Dispatch*, 18 November 1898.

22. *New York Herald*, 11 November 1898.

23. Elliott Rudwick, *Race Riot at East St. Louis July 2, 1927* (New York, 1972), 225–26.

24. *Wilmington Weekly Star*, 18 November 1898.

25. *Washington Post*, 11 November 1898; *Wilmington Messenger*, 11 November 1898.

26. Alfred M. Waddell, "The Story of the Wilmington, N.C., Race Riot," *Collier's Weekly*, 26 November 1898, 4.

27. *Brooklyn (N. Y.) Daily Eagle*, 11, 19 November 1898.

28. *Wilmington Messenger*, 11 November 1898.

29. Hayden Papers, 18.

30. *Washington Post*, 11 November 1898; *New York Sun*, 11 November 1898.

31. *Wilmington Messenger*, 11 November 1898.

32. Hayden Papers, 18.

33. *Wilmington Messenger*, 3, 14 August 1897.

34. Ibid., 19 November 1898.

35. Waddell, "Story of the Wilmington Riot," 4.

36. Red Buck, "A Pure-Bred Negro Relate It—The Head Waiter at the Hotel Lafayette, the Jack Falstaff of the Race-Political Riot at Wilmington in 1898," *Charlotte Observer*, 24 May 1908, in a scrapbook of clippings, *The Wilmington Race Riot, November 1898*, University of North Carolina.

37. Rountree, "Memorandum," 14.

38. *New York World*, 11 November 1898.

39. Association of the Wilmington Light Infantry, Minutes, 14 December 1905, Personal Accounts of Members' Experiences in the Wilmington Riot, 8–9, University of North Carolina.

40. [Jane Murphy Cronly?], "An Account of the Race Riot in Wilmington, N.C., in 1898," 2, Cronly Family Papers, Duke University.

41. Rountree, "Memorandum," 14.

42. *Wilmington Messenger*, 11 November 1898.

43. Rountree, "Memorandum," 14–15.

44. Wilmington Light Infantry, Personal Accounts, 9.

45. Helen G. Edmonds, *The Negro and Fusion Politics in North Carolina, 1894–1901* (Chapel Hill, N.C., 1951), 169.

46. Cronly, "Account of the Race Riot," 3.

47. Hayden Papers, 22.

48. Wilmington Light Infantry, Personal Accounts, 10.

49. *Wilmington Messenger*, 11 November 1898.

50. Hayden Papers, 20.

51. *Wilmington Messenger*, 11 November 1898.

52. Ibid.

53. *Raleigh News and Observer*, 11 November 1898.

54. Ibid.

55. *Wilmington Messenger*, 12 November 1898.

56. *Raleigh News and Observer*, 27 April 1900.

57. *Wilmington Messenger*, 11 November 1898.

58. Ibid.

59. *Brooklyn (N. Y.) Daily Eagle*, 11 November 1898; *Wilmington Weekly Star*, 8 November 1898.

60. Hayden Papers, 24.

61. Wilmington Light Infantry, Personal Accounts, 8.

62. J. Allen Kirk, *Facts concerning the Bloody Race Riot in Wilmington, N.C., November 10, 1898* (n.p., n.d.), 8.

63. Wilmington Light Infantry, Personal Accounts, 6.

64. Thomas W. Clawson, "The Wilmington Race Riot of 1898," 8, Clawson Papers in the Louis T. Moore Collection, North Carolina Department of Archives and History, Raleigh.

65. *Collier's Weekly*, 26 November 1898, 16.

66. Ibid.

67. *New York Times*, 11 November 1898; *Atlanta Constitution*, 11 November 1898.

68. Anonymous letter to McKinley, 13 November 1898, Department of Justice, file 17743-1898, National Archives.

69. Cronly, "Account of the Race Riot," 3.

70. Wilmington Light Infantry, Personal Accounts, 5.

71. Some evidence suggests that Wright had tried to inspire courage in the frightened blacks, who had left their wives and children at the mercy of the mob and were fleeing toward the forest. Death was his penalty.

72. Edmonds, *Negro and Fusion Politics*, 169.

73. Wilmington Light Infantry, Personal Accounts, 10.

74. *Wilmington Messenger*, 11 November 1898.

75. Wilmington Light Infantry, Personal Accounts, 16.

76. *Collier's Weekly*, 26 November 1898, 16.

77. *Wilmington Messenger*, 11 November 1898.

78. Hayden Papers, 22–23.

79. Ibid.

80. *Wilmington Messenger*, 11 November 1898.

81. Rudwick, *Race Riot at East St. Louis*, 225.

82. Hayden Papers, 21.

83. *Raleigh News and Observer*, 11 November 1898.

84. Cronly, "Account of the Race Riot," 2–3.

85. Ibid.

86. Anonymous letter to McKinley, 13 November 1898, "Please send relief as soon as possible or we perish," National Archives.

87. Louis N. Megaree, *Seen and Heard* (n.p., 1903), Schomburg, Center for Research in Black Culture, New York, 14.

88. *Atlanta Constitution*, 11 November 1898.

89. Hayden Papers, 27.

90. Rountree, "Memorandum," 16.

91. Hayden Papers, 20.

92. *Collier's Weekly*, 26 November 1898, 16.

93. *Wilmington Messenger*, 11 November 1898.

94. Ibid.

95. Bassett to Adams, 15 November 1898, in W. Stull Holt, ed., *Historical Scholarship in the United States, 1876–1901*, John Hopkins University Studies in Historical and Political Science, vol. 56 (Baltimore, Md., 1938), 259.

96. Ibid., 256 and 258.

97. *Wilmington Messenger*, 11 November 1898.

98. Wilmington Light Infantry, Personal Accounts, 5.

99. Buck, "Jack Flagstaff of Wilmington."

100. Ibid.

101. Ibid.

102. *Baltimore Sun*, 11 November 1898; *New York Herald*, 12 November 1898.

103. *Atlanta Constitution*, 11 November 1898.

104. *Wilmington Messenger*, 11 November 1898.

105. *Wilmington Morning Star*, 11 November 1898; *New York Times*, 11, 12 November 1898; *New York Herald*, 20 November 1898; *Richmond Daily Times*, November 11, 1898.

106. Alfred M. Waddell, *Some Memories of My Life* (Raleigh, N.C., 1908), 243.

107. *Wilmington Messenger*, 11 November 1898.

108. *Raleigh News and Observer*, 13 November 1898.

109. *Wilmington Messenger*, 11 November 1898.

110. Hayden Papers, 22.

111. Ibid., 21.

112. June Nash, "The Cost of Violence," *Journal of Black Studies* (December 1973), 164–65.

113. Kirk, *Statement of Facts*, 17.

114. Nash, "Cost of Violence," 165.

115. Felice Sadgwar and Mabel Sadgwar, interview with author, Wilmington, North Carolina.

116. *Wilmington Messenger*, 11 November 1898.

117. *Raleigh Caucasian*, 17 November 1898.

118. *Collier's Weekly*, 26 November 1898, 6.

119. Ibid.

120. Hayden Papers, 23.

121. *New York Herald*, 11 November 1898.

Chapter 5

1. *Minutes* of the City Council of Wilmington, New Hanover County, N.C., 10 November 1898, North Carolina Department of Archives and History, Raleigh.

2. Ibid.

3. Ibid.

4. George Rountree, "Memorandum of My Personal Recollection of the Election of 1898,"

17, Henry G. Connor Papers, Southern Historical Collection, Wilson Library, University of North Carolina, Chapel Hill.

5. Harry Hayden Papers, Duke University, 24.

6. *Collier's Weekly*, 26 November 1898, 5.

7. Wilmington Town Council, Minutes, 10 November 1898.

8. Ibid.

9. *Wilmington Messenger*, 11 November 1898.

10. Wilmington Town Council, Minutes, 10 November 1898.

11. *New York Herald*, 11 November 1898; *New York Times*, November 11 and 12, 1898.

12. Hayden Papers, 26.

13. Association of the Wilmington Light Infantry, Minutes, 14 December 1905, Personal Accounts of Members' Experiences in the Wilmington Riot, 4, University of North Carolina.

14. Hayden Papers, 25–26.

15. Wilmington Light Infantry, Personal Accounts, 4.

16. *Fayetteville Observer*, 11 November 1898.

17. *Baltimore Sun*, 12 November 1898.

18. *New York Sun*, 12 November 1898; *Atlanta Constitution*, 11 November 1898; *New York Times*, 12 November 1898.

19. *Wilmington Evening Dispatch*, 10 November 1898.

20. Hayden Papers, 26.

21. Ibid.

22. *Wilmington Messenger*, 11 November 1898.

23. *New York Herald*, 12 November 1898.

24. *New York Herald*, 17 November 1898; *Atlanta Constitution*, 12 November 1898.

25. *Raleigh News and Observer*, 13 November 1898.

26. Ibid.

27. *New York Times*, 12 November 1898; *Atlanta Constitution*, 12 November 1898; *New York Herald*, 12 November 1898; Hayden Papers, 27.

28. *Raleigh News and Observer*, 13 November 1898.

29. Ibid.

30. Jack Thorne [David Bryant Fulton], *Hanover; or, The Persecution of the Lowly* (n.d., n.p. reprint, New York, 1969), 17.

31. Hayden Papers, 24.

32. Wilmington Town Council, Minutes, 14 November 1898.

33. Ibid.

34. *Wilmington Messenger*, 12 November 1898.

35. Ibid., 4, 16, 18 October 1898.

36. *Wilmington Morning Star*, 28 October 1898.

37. Ibid., 2, 4 November 1898.

38. Ibid.

39. Hayden Papers, 38.

40. *Raleigh News and Observer*, 13 November 1898.

41. Wilmington Town Council, Minutes, March 1899.

42. June Nash, "The Cost of Violence," *Journal of Black Studies* (December 1973), 164–65.

43. Thorne, *Hanover*, 106.

44. U.S. Bureau of the Census, *Eleventh Census of the United States, 1890*, 1:473; *Twelfth Census, 1900*, 1:633.

45. *Raleigh News and Observer*, 13 November 1898.

46. Anonymous letter to McKinley, 13 November 1898, "Please send relief as soon as possible or we perish," National Archives.

47. *Collier's Weekly*, 26 November 1898, 16.

48. Hayden Papers, 28.

49. *Collier's Weekly*, 26 November 1898, 16.

Chapter 6

1. *New York Times*, 11, 12 November 1898.
2. *New York Herald*, 11, 12 November 1898.
3. Ibid., 12 November 1898; *New York Times*, 12 November 1898.
4. *New York Herald*, 12 November 1898.
5. *Atlanta Constitution*, 10 November 1898.
6. Keith to Butler, 7 November 1898, in Marion Butler Papers, Southern Historical Collection, Wilson Library, University of North Carolina, Chapel Hill.
7. McLean to Griggs, 9 November 1898, 3 December 1898, Department of Justice, file 17743-1898, National Archives.
8. Bernard to Griggs, 5 December 1898, Department of Justice, file 17743-1898, National Archives.
9. Bernard to Griggs, 1 April 1899, Department of Justice, file 17743-1898, National Archives.
10. Bernard to Griggs, 22 April 1899, Department of Justice, file 17743-1898, National Archives.
11. *New York Times*, 11, 12 November 1898.
12. Ibid.
13. Bunting and Melton to McKinley, 24 December 1898, Department of Justice, file 17743-1898, National Archives.
14. Della V. Johnson to McKinley, 14 November 1898, Department of Justice, file 17743-1898, National Archives.
15. Anonymous letter to McKinley, 15 November 1898, Department of Justice, file 17743-1898, National Archives.
16. Anonymous letter to President McKinley, 14 December 1898, Department of Justice, file 17743-1898, National Archives.
17. Wilhemena Anderson to President McKinley, ibid., 14 November 1898, Department of Justice, file 17743-1898, National Archives.
18. Anonymous letter to McKinley, 13 November 1898, "Please send relief as soon as possible or we perish," National Archives.
19. Ibid.
20. *Cleveland Gazette*, 19 November 1898.
21. *Richmond Planet*, 26 November 1898.
22. Booker T. Washington Papers, 14: Library of Congress; Benjamin Quarles, *The Negro in the Making of America* (New York, 1964), 173.
23. Herbert Aptheker, *Documentary History of the Negro People in the United States*, 3 vols. (New York, 1951–74), 1:778.
24. Numerous letters, telegrams, petitions, and resolutions from blacks in the files of the attorney general, 12, 14, 16, 24, 25, 29 November 1898, Department of Justice, file 17743-1898, National Archives.
25. Samuel E. Huffman to Hanna, 29 November 1898, Department of Justice, file 17743-1898, National Archives.
26. Kelly Miller, "The Race Problem in the South," *Outlook*, 31 December 1898, 106.
27. Josephus Daniels, *Editor in Politics* (Chapel Hill, N.C., 1936), 309.
28. Milo Manly, interview with author, Philadelphia, Pennsylvania, 25 May 1977.
29. *Literary Digest*, "Race Troubles in the Carolinas," 26 November 1898, 625–26.
30. Ibid.
31. Milo Manly, interview with author, Philadelphia, Pennsylvania, 25 May 1977.
32. Ibid.
33. Aptheker, *Documentary History*, 778.
34. John Campbell Dancy, *Sands against the Wind: Memoirs of John C. Dancy* (Detroit, 1966), 69–70.

35. Wilbur J. Cash, *The Mind of the South* (New York, 1941), 39.

36. Milo Manly, interview with author, Philadelphia, Pennsylvania, 25 May 1977.

37. Ibid.

38. Lewin R. Manly, interview with author, Atlanta, Georgia, 27 March 1981.

39. National Veteran's Boxing Association, souvenier convention program, 1965.

40. Carrie Manly, "Love Letter to My Sons," 4 January 1954 (in possession of Milo Manly, Philadelphia, Pennsylvania).

Chapter 7

1. Bobby L. Lovett, "Memphis Riots: White Reaction to Blacks in Memphis, May 1865–July 1866," *Tennessee Historical Quarterly* (Spring 1979), 9–10, 12–18, 20.

2. In 1868, riots erupted in the state of Louisiana and again at New Orleans, and in Mississippi at Meridian (1870), Vicksburg (1874) and Yazoo City and environs (1875). Richard Maxwell Brown, *Strain of Violence: Historical Studies of American Violence and Vigilantism* (New York, 1975), 323.

3. John Hope Franklin, *From Slavery to Freedom* (New York, 1966), 330.

4. James M. McPherson, *Ordeal by Fire: The Civil War and Reconstruction* (New York, 1982), 592.

5. Ibid., 598.

6. C. Vann Woodward, *The Strange Career of Jim Crow* (New York, 1966), 53–54.

7. McPherson, *Ordeal by Fire*, 607–8.

8. Thomas R. Cripps, introduction to *Hanover: or, The Persecution of the Lowly*, by Jack Thorne [David Bryant Fulton] (n.d., n.p.; reprint, New York, 1969), i.

9. Charles Crowe, "Racial Massacre in Atlanta, September 22, 1906," *Journal of Negro History* (April 1969), 164. See also J. Saunders Redding, *They Came in Chains* (New York, 1950), 221–28.

10. Elliott M. Rudwick, *Race Riot at East St. Louis, July 2, 1917* (New York, 1972), 41–54. See also, August Meier and Elliot M. Rudwick, *From Plantation to Ghetto* (New York, 1966), 194.

11. Franklin, *From Slavery to Freedom*, 460; see also Robert Y. Haynes, *A Night of Violence: The Houston Race Riot of 1917* (Baton Rouge, La., 1976).

12. James Weldon Johnson, *Along This Way* (New York, 1933), 341.

13. William M. Tuttle, Jr., *Race Riot: Chicago in the Red Summer of 1919* (New York, 1974), 57–64.

14. Arthur I. Waskow, *From Race Riot to Sit-In: 1919 and the 1960s* (New York, 1966), 121–29.

15. Tuttle, *Race Riot*, 14n.

16. George B. Tindall, *The Emergence of the New South, 1913–1945* (Baton Rogue, La., 1967), 154, 192.

17. Ibid., 155.

18. R. Halliburton, Jr., *The Tulsa Race War of 1921* (San Francisco, 1975), vii.

19. Ibid., 3–6.

20. Ibid., 12.

21. Scott Ellsworth, *Death in a Promised Land: The Tulsa Race Riot of 1921* (Baton Rouge, La., 1982), 66–70.

22. Halliburton, *The Tulsa Race War of 1921*, 32.

23. Meier and Rudwick, *From Plantation to Ghetto*, 247.

24. Joseph Boskin, *Urban Racial Violence in the Twentieth Century* (Beverly Hills, Calif., 1969), 66.

25. Tuttle, *Race Riot*, 258.

26. *New York Times*, 6, 7, 8, 9, 10, 11, 12 April 1968.

27. *Time,* 2 June 1980, 10–20; *Newsweek,* 2 June 1980, 32–39.

28. Quoted in Barbara W. Tuchman, *A Distant Mirror: The Calamitous 14th Century* (New York, 1978), xiv.

29. Tuttle, *Race Riot,* 249.

30. Ibid., 264.

31. Ibid.

32. Rudwick, *Race Riot at East St. Louis,* 217–18, 228.

33. Crowe, "Racial Massacre in Atlanta," 164.

34. Rudwick, *Race Riot at East St. Louis,* 50 and 217.

35. Tuttle, *Race Riot,* 242.

36. Brown, *Strain of Violence,* 208.

37. Gunnar Myrdal, *An American Dilemma: The Negro Problem in Modern Democracy* (New York, 1944), 559.

Epilogue

1. Alexander J. McKelway, "North Carolina Revolution Justified," *Outlook,* 31 December 1898, 1057–58.

2. *Biblical Recorder,* 16 November 1898.

3. *Harper's Weekly,* 19 November 1898.

4. Josephus Daniels, *Editor in Politics* (Chapel Hill, N.C., 1941), 307–8.

5. *Raleigh News and Observer,* 13 November 1898.

6. Ibid., 16 November 1898.

7. Henry L. West, "The Race War in North Carolina," *Forum* 26 (January 1899): 582.

8. *Literary Digest,* "Race Troubles in The Carolinas," 26 November 1898, 623.

9. Charles W. Chesnutt, *The Marrow of Tradition* (Ann Arbor, Mich., 1969), 243.

10. [Jane Murphy Cronly?], "An Account of the Race Riot in Wilmington, N.C., in 1898," 1, Cronly Family Papers, Duke University.

11. Bassett to Adams, 15 November 1898, in W. Stull Holt, ed., *Historical Scholarship in the United States, 1876–1901,* Johns Hopkins University Studies in Historical and Political Science, vol. 56 (Baltimore, Md., 1938), 256.

12. Keith to Butler, 17 November 1898, Marion Butler Papers, Southern Historical Collection, Wilson Library, University of North Carolina, Chapel Hill.

13. *Collier's Weekly,* 26 November 1898, p. 16.

14. Waddell to Page, 1 December 1898, Thomas Nelson Page Papers, Duke University.

15. Alfred M. Waddell, "The Story of the Wilmington, N.C., Race Riot," *Collier's Weekly,* 26 November, 1898, 4.

16. Waddell to Oldham, 29 November 1898, Edward A. Oldham Papers, Duke University.

17. *Wilmington Messenger,* 11 March 1899.

18. *Wilmington Morning Star,* 1 April 1903.

19. Alfred M. Waddell Papers, Southern Historical Collection, University of North Carolina.

20. George Rountree, "Memorandum of My Personal Reason for the Passage of the Suffrage Amendment to the Constitution (Grandfather Clause)," 1–2, Henry G. Connor Papers, Southern Historical Collection, Wilson Library, University of North Carolina, Chapel Hill.

21. Ibid.

22. *Wilmington Messenger,* 3 August 1898.

23. C. Vann Woodward, *Origins of the New South 1877–1913* (Baton Rouge, La., 1951), 325.

24. James M. McPherson, *Ordeal By Fire: The Civil War and Reconstruction* (New York, 1982), 618.

25. Every logical generalization cannot be documented. A major goal of the progressives was to make the government more democratic. Devices such as the grandfather clauses asserted a principle of democracy among white men and established a chasm between them and black men

which was removed by the Supreme Court decision of *Guin* v. *United States* (1915). Sources on the progressive era, including textbooks, seldom mention this significant case.

26. Rayford Logan, *The Negro in American Life and Thought: The Nadir 1877–1901* (New York, 1954), 162; see also Logan, *The Betrayal of the Negro: From Rutherford B. Hayes to Woodrow Wilson* (New York, 1967).

27. John Hope Franklin, *From Slavery to Freedom* (New York, 1966), 439.

28. C. Vann Woodward, *Origins of the New South*, 324–25.

29. C. Vann Woodward, *The Strange Career of Jim Crow* (New York, 1966), 93–94.

30. Nancy J. Weiss, "The Negro and the New Freedom," in Allen Weinstein and Frank Otto Gatell, eds., *The Segregation Era 1863–1954* (New York, 1970), 130.

31. Ibid., 133.

32. Ibid., 131.

33. John Wideman, "Charles W. Chesnutt: The Marrow of Tradition," *American Scholar* (Winter 1972–73), 129.

34. Jack Bass and Walter De Vries, *The Transformation of Southern Politics* (New York, 1976), 8–10.

35. *Outlook,* "North Carolina Race Conflict," November 19, 1898, 708–09.

36. George Simpler, *The Racial Attitudes of American Presidents: From Abraham to Theodore Roosevelt* (New York, 1971), 304.

37. Ibid., 374–75.

38. Ibid., 305–06.

39. *Outlook,* "North Carolina Race Conflict," November 19, 1898, 709.

Bibliographical Essay

The literature relevant to this study is both scattered and meager. The following essay is selective and makes no attempt to list all sources consulted in the writing of this book. Those interested in a more comprehensive examination of a particular aspect of this study should consult the sources mentioned in the appropriate notes.

Interviews

Because the Wilmington race riot occurred several generations ago, I had little hope of supplementing the documentary sources with interviews of members of the riot generation. Moreover, contemporary Wilmingtonians were in general reluctant to talk about the event. The recollections by those whose families had not actually witnessed the riot had faded to include only selective dramatic events. Accordingly, I exercised caution in recording what people of different generations believed to have happened.

The most indispensable and fascinating informant was Milo Manly (interview with author, Philadelphia, Pennsylvania, 25 May 1977). I am deeply grateful to Manly for his candor and cooperation in relating information about his father, other key persons, and background material, as well as for offering some insights. He also made it possible for me to contact his two aunts, Mabel Sadgwar and Felice Sadgwar of Wilmington. The Sadgwars gave valuable observations on a relative who had the courage to write the most controversial editorial of that era (interview with author, Wilmington, North Carolina, 6–8 April 1977). It is worth noting that all persons I interviewed shared a common characteristic—their voices reflected no anger about what had happened.

Archives

One of the most valuable archival sources for this study is located in the National Archives in Washington, D.C. File 17743-1898 of the Department of Justice contains a mass of data, including several letters to Attorney

General John W. Griggs from two members of the Department of Justice of Eastern North Carolina. The larger part of these materials, however (addressed to both Attorney General Griggs and President McKinley), is letters and telegrams from blacks and appeals from civil rights groups. All in all, this correspondence shows that blacks were looking to the national government for help. Despite their great historical value, these documents are unknown or have been neglected by scholars.

Still another valuable source of archival data for this study was discovered at the North Carolina Department of Archives and History in Raleigh. *Minutes* of the City Council of Wilmington, New Hanover County, *Wilmington, N.C., 1898–1911*, vol. F.G. All serious students of the Wilmington event of 1898 should consult this source. These minutes take the scholar behind the scene of the coup and provide information not found in newspapers or manuscripts (and certainly not in secondary sources). The minutes are in longhand and are available on microfilm, but they have been completely ignored by historians.

The Daniel L. Russell Papers are also located in the North Carolina Department of Archives and History. They are of limited value to this study. The same is true of the Edmund Smithwick Papers, among which was found a newspaper sheet by Iredell Meares entitled "The Wilmington Revolution." It has no date, and evidence suggests that it was printed privately. Some of its contents cannot be found elsewhere, and it follows closely and defends the Democratic version of the story.

Manuscripts

Although the Wilmington race riot gained the attention of President McKinley and his cabinet, only one telegram (from J. S. Carr, 12 November 1898) was found among the McKinley Papers. Carr's lengthy telegram served as the rationale for federal nonintervention in the affairs of North Carolina. While cabinet-level officials were informed about and discussed the Wilmington riot, there is virtually no information available as to how they viewed the event. According to *A Guide to Archives and Manuscripts in the United States* (New Haven, Conn., 1961), edited by Philip M. Hamer, the Sussex County Historical Society, Newton, New Jersey, holds a small body of the papers of the family of Attorney General John W. Griggs. I did not examine these papers.

The Booker T. Washington Papers (particularly the volume entitled "Personal and Office Correspondence, 1890–1905") include some interesting information on the disfranchisement movement in North Carolina and elsewhere. There is also an interesting reference to the Manly editorial in Louis R. Harlan's *Booker T. Washington Papers*, volume 4 (Urbana, Ill., 1975).

In the Schomburg Center for Research in Black Culture (New York) are a few items on the Wilmington race riot. In the John Edward Bruce Collection is a letter dated 30 July 1898, written by John Campbell Dancy, very critical of Alexander L. Manly and his editorial.

In using the Manuscript Division, William R. Perkins Library, Duke University, historians should start with *Guide to the Manuscript Collection in the Duke University Library,* by Nannie A. Tilley and Norma Lee Goodwin (Durham, N.C., 1947). Here I located several important manuscript collections. I have relied heavily on the Harry Hayden Papers, because there is no other source to replace them. These documents are contained in a typescript from an unpublished manuscript entitled "Hell, Heaven or Home," revised up to 25 June 1942. A shorter version of it was published in 1936 under the title *The Story of the Wilmington Rebellion* (see below, Secondary Sources). While I accepted the facts as correct, I exercised caution in interpretation, because of Hayden's propensity to support white supremacy and his defense of the actions of the Democrats.

The Cronly Family Papers are another source of data I found indispensable. This unique collection is comprised of a diary, letters to newspaper editors, pictures, and genealogical information. Because the original account is in poor condition, its most important document has been retranscribed for preservation, which also greatly facilitates reading. Entitled "Account of the Race Riot in Wilmington, N.C., in 1898," it appears to have been written by Jane Murphy Cronly. She is very critical of the white residents of Wilmington and condemns Democratic partisans as persecutors and murderers of innocent blacks.

Of some value are the Thomas W. Clawson Papers in the Louis T. Moore Collection of the North Carolina Department of Archives and History (also available at Duke University). In 1898, Clawson was city editor of the *Wilmington Messenger,* and he was later editor of the *Wilmington Morning Star.* His recital of the events of the riot is entitled "The Wilmington Race Riot of 1898: Recollections and Memories." If free from mistakes or errors in recording the violent confrontation that occurred between the whites and blacks, then Clawson offers a glowing, heroic account of it from the white point of view.

John Spencer Bassett's letters to Herbert Baxter Adams, at John Hopkins University (available in photostatic copies at Duke University), are a must for a scholarly interpretation of the white supremacy movement, the Wilmington race riot, and black disfranchisement. On the same subject, see W. Stull Holt, ed., *Historical Scholarship in the United States, 1876–1901,* Johns Hopkins University Studies in Historical and Political Science, vol. 56 (Baltimore, Md., 1938).

The following collections contain several illuminating letters that were useful for the study: Edward A. Oldham Papers, Thomas Nelson Page

Papers, Hinsdale Family Papers, and the Alexander Sprunt and Son Papers (office files 6138–6410 [1898] and political correspondence and other papers [7 September 1906–April 1906]).

Another major respository of manuscripts is the Southern Historical Collection in the Wilson Library of the University of North Carolina at Chapel Hill. I examined first the Alfred M. Waddell Papers. Because he played a pivotal role in the riot, I anticipated a wealth of valuable data in his papers. The disappointment, however, was equal to the anticipation—his bulky papers contain mostly newspaper clippings, and Waddell had exorcised all incriminating information from his collection. The Marion Butler Papers include two valuable letters from Benjamin F. Keith. The George G. Rountree typescript monograph entitled "Memorandum of My Personal Recollection of the Election of 1898" is located in the Henry G. Connor Papers. Although it is sympathetic to the riot planners and does not follow the sequence of events, it was valuable in my research. No historian interested in the disfranchisement movement should neglect Rountree's "Memorandum of My Personal Reasons for Passage of the Suffrage Amendment to the Constitution (Grandfather Clause)," also located in the Connor Papers. An analysis of this monograph and the Hayden Papers strongly suggests that the clarion call for black disfranchisement came from Wilmington. The Louis Henry Meares-DeRossett Papers, under seal until 1975, proved of little value.

Available in the North Carolina History Room is an important source: Association of the Wilmington Light Infantry Minutes, 14 December 1905, Personal Accounts of Members' Experiences in the Wilmington Riot. The minutes are a typescript of the organization's meetings at Lumina at Wrightsville Beach. They do not follow the sequence of events, are very limited in accounts, and not very well written. "All these papers," according to Walker Taylor, "are official reports of what happened prior [to] and during that time." They were useful both for the insights and for data not discovered elsewhere.

State and City Publications

Under this heading, the record of the North Carolina Supreme Court case, Van Bokkelen v. Canady (10 June 1875), located at the University of North Carolina, proved useful.

Wilmington Business Directory, 1897 (Richmond, Va., 1897) is a good source of names of both white and black businesses and churches. Anyone interested in the economic life of Wilmington on the eve of the race riot should not neglect this source. For an early account of blacks engaged in business, see Frank D. Smog, Jr., *Smog's Wilmington Directory* (Wilmington, N.C., 1866).

Newspapers

Newspapers are the best source for movements, developments, and events concerning the Wilmington race riot. All newspapers consulted are available on microfilm at the University of North Carolina Library, Chapel Hill; the North Carolina Department of Archives and History, Raleigh; the Library of Congress; and the New York City Public Library.

The Wilmington affairs and the statewide white supremacy campaign of 1898 attracted magazine and newspaper correspondents from both the South and the North. They provided the nation with daily interpretations of what was going on in the city. In spite of the violence by whites, the Southern papers were in sympathy with the doctrines of white supremacy, and with the exception of Baltimore, the Potomac River was the boundary between Southern approval and Northern criticism. For example, the *Washington Post* was conspicuously sympathetic with Wilmington's *White Supremacy Movement,* but it did condemn the riot. The *New York Times* gave modest coverage to the event. In contrast, the *New York Herald* reflected an attitude of condemnation and is the most valuable Northern source of information about the riot. Finally, there are several clipping books located in the North Carolina History Room at Chapel Hill.

Of the Southern newspapers consulted, I gave top priority to the *Wilmington Messenger,* the best source for studying the political developments, the white labor movements, and the mounting racial tensions of Wilmington during the several months preceeding the riot. Its editor, Thomas W. Clawson, was very sympathetic toward the Wilmington rebellion, however, and I was cautious in the utilization of interpretations from this paper. The same prudence had to be exercised in the use of data from the *Wilmington Morning Star.* Especially useful was the bicentennial issue of the *Wilmington Star-News* (11 January 1976), which has some excellent articles on the antebellum era.

The *Raleigh News and Observer* gave wide coverage to politics, but the accuracy of its information was often marred by the propaganda crusades it carried on against Republicans, Populists, and blacks. The *News and Observer* remains the best source for studying the statewide white supremacy campaigns of 1898 and 1900.

Other papers I found useful are the *Wilmington Evening Dispatch, Fayetteville Observer, Raleigh Caucasian,* and the *Atlanta Constitution.* Two significant black newspapers are the *Richmond Planet* and the *Cleveland Gazette.*

Memoirs, Biographies, and Autobiographies

The works of Alfred M. Waddell and John D. Bellamy deserve attention because of the significant involvement of these two men in the Wilmington race riot. Waddell played a pivotal role in the riot and the abolishment of the city government, yet in his memoirs, *Some Memories of My Life* (Raleigh, N.C., 1908), he devoted less than two pages to these events. Bellamy wrote in the preface of his book, *Memoirs of an Octogenarian* (Charlotte, N.C. 1942): "These narratives and memoirs are truthful and faithful portrayals of events occurring between the years 1839 and 1942, divided into several respective periods." Ironically, he included no reference to the events of 1898. Josephus Daniels, editor of the Raleigh *News and Observer,* was a skilled writer and a dedicated supporter of the Democratic Party. His memoirs, *Editor in Politics,* contain valuable information and insights. Highly recommended for its penetrating insights into the political activities of Wilmington is Benjamin F. Keith's *Memories* (Raleigh, N.C., 1902). Keith did not identify any people by name, but anyone familiar with the events should have no trouble in singling out the involvement of prominent individuals. A work that should not be neglected is John C. Dancy's *Sands Against the Wind: Memoirs of John C. Dancy* (Detroit, 1966).

Books

Valuable for its background of state politics and socioeconomic forces is H. Leon Prather, Sr., *Resurgent Politics and Educational Progressivism in the New South: North Carolina, 1890–1913* (Rutherford, N. J., 1979).

The Democrats' interpretation of the Wilmington race riot persisted until the publication of Helen G. Edmonds's *The Negro and Fusion Politics in North Carolina, 1894–1901* (Chapel Hill, N.C., 1951). While she gives only a few pages to the actual riot (see chapter 11, "The Wilmington Race Riot"), it is the essential starting point for any study of the event. I only wish she had interviewed some of the rank and file people living at that time who actually experienced the trauma of the massacre. This is not intended as a criticism of Professor Edmonds: her major theme is reflected in the title of her book. A most informative small volume of thirty-two pages is Harry Hayden's *The Story of the Wilmington Rebellion* (Wilmington, N.C. 1936). This work was cited infrequently because the Hayden Papers were more comprehensive. In any event, this work is useful, but caution must be employed because of the author's penchant for white supremacy. A still smaller work, by the Reverend J. Allen Kirk, *A Statement of Facts Concerning the Bloody Riot in Wilmington, N.C., November 10, 1898,* is an emotional account, allegedly written by an eyewitness. The Reverend Mr. Kirk was one of the numerous blacks who were forced to flee the city; some of the facts he reports appear to have been taken from the *Wilmington Evening Dispatch.*

Novels can provide sociological insights into human experiences that go beyond the historian's objective analysis. As pointed out in the Preface, the Wilmington event influenced two works of fiction: *Jack Thorne [David Bryant Fulton],* Hanover; or, *The Persecution of the Lowly* (n.d., n.p.; reprint,

New York, 1969); and Charles W. Chesnutt, *The Marrow of Tradition* (n.d.; reprint, Ann Arbor, Mich., 1969). *Hanover* is a novella, and Professor Thomas R. Cripps of Morgan State University has written a scholarly and documented introduction to it. He writes, "This is the work of one who was reared in Wil[mington] and knows . . . the victims of the mob's fury." Thorne, in his own introductory statement, also writes authoritatively about some aspects of the riots, but he does make some factual errors.

A scholar familiar with the Wilmington event who reads Charles W. Chesnutt's *Marrow of Tradition* may think that he is reading real history. During both the white supremacy campaign and the race riot, Chesnutt had firsthand reports from friends and relatives in the state. "In the spring and summer of 1901, at the height of his fame as a fiction writer," wrote John Wideman (*American Scholar*, Winter 1972–73, 128), "Chesnutt was working on the novel, originally based on a race riot in the state where he had grown up and taught school. During a lecture tour of the South that year, he assiduously gathered firsthand accounts of the Wilmington, North Carolina, massacre." While I found *The Marrow of Tradition* interesting and illuminating, it was Professor Wideman's interpretations that were most informative.

Articles, Editorials, and Theses

The best report of the Wilmington race riot is offered by H. L. West in "The Race War in North Carolina," *Forum* 26 (January 1899). Indispensable are the articles and photos in *Collier's Weekly* (26 November 1898). The most recent work based on interviews is June Nash, "The Cost of Violence," *Journal of Negro Studies* (December 1973). Other editorials that should be consulted are: *Outlook, The*, "North Carolina Race Conflict," November 19, 1898; Alexander J. McKelway, "The Cause of the Trouble in North Carolina" *Independent* (July–December, 1898); *Literary Digest*, "Race Trouble in the Carolinas" (November 26, 1898); Ibid., "The North Carolina Suffrage Amendment" (May–August, 1900). Two recently completed theses are: Hayumi Higuchi, "White Supremacy on the Cape Fear: Wilmington Affair of 1898," M.A. thesis, University of North Carolina, 1980; and Jerome A. McDuffie, "Politics in Wilmington and New Hanover County, N.C. 1865–1900: The Genesis of a Race Riot," Ph.D. dissertation, Kent State University, 1979. McDuffie's bulky work (viii, 843 pp.) is well documented, but lacks coordination and analysis of key issues and is weak on interpretation. Neither of these two studies was used in my research, but historians and others should know of their existence.

Index

Index

Printed in the USA
CPSIA information can be obtained
at www.ICGtesting.com
LVHW010002220324
775187LV00033B/974